Why Women Protest

Why do women protest? Under what conditions do women protest on the basis of their gender identity? Lisa Baldez answers this question in terms of three concepts: tipping, timing, and framing. She relies on the concept of tipping to identify the main object of study – the point at which diverse organizations converge to form a women's movement. She argues that two conditions trigger this cascade of mobilization among women: partisan realignment, understood as the emergence of a new set of issues around which political elites define themselves, and women's decision to frame realignment in terms of widely held norms about gender difference. To illustrate these claims, she compares two very different women's movements in Chile: the mobilization of women against President Salvador Allende (1970–3) and that against General Augusto Pinochet (1973–90). Despite important differences between these two movements, both emerged amidst a context of partisan realignment and framed their concerns in terms of women's exclusion from the political arena.

Lisa Baldez is Assistant Professor of Political Science and Harbison Faculty Fellow at Washington University in St. Louis.

Cambridge Studies in Comparative Politics

General Editor

Margaret Levi   *University of Washington, Seattle*

Assistant General Editor

Stephen Hanson   *University of Washington, Seattle*

Associate Editors

Robert H. Bates   *Harvard University*
Peter Hall   *Harvard University*
Peter Lange   *Duke University*
Helen Milner   *Columbia University*
Frances Rosenbluth   *Yale University*
Susan Stokes   *University of Chicago*
Sidney Tarrow   *Cornell University*

Other Books in the Series

Stefano Bartolini, *The Political Mobilization of the European Left, 1860–1980: The Class Cleavage*
Carles Boix, *Political Parties, Growth and Equality: Conservative and Social Democratic Economic Strategies in the World Economy*
Catherine Boone, *Merchant Capital and the Roots of State Power in Senegal, 1930–1985*
Michael Bratton and Nicolas van de Walle, *Democratic Experiments in Africa: Regime Transitions in Comparative Perspective*
Valerie Bunce, *Leaving Socialism and Leaving the State: The End of Yugoslavia, the Soviet Union and Czechoslovakia*
Ruth Berins Collier, *Paths Toward Democracy: The Working Class and Elites in Western Europe and South America*
Nancy Bermeo, ed., *Unemployment in the New Europe*
Donatella della Porta, *Social Movements, Political Violence, and the State*
Gerald Easter, *Reconstructing the State: Personal Networks and Elite Identity*
Roberto Franzosi, *The Puzzle of Strikes: Class and State Strategies in Postwar Italy*
Geoffrey Garrett, *Partisan Politics in the Global Economy*
Miriam Golden, *Heroic Defeats: The Politics of Job Loss*
Jeff Goodwin, *No Other Way Out: States and Revolutionary Movements, 1945–1991*
Merilee Serrill Grindle, *Changing the State*
Frances Hagopian, *Traditional Politics and Regime Change in Brazil*
J. Rogers Hollingsworth and Robert Boyer, eds., *Contemporary Capitalism: The Embeddedness of Institutions*
Ellen Immergut, *Health Politics: Interests and Institutions in Western Europe*
Torben Iversen, *Contested Economic Institutions*

Continued on page following the Index

Why Women Protest

WOMEN'S MOVEMENTS
IN CHILE

LISA BALDEZ
Washington University

CAMBRIDGE
UNIVERSITY PRESS

PUBLISHED BY THE PRESS SYNDICATE OF THE UNIVERSITY OF CAMBRIDGE
The Pitt Building, Trumpington Street, Cambridge, United Kingdom

CAMBRIDGE UNIVERSITY PRESS
The Edinburgh Building, Cambridge CB2 2RU, UK
40 West 20th Street, New York, NY 10011-4211, USA
477 Williamstown Road, Port Melbourne, VIC 3207, Australia
Ruiz de Alarcón 13, 28014 Madrid, Spain
Dock House, The Waterfront, Cape Town 8001, South Africa

http://www.cambridge.org

First published 2002

Printed in the United Kingdom at the University Press, Cambridge

Typeface Janson Text 10/13pt.   *System* QuarkXPress [BTS]

A catalog record for this book is available from the British Library.

Library of Congress Cataloging in Publication Data
Baldez, Lisa.
    Why women protest: women's movements in Chile / Lisa Baldez.
        p.   cm. – (Cambridge studies in comparative politics)
    Includes bibliographical references (p.) and index.
    ISBN 0-521-81150-3 – ISBN 0-521-01006-3 (pb.)
    1. Women in politics – Chile – History – 20th century.   2. Protest movements –
Chile – Case studies.   3. Women in politics.   4. Gender identity – Political aspects.
I. Title.   II. Series.
HQ1236.5.C5   B35   2002
305.42'0983 – dc21   2001052842

ISBN   0 521 81150 3   hardback
ISBN   0 521 01006 3   paperback

For John

Contents

Figures and Tables

Figures

Table

Preface

On October 16, 1998, British authorities arrested Chile's former military dictator, General Augusto Pinochet, as he recovered from back surgery at a private London clinic. Spanish judge Baltasar Garzón had requested that London police detain Pinochet so that he could be extradited to Spain and tried for human-rights violations. Just prior to the arrest, Pinochet seemed to be basking in glory and ease, symbolized by his friendship with Margaret Thatcher, Pinochet's free-market heroine. Pinochet's arrest focused the world's attention on Chile. In Chile, the event galvanized the dictator's old supporters into action. Scores of women flew to London on chartered jets to support the general. They held vigils to pray for Pinochet's return to Chile. Their speeches invoked the same rhetoric they had used against Chilean President Salvador Allende nearly three decades earlier. "We women will fight until the end so that a Marxist government never returns to power in this country," said Patricia Maldonado, leader of a group called "Women for the Dignity of Chile," according to the *Santiago Times* (December 16, 1998). In Santiago, pro-Pinochet women burned British flags outside the British and Spanish embassies to demand his return.

Women's fervor for Pinochet provides a stark contrast to the view of Latin American women as *supporters* of democracy. Most of the news about women in Latin America in the past two decades has highlighted women's efforts to promote the return to civilian rule and bring human-rights violators to justice. In Chile, for example, women formed a movement against the military in the late 1970s and 1980s. These two different perspectives on women's mobilization could not have been more clear to me than when I interviewed activists from both movements in the early 1990s. Before I left to do my fieldwork, I worried that activists from the anti-Allende movement would not want to talk with me. Given the international community's uniform condemnation of the dictatorship, I felt sure they would feel ashamed of having supported the 1973 coup. My fears proved to be unwarranted. Most of the anti-Allende women I contacted readily granted me interviews and recalled their activist past with fondness and enthusiasm. Several of them showed me miniature "empty pot" pins that had been made to commemorate their participation in the famous "March of the Empty Pots" against Allende. One of the women I interviewed gave me one that was made of bronze, but claimed to have one "made of solid gold, from Cartier in Paris." These women believed that Pinochet had saved Chile from ruin at the hands of a socialist leader. During one interview, activist María Correa choked back tears as she read aloud a poem about women's opposition to Allende. The poem, "Knocking on the Doors of the Barracks," starts like this:

Sobbing, we knocked on the doors of the barracks, calling to the blue sailors, begging the soldiers, the air force pilots, to those born here, by God rescue the country we once had from this ignominy![1]

Of the women I interviewed who were associated with the Right, not one expressed remorse about what had happened during the military regime. On the contrary: Pinochet's arrest reawakened women's passionate feelings of loyalty and gratitude for the dictator.

Certainly not all women in Chile supported the military dictatorship. Many of those who had helped bring Pinochet to power in 1973 later became involved in the mobilization of women *against* Pinochet. They felt deep shame for their role in anti-Allende activities. When I asked a former Christian Democratic congresswoman to talk about the March of the Empty Pots, she closed her eyes and said, "I don't want to remember all that. I never banged on empty pots. In reality, I never thought that a coup was the solution. . . . I went to the march to see what was happening, but I did not actually march. I tell you now, I did not go. I always thought that the thing to do was hold a plebiscite [on the Popular Unity]. In my memory, in my conscience, I was never a *golpista*." The pain my questions caused this woman gives eloquent testimony to her feelings of regret about the way the military regime turned out. In some ways it has only recently

[1] The complete text of this poem, "Golpeando las puertas de los cuarteles" by Nina Donoso, appears in María Correa, *Guerra de las mujeres* (Santiago: Editorial Universidad Técnica del Estado, 1974), 144–5.

become possible to consider these two movements dispassionately, after more than a decade of efforts to reconcile the past.

Methodology

This study forwards a general framework to explain the emergence and evolution of women's protest movements. I treat the two movements in question here as separate cases in order to generate multiple observations from a single country, and thus increase the validity of the inferences I draw about the conditions that foster mobilization among women. These movements constitute "most different cases" because of their distinct and mutually opposed ideological orientations. By comparing two such dramatically different cases, this study throws into relief the similarities they share. Within each case I examine failed and successful efforts to catalyze a movement, providing variation on the dependent variable. The research design and theoretical emphasis of this study represent an effort to enhance the fundamental claims of a literature that has been largely descriptive.

This research builds on fifty extensive interviews conducted with activists in the anti-Allende and anti-Pinochet movements (twenty-five each, from both leaders and followers) and more than twenty-five interviews with Chilean academics, party leaders, and government officials. These interviews took place during trips to Santiago in 1990, 1993–4, 1996, 1998, and 1999. This study also draws heavily from archival materials, particularly Chilean newspapers and magazines. Media coverage of women's activities provided me with information about the details of particular protests as well as the rhetorical "spin" that different groups put on these events. I also relied on movement documents provided to me by activists, and the excellent microfilm collection of pamphlets on Chilean women's organizations created by Peter T. Johnson, Bibliographer for Latin America, Spain, and Portugal at the Princeton University Library.

Acknowledgments

I gratefully acknowledge the many sources that funded the research on which this book is based. The bulk of the research was conducted in 1993–4 under the auspices of a dissertation grant from the Fulbright Commission. Additional funding for the project came from the Susan B. Anthony Center at the University of Rochester; the Center for Iberian and

Latin American Studies at the University of California, San Diego; and the Friends of the International Center at the University of California, San Diego.

The ideas presented in this book benefited a great deal from comments I received at conferences and seminars. I thank Norman Schofield, Itai Sened, and Sunita Parikh for giving me the opportunity to present my work at the annual conferences at the Center for Political Economy at Washington University. I first tried out the main argument of this book at the "Political Institutions, Cultural Norms and Mobilization" conference there in December 1999 and received astute suggestions from Randy Calvert, Ken Shepsle, and Margaret Levi. I have presented other parts of the book at the annual meetings of the Latin American Studies Association (LASA), the American Political Science Association, and the Midwest Political Science Association. I made substantial revisions to the manuscript during two stints at Harvard University in 1999 and 2001. I am grateful to Jorge Dominguez at the Weatherhead Center for International Affairs and to Jim Alt and Gary King at the Center for Basic Research in the Social Sciences at Harvard for providing all the resources I needed to think and write, as well as an intellectually stimulating environment.

I am grateful to Lewis Bateman at Cambridge University Press and to Margaret Levi, editor of the Cambridge Studies of Comparative Politics series, for their support of this project. Jane Jaquette and María Elena Valenzuela reviewed the manuscript with care and precision. Their incisive suggestions helped me articulate my ideas much more clearly. A special note of remembrance to Elsa Chaney, one of the first people with whom I discussed this project – while sitting around the swimming pool at a LASA meeting! Her warmth and enthusiasm melted away many of my fears about academia. I appreciate the advice and encouragement I have received from many friends and colleagues, including Pippa Norris, Temma Kaplan, Joyce Gelb, Sonia Alvarez, Karen Beckwith, Suzanne Marrilley, Sandra McGee Deutsch, Mary Fainsod Katzenstein, Kathy Jones, Katie Hite, Lee Ann Banaszak, Wendy Hunter, Richard Matland, Mark Jones, Mala Htun, Karin Rosemblatt, Mona Lyne, Liz Hutchison, Anna Greenberg, Annabelle Lever, Lorraine Bayard de Volo, Dave Auerswald, Elisabeth Friedman, Valerie Sperling, and Christian Davenport. My dissertation advisors at the University of California, San Diego – Paul Drake, Alan Houston, and Rebecca Klatch – guided this study in its first incarnation as a dissertation and continue to be treasured friends. Margaret Power has talked me through every step of this process, from our

Preface

very first day of fieldwork in Chile to the final editing. Our friendship and our weekly phonecalls have sustained me.

I consider myself privileged to be a part of the intellectual community at Washington University in St. Louis. Discussions with my colleagues in the Department of Political Science have improved the quality of my work immensely. I am particularly grateful to Lee Epstein and Jack Knight. They enthusiastically supported the book and patiently read many drafts. I developed many of the ideas presented in these chapters in response to interactions with the exceptional students in the classes I have taught at Washington University. The students who staged a revolution in "Revolution and Protest in Latin America" (Spring 1999) changed the way I think about social movements by showing me a "moment of madness" firsthand. A very special thanks to Ann Collins and Shelby Wolff, who are exceptionally good research assistants. They quickly won my trust and admiration for their competence and initiative.

In *Peer Gynt*, Henrik Ibsen wrote: "to live, that is to do battle with the trolls; to write, that is to sit in judgement on one's self." My friend Margaret Talcott used this as her senior quote in our college yearbook and it has resonated with me ever since. At times I judged myself quite harshly while writing this book, but my dad, Joe Baldez, intervened at a critical moment to rescue me from all that. Thanks Dad!

My Dad is just one of many, many people who held me aloft while working on this book: Edmundo Vargas, Pia Varela, Holly Johnson, Juan Vargas, Javier, Alejandra, Andrés Vargas Johnson, María Mendoza, Andrea Ansaldi, Marianne Tucker, Katharine Williams, Susan Jackson, Anne Tergesen, and Sara Singer.

I would never have been able to write this book without the love and support of my family, especially Clare and Bill Cumberland; Joe and Kris Baldez; Marion J. Cumberland; Kathy and Sonny Didden; and Bob and Mary Carey. My parents and my in-laws have given so generously of their time in order to help out with the hard work of being a working parent.

My children, Joe and Sam Carey, bring me so much joy. They celebrate my accomplishments and reward me for keeping work in proper perspective. Finally, no one is happier to see the publication of this book than my husband, John Carey. He has lovingly supported me in every imaginable way. He always knows how to make me laugh – well, almost always! Here's to all the fun we're going to have now that the book is finished.

1

Why Women Protest

TIPPING, TIMING, AND FRAMING

The socialist government of President Salvador Allende (1970–3) and the military government of General Augusto Pinochet (1973–90) represented two of the most divisive periods in the recent history of Chile. These two regimes differed in almost every respect. The Allende government attempted to pave a "peaceful road to socialism," implementing Marxist reforms within a democratic framework. Allende nationalized industries, accelerated the process of agrarian reform, and incorporated peasants and workers into the political system on a massive scale. When the military took power in a coup in 1973, the Pinochet regime put a decisive end to Chile's experiment with socialism, not only undoing Allende's reforms but implementing a new order altogether. Pinochet's efforts to reconstruct the country extended far beyond replacing civilian leaders with military officials. He opened the economy to the free market and built Chile's political institutions to establish order and stability. A fierce campaign of repression limited the expression of public opposition to these policies.

Despite the stark differences between these two regimes, they shared an important, even remarkable feature in a patriarchal culture such as Chile's: the mobilization of women. In both of these tumultuous periods, women mobilized to bring down the government in power and demanded a role in the new political order. The anti-Allende women organized the famous "March of the Empty Pots" and pressured the military to heed women's call for intervention. During the Pinochet regime, women organized around the slogan "Democracy in the Country and in the Home," punctuating the pro-democracy movement with demands for human rights, economic justice, and women's equality.

To be sure, the two cases of mobilization differed in fundamental ways. Activists mobilized in very different political contexts and espoused

1

radically distinct interests. The anti-Allende women protested against a democratically elected government and supported a military coup, while the anti-Pinochet women mobilized in the midst of a repressive military dictatorship and sought to restore democratic rule. These movements represent two opposing sides of a deep and enduring conflict in Chilean politics, one that centers on the legacies of the Allende government and the military regime. In one version of Chile's history, the Allende government epitomized the triumph of the Chilean *pueblo* over the bourgeoisie, and the military government represented a fascist dictatorship that systematically violated the basic human rights of its own citizens. This view characterizes the women who organized the March of the Empty Pots as the shrill harpies of the upper class, who complained about food shortages while hoarding goods and making profits on the black market. According to the other view of Chilean history, the Allende government unleashed a period of chaos, violence, and Marxist arrogance that threatened to destroy the entire nation, while the military government restored order, established economic prosperity, and vanquished the enemy in an internal war against subversion. From this vantage point, the women who protested against Pinochet emerge as communists in Gramscian disguise.[1]

Given these differences, drawing comparisons between these two movements may not seem appropriate; it may even be anathema to those who sympathize with one movement over the other. Yet striking similarities between them warrant explanation. The two closely resembled one another in terms of the timing of women's protest and the way in which women framed their demands. In each case, women mobilized amid a context of partisan realignment, as the political parties of the opposition formed a new coalition against the regime in power. Women perceived moments of realignment as uniquely gendered opportunities. Women framed their mobilization in terms of their status as political outsiders, in response to what they perceived as men's characteristic inability to overcome narrow partisan concerns. The groups that predominated within each movement argued that women "do politics" differently from men. Activists maintained that women possess a unique ability to transcend con-

---

[1] Chilean conservatives appear to have read quite a bit of Gramsci. Many of the conservative women I interviewed for this project described Gramscian theory as the current embodiment of the Marxist threat. As one woman explained to me, "It is another way of getting to Marxism, but by way of education. . . . People are calmer now, that the [Berlin] wall has fallen and Communism destroyed itself, but – watch out! (*Ojo!*) – even some of Aylwin's ministers are declared Gramscians" (Maturana 1993).

2

flict and forge unity within a male-dominated political order. Women organized across party lines in the hopes of setting an example for male politicians, who had been unable to coordinate their actions against the government. Both movements sought to forward the concerns of women in the context of more general demands for regime change. At the same time, women in both movements lobbied for the incorporation of their own issues and concerns on partisan agendas, with varying degrees of success.

Why did these two conditions – partisan realignment and gendered framing – lead to the emergence of mass mobilization among women? The decision of female political entrepreneurs to frame their actions in terms of women's status as political outsiders resonated within a broad spectrum of women, activists and nonactivists alike. Even women actively engaged in partisan politics framed their participation in these terms. Framing women's demands in terms of women's status as political outsiders allowed diverse groups to coalesce in a movement. Claims about the nonpartisan status of women distinguished them from numerous other movements active at the time (e.g., among workers, students, and peasants) and brought women to the forefront of the opposition struggle in each case.

The timing and framing of women's demands also appealed to male politicians. At periods of realignment, politicians try to portray their actions as a response to the will of the people, rather than as a bold effort to gain political power. Women's protests provided a way for male party leaders to recast their goals in credibly nonpartisan terms, as a response to the concerns expressed by female activists. This explains why male politicians acknowledged the emergence of women's mobilization and encouraged its development.

The parallels between these two "most different" cases raise important questions about women's mobilization more generally. Why do women protest? Under what conditions do women protest as women, on the basis of their gender identity? What prompts female political entrepreneurs to perceive certain situations in gendered terms? In what context will decisions made by a diverse array of women coalesce into a collective response, thus sparking the formation of a movement?

By raising these questions in the context of the two Chilean movements, I am focusing on points of similarity across women's movements rather than differences among them. To that extent, this book diverges significantly from most studies of women's movements, for which acknowledgment of the diversity of interests that women's movements represent has

3

proven fundamentally important. Studies of women's movements show that women have mobilized in diverse political environments. Recent research has emphasized national and regional differences across women's organizing (Nelson and Chowdhury 1994; Basu 1995; Marsh 1996; Threlfall 1996; Buckley, M. 1997; Buckley, S. 1997; Chatty and Rabo 1997; Kaplan 1997; Stephen 1997; Jaquette and Wolchik 1998; Rodríguez 1998; Bystydzienski and Sekhon 1999; Sperling 1999; Young 1999), as well as transnational mobilization among women (Rupp 1997; Alvarez, Dagnino et al. 1998; Clark 1998; Keck and Sikkink 1998). Women have mobilized within diverse political contexts, including stable democracies (Katzenstein and Mueller 1987; Black 1989; Gelb 1989; Bashevkin 1998), revolutions (Tétreault 1994; Gilmartin 1995), nationalist movements (Ackelsberg 1991; Kaplan 1992; West 1997), fascism (Koonz 1987; De Grazia 1992), and transitions to democracy (Alvarez 1990; Jelín 1991; Feijoo 1994; Jaquette 1994; Friedman 2000) as well as around a diverse set of substantive interests, from suffrage (Hahner 1990; Lavrín 1995; Banaszak 1996; Marilley 1997; Marshall 1997; Terborg-Penn 1998) to peace (Kaplan 1997) to economic justice (West and Blumberg 1990). Even the term *feminist movement* encompasses tremendous diversity. Recent studies affirm that feminist movements come in various forms – liberal; radical; socialist; African-American; Chicana; Latina; lesbian; third-world; multicultural; nationalist; indigenous; pan-Asian; or first-, second-, or third-wave (Jayawardena 1986; Mohanty, Russo et al. 1991; Cohen, Jones et al. 1997). As Sonia Alvarez (1990: 23) observes,

When one considers that women span all social classes, ethnicities, religions, nationalities, political ideologies and so on, then an infinite array of interests could be construed as women's interests. Gender, class, race, ethnicity, sexual preference and other social characteristics determine women's social positioning and shape women's interests.

In the effort to highlight difference, however, scholars have neglected the question of what women's movements have in common. A focus on diversity across and within women's movements provides little leverage on the question of why women mobilize as *women*. This book argues that all women's movements share the decision to mobilize as women, on the basis of what I maintain are widely held norms about female identity. These norms constitute a set of understandings that reflect women's widespread exclusion from political power. At certain historical moments, women have bridged myriad differences among them to stage mass demonstrations that

4

have set in motion profound transformations both in women's lives and within the political system overall. If women represent so many different interests, then what prompts them to mobilize on the basis of a shared identity that allows them to transcend those differences? Under what conditions are women likely to protest as women?

This book forwards a general theoretical framework to address these questions. I explain why women protest in terms of three theoretical concepts: tipping, timing, and framing. I rely on the concept of tipping to identify the dependent variable in this study, which I define as the point at which diverse organizations converge to form a women's movement. Tipping, a cascade of mobilization among women, is the main object of study. Timing and framing constitute the main independent variables in this study. I argue that two conditions must be in place in order for widespread mobilization to emerge among women: partisan realignment, understood as the formation of new coalitions among political parties, and women's decision to frame realignment in terms of widely held cultural norms about gender difference. At moments of realignment among political elites, women have mobilized around the idea that the male political elites care more about preserving their power than addressing pressing substantive issues.

Tipping

This study focuses on the precise point at which social movements coalesce as movements. I aim to identify the moment when diverse groups and individuals join together under a common rubric to challenge the status quo. Scholars of social movements have long recognized the importance of particular protests that change the course of future events in profound ways – the civil-rights march on Selma, the first protest of the Berkeley Free Speech movement, and the student protests at Tienanmen Square, for example. Yet people tend to talk about such protests in somewhat metaphysical terms. Numerous firsthand accounts of protests such as these attest to the existence of transcendental moments in the evolution of protest, or a point during which everything seems possible and after which "nothing remains the same." These "moments of madness," as Aristide Zolberg (1972) calls them, mark the point at which disparate organizations and individuals converge to forge a common identity and to confront a common opponent. Such moments catalyze the formation of a social movement. As I shall show, the conditions that shape a movement's emergence also constrain its evolution and outcomes in significant, although not determinant, ways.

The tipping model describes movement emergence in analytically tractable terms. Mobilization among women emerges as the result of a tipping process in which participation in protest activities starts out small, builds gradually as more people become involved, and then suddenly reaches a critical mass of momentum. A tip occurs when political entrepreneurs frame the need for mobilization in terms that resonate with an array of people, at a particular point in time.

In a tipping model, the probability that any given individual will participate depends on the likelihood that a person thinks others will participate (Schelling 1978). Whether individual actions reach a critical mass and tip or cascade toward a collective outcome, in other words, depends on a particular individual's perceptions of what others appear ready to do. A tip occurs when a sufficiently large number of people believe that other people will also participate. In the strongest case, a tip will occur when people come to believe that their participation becomes necessary or even required (Chong 1991; Laitin 1998). Tips occur as the result of individual decisions made by activists and members of the general population about whether or not to participate in a protest. The tipping model explains mobilization in terms of how people respond to each other, rather than how they respond to selective incentives, or some kind of material benefit. Whether someone participates does not hinge on thinking "what do I get out of it?" but "what will you think of me if I don't participate?" In other words, your decision to participate in an act of protest hinges on your beliefs about what others are likely to do.

The tipping model thus points to cognition and perception as the triggers that set off the process of mobilization. An appeal to common knowledge or widely held cultural norms often sets the tipping process in motion. Movement entrepreneurs can draw upon these norms in a variety of contexts (Taylor 1987; Chai 1997; Laitin 1998; Petersen 2001). *Cultural norms*, defined as sets of common beliefs and practices in a particular society, can provide the kinds of focal points that trigger collective action. Mobilizing as women entails framing activism in terms of readily understood cultural norms about female behavior.

Yet entrepreneurs cannot expect to issue a call to women any old time and expect tens of thousands to take to the streets. A rhetorical appeal will trigger a collective response only under certain conditions. My approach focuses on the macroconditions under which tipping is likely to occur, and thus differs from studies that employ the tipping model to explain the microfoundations of protest, that is, to illustrate the process by which individual decisions are coordinated into collective outcomes (Chong 1991; Lohmann 1994; Parikh and Cameron 1999). My study explains the conditions that set off mobilizational cascades among women in particular and identifies the conditions that activate this process, or cause it to be "switched on," to use Jon Elster's terminology (Elster 1989). I argue that two conditions – timing and framing – evoke a desire to participate, and evince participation from a particular group of people, setting the tipping process in motion.

Timing

The timing of women's mobilization can be explained in terms of partisan realignment. Women's movements emerge in response to a realignment, understood here as the formation of new coalitions among political parties. Political scientists have tended to define partisan realignment as enduring shifts in partisan attachments *within the electorate* (Sundquist 1983; Gates 1987; Kawato 1987; Hurley 1991; Nardulli 1995; for a review see Brady, Ferejohn et al. 2000). Yet defining realignment in terms of voting behavior need not be the only way to identify realignment. I define *realignment* as fundamental changes in the issues that political parties represent, similar to the approach followed by Robert Rohrschneider (1993). In multiparty political systems, the formation of a new coalition among political parties also constitutes a realignment. New coalitions indicate evidence of a realignment even in cases (such as Chile) where voting behavior for particular political parties remains fairly stable over time (but see Valenzuela and Scully 1997). In addition, most studies assert that realignments must be long-lasting in order to count as legitimate realignments, rather than temporary blips in voting behavior. I would argue that the temporal dimension of this definition is unnecessary. A long-term pattern may be appropriate for stable democracies such as the United States, but realignments have occurred with far greater frequency in Latin American countries. The short duration of cleavage patterns in Latin America should not mean that they are any less significant.

At moments of realignment, political parties establish a new political agenda. They also cast about for new bases of popular support and seek to legitimate their actions in the public eye. To do so, they often seek to portray their new alliance as representing national interests over sectarian ones. This strategy often involves masking partisan interests in appeals to unity, nonpartisanship, and the spirit of cooperation – precisely the characteristics commonly associated with cultural norms about women. Political elites frequently look to women as a quintessentially "neutral" constituency to lend legitimacy to the new coalition. In many cases, women do not represent the only organized groups mobilizing at these moments; other groups may be trying to gain concessions from political leaders at the same time. Nonetheless, women's appeal to their status as political outsiders makes them a particularly desirable constituency for parties negotiating the terms of alliance with one another. Gender cuts across all other political cleavages and enhances the degree to which a coalition can be seen as representing national rather than narrow, partisan interests. Thus, partisan realignment provides a political opportunity that is uniquely propitious for the mobilization of women.

This focus on realignment as a necessary condition for the emergence of women's movements links claims within the literature on social movements to predictions about elite behavior drawn from the literature on political institutions. Social movement scholars concur that movements rise and fall in part in response to changes within the political arena, known as changes in political opportunities (Tilly 1978; McAdam 1982; Kitschelt 1986; Gelb 1989; Costain 1992; Tarrow 1994; Hipsher 1997). The political opportunities approach points, correctly so, to the state as the central interlocutor of collective action in many cases. Recent scholarship has sought to narrow the concept of political opportunities in order to increase the possibilities for generating predictions about future outcomes (McAdam, Tarrow et al. 1996). Tarrow (1994: 86), for example, focuses specifically on realignment as a key variable. My approach builds on this perspective by not only identifying what political opportunities are relevant, but explaining when we might expect them to emerge.

The approach I have described uses the insights of the literature on political institutions to explain when political opportunities emerge and to explain *why* certain conditions are more favorable for protest than others. The formal rules of political engagement shape the incentives of political actors and define the points at which elites become vulnerable to challenges issued by activists. Divisions among political elites arise somewhat predictably as a consequence of the rules that structure their behavior. An institutional explanation can identify when a political system is ripe for realignment.

Institutional arrangements are sets of rules, both formal and informal, that structure social interactions in predictable ways (Knight 1992). Formal political institutions such as constitutions, laws, and electoral systems shape the range of possible outcomes in a given situation. Institutions facilitate coordination among political actors because they shape people's expectations about the future in ways that people can anticipate, by providing a common frame of reference. The "establishment of clear mutual expectations" makes institutions binding, even when they generate outcomes that run counter to the interests of those who abide by them (Carey 2000: 13, see also Levi 1988; Hardin 1989; North 1990). Recent literature on political institutions has focused primarily on the actions of presumably rational elites who pursue their interests within the formal political arena, particularly the courts, legislatures, and the executive branch (for a review of this literature see Carey 2000). Some recent work examines how formal institutions structure strategic interaction among voters (Cox 1997; Harvey 1998; Lyne 2000). My study extends this research by determining how the design of formal political institutions affects decisions made by groups within civil society.

The Chilean Institutional Context

In the past, the institutional design of the Chilean political system created (regular) opportunities for "outsider" appeals by those who criticized the extent to which negotiations for power within a particular coalition prevented the parties from uniting around national interests. Prior to the 1973 coup, Chile was governed by a moderately strong presidential system characterized by two contradictory tendencies. The formal rules that structured engagement among political elites led them in two conflicting directions. On the one hand, the electoral system for congressional elections fostered the development of strong, ideologically distinct parties, rather than "catchall" parties that encompassed a broad spectrum of issues. On the other hand, the political system required the parties to form coalitions with one another in order to win control of the powerful executive branch. For presidential elections, institutional rules favored the formation of broad cross-partisan coalitions (Valenzuela 1978; Linz and Valenzuela 1994). Realignment in this kind of environment sometimes proved to be a tricky business, as it occasionally required parties to enter into coalitions with those who previously had been sworn enemies. These contradictory tendencies required parties to engage in competition on two fronts simultaneously: to enhance their own base of support in order to establish dominance within a particular coalition and to elicit support for the coalition as a whole in order to beat their opponents. This feature made the Chilean parties persistently vulnerable to realignment.

As I discuss in the chapters that follow, women's movements formed at three precise moments over the course of the twentieth century: the women's suffrage movement (1935), the anti-Allende women's movement (1971), and the anti-Pinochet women's movement (1983). The formation of these movements corresponds with major realignments among the political parties of the opposition: the formation of the Popular Front, an alliance of center-left parties (1935); the formation of the Democratic Confederation (CODE), an alliance of center-right parties (1971); and the Democratic Alliance (AD), a coalition of center-left parties (1983).[2] The parallels among these instances in terms of timing provides suggestive evidence for a correlation between the emergence of women's movements and partisan realignment. But an important question remains: why did women perceive these institutional moments in gendered terms?

Framing

It is not enough to identify the conditions under which protest occurs, even if we can anticipate those conditions with some precision. The third component of my argument explains why women *perceive* these conditions as opportunities, why they perceive them *in gendered terms*, and why they perceive these conditions *as requiring them to take action*. Social movement scholars refer to this as cultural framing (Snow and Benford 1988; Snow 1992; McAdam, McCarthy et al. 1996). Rational-choice theorists would argue that women's movements engage in what William Riker termed *heresthetics*, the rhetorical restructuring of political situations in ways that change the possible outcomes (Riker 1986; Riker, Calvert et al. 1996). The term *heresthetic* remains obscure, but Riker (1986: ix) provides a straightforward definition:

---

[2] The Democratic Alliance (Alianza Democrática) formed the basis of what would later become the Coalition of Parties for Democracy (Concertación de Partidos por la Democracia), the coalition that would defeat the pro-military candidate in the 1989 presidential elections and has controlled the executive branch in three consecutive administrations since then.

[People] win because they have set up the situation in such a way that other people will want to join them – or will feel forced by circumstances to join them – even without any persuasion at all. And this is what heresthetic is about: structuring the world so you can win.

In a successful heresthetic move, political actors achieve their goals not by superior resources, but by introducing a new dimension that reframes a particular issue to their advantage.

A women's movement will emerge during partisan realignment if female political entrepreneurs respond to such moments in gendered terms, particularly in terms of women's exclusion from political decision making. I argue that they will do so in response to the exclusion of women and women's interests during moments of realignment by framing their activities in terms of cultural norms that portray women as political outsiders. Framing realignment in terms of gender appeals to one characteristic that all women share. Appeals to gender identity bridge women's different and sometimes contradictory interests: exclusion from political power. No matter what specific agenda women's organizations wish to pursue, they cannot pursue it efficiently without political access. This frame permits a diverse array of women's groups to organize under a common rubric.

The prior existence of networks of women's organizations constitutes a necessary but not sufficient condition for the emergence of a women's movement, consistent with the prediction of a resource mobilization approach to social movements (McCarthy and Zald 1973; Zald and McCarthy 1979; McCarthy and Zald 1987). In other words, my argument rests on an assumption that women's organizations already exist. It is beyond the scope of the present work to identify the general conditions that foster the creation of such networks. In the Chilean case, however, I demonstrate the specific conditions that led to the formation of various kinds of women's organizations, including support from the Catholic Church, the media, and international organizations. Nonetheless, these factors occupy a secondary role in the overall theory presented in this book. My main focus is to explain what happens in order for women's organizations to coalesce and act in a coordinated way.

Gender functions as a source of collective identity in ways that are similar to other sources of identity, such as race, ethnicity, or nationality. Nonetheless, gender differs from other categories in at least one important way. Most societies have defined women's roles in terms of the domestic or household sphere, as mothers and housewives (Rosaldo, Bamberger et al. 1974). Gender norms tend to define women as political outsiders, as inherently *nonpolitical* or *apolitical*. Mobilizing as women, therefore, politicizes a source of identity that by definition has no place in the political arena. Although seemingly a contradiction in terms, this dynamic holds central importance in understanding the conditions and consequences of mobilization among women.

At the same time, cultural norms about gender are not static or eternal; people continuously reconstruct and resignify them. The very term *gender*, as opposed to the term *sex*, reflects the idea that differences between men and women are not biologically determined but socially constructed (Scott 1988; Lorber 1997). What it means to be male and female, in other words, differs in different societies, and varies over time (Kessler and McKenna 1978). Yet part of the appeal and persuasiveness of *woman* as a category centers on its appearance of being universal. Dichotomous gender differences permeate most societies and the two categories *feminine* and *masculine* still constitute meaningful, universally recognized categories of identity in most contexts. They function like two containers that people fill up with different contents.

The way in which cultural norms about gender are defined varies according to context. In Latin America, long-standing gender norms have portrayed men as *macho*, dominant and sexually aggressive, and women as weak, submissive, and requiring men's protection. In Chile, gender norms portray women primarily as political outsiders. Whether women are seen as mothers, as housewives, as feminists, or as saints, they are all considered to belong appropriately outside the arena of politics. These norms have been continuously present in public discourse throughout Chile's history as a nation, since the Wars of Independence in the early 1800s. Despite the significant ideological and political differences between the movements examined in this study, activists in both of them appealed to the same set of norms about the role of women. While these stereotypes appear to be eternal and unchanging, however, they are actually continuously reconstituted and redefined, both by political elites and by ordinary men and women.

Women's Movements and Women's Interests

Conventional wisdom suggests that women organize around shared interests such as the right to vote, equal pay, or concern for the safety of their children. I suggest, however, that focusing on women's specific, policy-oriented interests leads us *away* from understanding why women protest as women – that is, on the basis of their gender identity. I argue that all women's movements invoke their identity as women in order to emphasize two things: their uniqueness in relation to men and their interest in having greater access to decision making. Women mobilize on the basis of their gender identity in the hopes of influencing political outcomes determined primarily by male elites. Framing their concerns in terms of gender difference proves more successful at some points than at others. I develop this perspective through an analysis of the strengths and weaknesses of two other approaches that explain women's mobilization in terms of interests – structural models and accounts that highlight the differences between *feminine* and *feminist* movements.

Studies of women's movements often begin with an account of how structural change shapes women's interests. Structural explanations account for the emergence of mobilization in terms of broad socioeconomic, material conditions – "big-picture" variables such as demographic change, economic distribution, and class conflict (Davies 1962; Smelser 1963; Gurr 1970).[3] The correlations suggested by structural studies of women's movements make intuitive sense: the impact of structural changes that occurred during the past century on women's lives proves impossible to ignore. Increased access to education, higher rates of participation in the workforce, and the availability of new technologies (such as the washing machine and the birth control pill) have transformed the status of many of the world's women. The widespread emergence of mass-based struggles for women's emancipation cannot be imagined without these advances. Studies of feminist movements, however, seldom consider the possibility that the same changes in women's status that prompted the emergence of feminism may also have fueled activism among conservative or nonfeminist women. Structural explanations tend to presume a causal relationship between structural change and *progressive* movements. Yet conservative or reactionary women may also organize in response to the same kinds of structural changes as their progressive counterparts. As Rebecca Klatch suggests in *A Generation Divided* (1999), a study of the new Right and new Left in the United States, not all the activists in the 1960s could be considered hippies.

---

[3] Social scientists have used the term *structure* in a variety of ways. Theda Skocpol (1979; 1994) uses the term *structural* to identify state-centered approaches to revolution. I categorize state-centric approaches as institutional.

Scholars have also conceived of the relationship between gender interests and women's movements in terms of feminine or feminist movements, a dichotomy that categorizes movements according to whether activists seek to preserve the status quo or aim to change it. This perspective emphasizes the goals that women pursue. Feminine movements mobilize on the basis of women's traditional roles in the domestic sphere, usually as mothers and wives, while feminist movements explicitly challenge conventional gender roles (Alvarez 1990; Jaquette 1994). Others have described the same dichotomy in terms of practical or strategic gender interests (Molyneux 1985), maternalist movements (Jetter, Orleck et al. 1997), or movements that embody female consciousness (Kaplan 1982).

The feminine/feminist distinction highlights the differences between gender and other collective categories, such as race, ethnicity, or class. Standard approaches to the study of women in politics (i.e., those that do not take gender ideology into account) often fail to "get at" the sources of gender discrimination and do not problematize the sexist nature of political institutions (Jónasdóttir and Jones 1988). Drawing a distinction between feminine and feminist mobilization also acknowledges that not all women organize along feminist lines and thus legitimates the contributions of women who do not necessarily or explicitly support gender equality.

To be fair, the distinction between feminine and feminist movements has been forwarded more as a mode of classification than as an *explanation* for why women protest. But this typology implies that women protest in response to their interests as women, either to defend "traditional" interests centering on children and the family or to promote women's interests in achieving equality. In reducing women's interests to two categories, however, this approach obscures more than it explains. Many movements do not fit easily into either category. Some are feminine and feminist at the same time (Kaplan 1997; Stephen 1997). Studies of conservative and reactionary women have convincingly demonstrated that women's political participation cannot necessarily be explained simply in terms of women's adherence to or defense of traditional gender roles (Luker 1984; Klatch 1987; Koonz 1987; Blee 1991; De Grazia 1992; Power 1996; Blee 1998; Klatch 1999; Kampwirth and Gonzalez 2001). Women who participated in the Ku Klux Klan in the 1920s, for example, formed a unique ideology that joined racism, motherhood, and support for women's rights (Blee 1991). More importantly, *feminine* mobilization presents a contradiction in terms: *if women acted in accord with traditional views of women's*

14

roles, they would not mobilize at all. We might expect truly feminine-minded women to stay home. Linking female identity with a particular set of interests more often than not leads us to portray women's interests inaccurately and makes them susceptible to the charge of false consciousness, in the sense of attributing interests to women that they do not actually hold.

So what interests do women share in common? What unites women is their exclusion from the political process and their collective status as political outsiders. There are important individual exceptions, but they do not challenge the existence of widespread patterns of marginalization among women (Williams 1998). Mobilizing as women provides a rhetorical frame that permits women with diverse substantive interests to engage in collective action to pursue their ends under the rubric of having access to political decision making. Whatever women's specific concerns may be, they cannot pursue them if they lack the ability to voice their concerns and have them taken seriously in the political arena. Women protest as women not necessarily because they share mutual interests (although they may) but because mobilizing as women frames their actions in a way that facilitates coordination among them.

While women's movements diverge widely in terms of substantive concerns, they share an appeal to "women" as a source of collective identity. In any particular context, and to a certain extent universally, the term *woman* conveys a set of shared meanings and readily understood norms about behavior. Gender is constructed, but it is constructed in ways that are more or less readily understood in any given society at any given point in time. When women mobilize as women, they tap into common knowledge about gender norms that portray men and women as categorically different.

Using norms strategically may or may not be consistent with activists' "real" beliefs, and may or may not result from a conscious decision-making process in which other strategies are explicitly suggested, considered, and rejected. Women do not inevitably mobilize on the basis of their identity as women simply because they are women. Framing mobilization in terms of conventional gender roles may seem to be an obvious or inevitable move, especially for women in Latin America, where *machismo* and *marianismo* (the cult of the Virgin Mary) run deep and appear to constitute an essential component of the culture. But women have choices about how to frame their actions. Women may also mobilize as students, workers, members of a socioeconomic class, or any one of a host of nongender-specific categories. Women comprised a significant percentage of activists

15

Why Women Protest

in the Polish Solidarity movement, for example, but they did not raise gender-specific demands until well into Poland's transition to democracy (Bernhard 1993). Moreover, of the numerous women who participated in the New Left movement in the United States, a relatively small percentage joined women's liberation (Klatch 1999). Even if activists consider mobilizing as women to be the obvious choice in a given situation, however, there are some conditions in which it makes more sense to do so than others. There are some situations in which mobilizing on the basis of gender identity will prove more persuasive and more successful than others, in terms of generating popular support or eliciting a response from political authorities.

When women do mobilize as women, they often use gender roles *strategically* to further certain political goals. When activists in a particular movement engage in practices associated with women's traditional roles, such as banging on empty pots and pans, they may in fact be exploiting conventional gender norms in the service of strategic political goals. Women's appeal to motherhood as the basis for mobilization does not necessarily evolve because society literally relegates women to the domestic realm. Women do rely upon conventional gender roles as the basis for mobilization, and they do so for a number of different reasons. In some situations, women's decision to articulate their demands in terms of motherhood may prove politically advantageous, because motherhood affords women a political space not available to men. Karen Beckwith (1996: 1055) maintains, for example, that "where women's standing emphasize[s] their relationships as mothers and wives, it serve[s] as a resource that protects them against certain kinds of reprisals" and enables women to do things that would be "unimaginable" for other groups to undertake. In this sense, one might say that activists in women's movements *perform* gender identity (Butler 1990). When women mobilize as women, they appeal to a certain set of expectations about women's behavior and tap into widely held and commonly recognized cultural norms about women's status in society. Yet they do so in order to highlight women's shared experience of exclusion from political power.

Conclusion

My study predicts that women's movements will emerge under two conditions: partisan realignment and framing conflict in terms of widely held cultural norms about gender difference. Women's movements are most

16

likely to generate a tip, in terms of winning popular support and influencing political outcomes, when their mobilization coincides with the formation of new coalitions and when they frame their mobilization in terms of their status as political outsiders. The conditions under which political realignment occurs can be determined by examining the institutional rules that structure engagement among political elites. Understanding institutional design in a particular context not only helps to clarify the conditions under which these outcomes are likely to occur, but also explains why they occur. Women's proclivity to perceive these conditions in gendered terms, and their likelihood to take action in response to them, stems from the way in which differences between men and women become salient in the political arena. Convergence between the precise institutional moment when particular protests occurred and the way in which women framed their actions set in process a series of events that changed the entire political landscape – for the women in the movement as well as for political actors outside the movement. Once the movement coalesces, politicians are likely to address its concerns in their efforts to build popular support for their new coalition.

The argument presented here about why women protest joins "bottom-up" and "top-down" approaches to the study of social movements. That is, this book accounts for the role that individual people play in initiating mobilization, as well as the broad conditions under which they do so. Karl Marx (1987) expressed this idea in *The Eighteenth Brumaire of Louis Bonaparte* when he wrote "men [*sic*] make their own history, but they do not make it just as they please; they do not make it under circumstances chosen by themselves, but under circumstances directly encountered, given and transmitted from the past." Collective political outcomes must be explained in terms of individual actions, on what some have called a "microfoundational" level. I start from this assumption, which is a central premise of rational choice theory, not only because I find it logically persuasive, but also because it acknowledges the potential for human agency and creativity. At the same time, people make choices and take action within a particular context, or set of "macrolevel" conditions, that limits them in significant and, to a certain extent, identifiable ways.

The three general concepts presented in this book – tipping, timing, and framing – constitute a general framework from which to understand why women protest. In and of themselves, however, these concepts do not constitute an explanation. In order to employ these concepts to generate predictive explanations, they must be linked to empirical details from specific cases. The precise parameters of these variables will be defined differently from case to case, depending on the institutional design and historical details of a particular political system. Thus the remaining chapters in this book delve deep into the substantive details of Chilean history. Ultimately, as I suggest in the final chapter, the generalizability of the claims I make here merits examination across an array of different cases.

Overview of the Book

This chapter provides a general framework from which to understand mobilization among women, one that points toward institutional dynamics and cultural norms as the key variables. The balance of the book examines these theoretical claims against empirical detail drawn from Chile. Chapter Two provides a historical overview of women's participation in the Chilean political process. It begins by explaining the women's suffrage in terms of tipping. In the 1930s, a diverse array of women's organizations united around the demand for suffrage in the context of partisan realignment: the formation of the center-left coalition known as the Popular Front. They framed their demands in terms of women's status outside the parties, but the movement collapsed when women's claims to transcend party politics proved unsustainable. The second half of the chapter shows how the Cold War politics of the 1960s shaped the reemergence of women's protest in the 1970s and 1980s.

I present the two main cases in separate parts. The three chapters in each part examine three distinct phases of women's mobilization: failed efforts to coalesce; successful efforts to coalesce; and the consequences of mobilization in each case. Chapter Three charts the initial efforts of female party leaders to mobilize Chilean women against the socialist government of President Allende – a failed tip. Conservative women began to protest just after the 1970 presidential election in the hopes of fomenting a mass women's movement against the new leftist government but they did not succeed. The female protesters framed their actions in terms of women's unique ability to transcend male partisanship. They believed that the opposition parties were poised to form a new alliance with one another, but this anticipated realignment did not occur and the protests failed to achieve their immediate objective. Nonetheless, these efforts established the tone for later demonstrations. Chapter Three also illustrates how political conditions changed over the course of Allende's first year in office. Gradually, the parties within the opposition began to converge and a realignment did occur, setting the stage for a women's movement to emerge.

Chapter Four examines the March of the Empty Pots, an example of successful mobilization that I identify as the tipping point for the anti-Allende movement. By November 1971, a climate of instability had prompted the opposition parties to join forces against the Allende government. Female opposition leaders responded by convening a mass demonstration of women against the government, an event that erupted in street violence and chaos. The March of the Empty Pots ignited women's mobilization because of the moment at which it occurred and the way in which the organizers framed women's actions. These two conditions – a realignment of the center right against the leftist Allende government, and an emphasis on women's status as political outsiders – triggered sustained mobilization among women. These events definitively shaped the events that occurred during the course of the remaining two years of the Allende government and influenced the Pinochet regime as well.

Chapter Five illustrates the lasting significance of the March of the Empty Pots – for women, for the opposition as a whole, for the Allende government, and for the military regime that followed it. Various constituencies within the opposition fought to monopolize the symbol of the empty pot. Chapter Five also illustrates the ways in which the military government of General Augusto Pinochet adopted the anti-Allende women's movement to serve its own purposes. When the armed forces seized power on September 11, 1973, they credited "the women of Chile" with liberating Chile from Marxism. Women became one of the military government's most important constituencies. Pinochet and his wife, Lucía Hiriart, continuously invoked women's opposition to Allende and incorporated hundreds of thousands of women into government-sponsored volunteer programs.

Part Two analyzes women's organizing against the Pinochet regime. Chapter Six traces the origins of a diverse array of women's organizations opposed to the military, beginning just after the coup and leading up to 1983. During this period, women formed groups centered on human rights, economic survival, and women's rights – the organizational base upon which a new women's movement would emerge. Most of this activity remained isolated and underground because of the fierce campaign against subversion being waged by the military. The few protests that women staged during this period tended to be small and easily repressed.

Chapter Seven illustrates how changes in the political context precipitated a mass women's movement. In 1983, the loose networks of women's organizations coalesced to produce a new movement of women opposed to Pinochet. The movement emerged in response to the formation of two competing crosspartisan coalitions within the opposition. These coalitions proved unable to agree on how best to bring about a return to civilian rule. Women representing the entire spectrum of the opposition came together in this setting, triggering the formation of a united women's movement. They framed the need to unite in terms of women's ability to transcend party politicking in the face of a dire political crisis. Their efforts emphasized women's defense of life against the "culture of death" represented by the military.

Chapter Eight evaluates the impact of the women's movement on the process of democratic transition and consolidation in Chile. Women's movement organizations played a critical role in the transition to democracy between 1987 and 1989, amidst a period of intense competition to monopolize women's electoral power. The second part of Chapter Eight focuses on the fate of the women's movement since the return of civilian rule in 1989.

Chapter Nine concludes by examining the extent to which the theoretical framework developed in this book can be used to explain other cases. I consider the "tipping, timing, framing" perspective in light of evidence drawn from three other countries that underwent transitions to democracy: Brazil, Russia, and the former East Germany.

2

Mothers of the Cold War, Daughters of the Revolution

A HISTORICAL OVERVIEW OF WOMEN AND CHILEAN POLITICS

Just like its counterparts elsewhere in the world, women's mobilization in Chile has been categorized primarily in terms of a first-wave suffrage movement in the first half of the twentieth century and a second-wave women's movement in the second half, with a period of relative quiescence in between. This chapter reexamines women's history in Chile and traces the relationship between women's organizations and political parties, starting with women's first attempts to vote in the late nineteenth century and ending with their participation in the student movements of the 1960s. This historical overview provides suggestive evidence for the central argument of the overall book, that the rise and fall of women's movements can be explained in terms of partisan realignment and gendered framing. In Chile, an independent women's movement emerged during the 1930s as the main cleavage in party politics shifted from religion to class. In 1953, the women's movement became tainted by scandal and collapsed suddenly, paving the way for parties to monopolize women's political involvement. The political incorporation of women during this period set the stage for the reemergence of autonomous women's mobilization in the 1970s and 1980s.

Realignment and the Rise of the Women's Suffrage Movement

This account of women's incorporation into the Chilean political system begins in November 1875, in San Felipe, a small town sixty miles north of Santiago. By a vote of four to one, the Electoral Registry Board of San Felipe decided to allow Señora Domitila Silva y Lepe, the widow of a former provincial governor, to register to vote. Señora Silva y Lepe was one of several women who attempted to register that year, in the hope of

21

taking advantage of an electoral reform passed the previous year. The new law did not expressly include women, but it did not exclude them either; it merely stated that all literate Chileans with sufficient income could vote. As historian Erika Maza (1995: 17) explains, "the [Electoral] Board noted that [Silva y Lepe] met the requirements demanded by the law to vote (she was Chilean and she knew how to read and write), and that she did not fall into any of the categories of individuals who were barred from voting (such as those who were insane or who had been condemned to jail terms of more than three years)." Señora Silva y Lepe's actions aroused considerable controversy, particularly among incumbent legislators. In the next round of electoral law reforms (required to be held every ten years) Congress changed the law to deny women the right to vote: the 1884 electoral reform permitted only male citizens to vote. With this change, Chilean congressmen formalized an understanding of politics as the domain of men.

Nonetheless, male legislators did not uniformly oppose women's suffrage. The pro-Catholic Conservative Party supported giving women the right to vote, while the anticlerical Liberal and Radical parties vehemently opposed it. The Conservative Party represented the views of the Catholic Church and the *latifundistas*, the powerful landowners of Chile's central valley region. Both the Liberal and Radical parties advocated the separation of church and state. The religious-secular cleavage had dominated Chilean politics since these parties formed in 1865 in response to the "sacristan question," a conflict that emerged regarding the jurisdiction of civil courts in church affairs. The Liberals held a majority of seats in Congress throughout this era, but the Conservatives still wielded power by virtue of their ties to the church. Conservatives and clergy encouraged the participation of women in public life and supported equal political rights for women, and beginning in the 1850s Catholic women fought actively against anticlerical reforms. Conservative Party leaders ostensibly believed that allowing women to vote would strengthen their position with regard to the Liberals, a view that reflected strategic concerns more than support for the extension of women's rights per se. Maza (1995) identifies the women who had registered to vote in San Felipe, for example, as "part of a Conservative Party strategy to enhance its electoral base." The anticlericals opposed women's suffrage on these same grounds, for fear of ceding a potential base of support to their opponents, even as they promoted equal rights for women in other arenas. Liberal politicians anticipated that the incorporation of women would shift the balance of power toward the

22

Conservatives. Suffrage for women would have doubled the size of the electorate, introducing considerable uncertainty into already tightly contested elections. Conflicts among male politicians on this issue obviate arguments that explain the relatively late extension of suffrage to Chilean women in terms of traditional gender ideology: men did not uniformly espouse views of women as unfit to vote. Rather, anticlerical opposition and intense electoral competition along the secular-religious divide prevented women's political incorporation from being seriously considered for many decades. As long as the divide between Liberals and Conservatives constituted the primary axis around which politics revolved, women's efforts to gain political enfranchisement remained on hold.

The collapse of the economy in 1910 initiated a slow and rocky process of realignment that fostered women's political mobilization. In 1915, voters' central concerns began to shift away from religion and toward class, precipitating "an incipient leftward movement of the Chilean electorate" (Drake 1978). This marked the beginning of a period of partisan realignment, away from the oligarchic politics of the landed elites in favor of politics centered on conflicts between the bourgeoisie and workers.

Once the religious cleavage began to lose salience, women's issues gained a more prominent place on the political agenda. Women's organizations began to proliferate in the 1910s and 1920s, both Catholic (the League of Chilean Women in 1912 and the Association of Catholic Youth Women in 1921) and secular (the Women's Reading Circle in 1915, the National Women's Council in 1919, and the Civic Feminine Party in 1922) (Verba 1999). Members of Congress introduced women's suffrage bills in 1917 and 1922 and a women's organization lobbied the constitutional commission of 1925 to include a female-suffrage plank in the new charter. These efforts failed, but they sparked debate on the issue in Chilean society (Lavrín 1995). The suffrage issue became eclipsed by the climate of political instability that reigned in the 1920s – the constitutional crisis of 1924–5 and military regime of General Carlos Ibañez del Campo (1925–31). But in 1931, President Ibañez issued a decree-law that permitted property-owning women to vote in municipal elections.

In the presidential elections of 1932, (male) voters distributed their support fairly evenly across the Left, Center, and Right, establishing the "three-thirds" pattern of voting behavior that would continue for decades (Valenzuela and Scully 1997). For the first time, the Left emerged as a contender in the electoral arena (Fernandez 1996: 39). The cementing of this new alignment fueled the formation of autonomous organizations that joined women across the political spectrum. With the return to civilian rule, suffrage was at the top of their agenda. Women's groups lobbied Congress to confirm Ibañez's earlier decree – and to eliminate the property requirement. In 1934, Congress voted to affirm women's right to vote in municipal elections. The new law gave women the right to vote in elections for *regidores* (the equivalent of members of the city council) and *alcaldes* (mayors), as well as to run for these offices. This represented a very limited extension of women's political rights, particularly given that the mayors in large cities (those with more than 100,000 residents) were not elected but rather appointed by the President of the Republic (Klimpel 1962: 116 n. 63). Importantly, the government created separate registries for female voters and established separate polling places for them.

Women's mobilization peaked with the formation of the Popular Front in 1935, a coalition of the Socialists, Communists, and the reformist Radical Party, headed by President Pedro Aguirre Cerda (Antezana-Pernet 1994; Fernandez 1996). Women's participation in politics during this era confirms the argument that parties previously engaged in fierce competition with one another look to women to legitimize the formation of coalitions among them. In the case of the Popular Front, the new alliance included three parties whose relationships with one another had been – and would continue to be – fraught with conflict. Until 1936, the Communists espoused a hard-line, doctrinaire Marxist agenda. The Socialist Party sought to incorporate workers and the middle classes in a "creole" alliance that respected Chile's democratic traditions. The Radicals, on the other hand, represented the middle classes and white collar workers, who had been hesitant to ally with the Left (Drake 1978). These conflicts proved particularly divisive within the Left. As historian Karin Rosemblatt (2000: 34) avers:

Left political parties frequently debated whether the governing coalition actually favored the poor and whether leftist participation in the popular fronts was warranted. Differing positions on this question caused successive ruptures between Communists and Socialist and within the Socialist Party.... Parties, party splinters, movements, and groups participated in and withdrew from the popular fronts often; the coalitions were never monolithic blocs.

Female political entrepreneurs perceived this climate of conflict as an opportune moment to press for gender-specific demands. In 1935, the Movement for the Emancipation of Chilean Women (MEMCh) joined middle-class and working-class women in a broad, cross-partisan coalition.

As Rosemblatt (2000: 100) affirms, "According to [MEMCh founder] Elena Caffarena, MEMCh 'achieved something that, until then, seemed incredible: to see women of all social classes acting together in perfect harmony: white-collar workers alongside doctors, lawyers alongside *campesinas*, *la señora* alongside domestic servants, artists, writers, alongside women of the people.' MEMCh would become the first mass women's organization." In part, MEMCh hoped to take advantage of the progressive political climate to press for the "economic, juridical, biological and political emancipation of women" (Lavrín 1995: 311). At the same time, however, women's demands sometimes conflicted with those of male workers. In one instance, women's organizations united across the political spectrum to lobby against legislation that sought to limit women's rights in the workplace, a bill that would have advantaged male workers at the expense of their female counterparts (Lavrín 1995: 315; see also Rosemblatt 2000). Conflicts between the demands of women's groups and the Popular Front agenda make it difficult to argue that women's mobilization and class mobilization naturally go hand in hand.

MEMCh's political influence waned with the premature death of Popular Front President Pedro Aguirre Cerda in 1941. That same year, María Correa de Irarrazaval, president of the women's division of the Liberal Party, formed the Committee for Women's Rights in an effort to step up pressure for granting women the right to vote. This organization focused exclusively on women's suffrage and incorporated women from a wide array of parties. The discourse of the committee presaged the kinds of arguments that women would make in the context of political opposition several decades later. "At a rally in the Municipal Theater in Santiago in October 1941, Correa de Irarrazaval . . . appealed to the legislators to overcome their 'selfish partisanship' and approve the [suffrage] legislation" (Antezana-Pernet 1994: 172).

World War II galvanized the women's movement once again. In 1942, a larger coalition of women joined together to demand the right to vote (Antezana-Pernet 1994: 173; Rosemblatt 2000: 115). Two organizations that united women across class and partisan lines formed during the War: the Chilean Federation of Feminine Institutions (FECHIF) and the Chilean Women's Party, *Partido Femenino Chileno*. Suffrage organizations frequently framed their demands in terms of women's ability to unite against men's partisan divisiveness. As Women's Party leader María de la Cruz quipped, "men disagree because of ideas; women unite because of their feelings" (cited in Antezana-Pernet 1994: 177; Fernandez 1996: 294).

Rosemblatt (2000: 245) identifies this discursive strategy as part of a historical trajectory:

Because of their long-standing defense of political transparency and the expansion of political rights, women on the Left were particularly well positioned to highlight the value of democratic procedures. Since at least the 1920s, women had organized to oppose electoral fraud. In the countryside, women had denounced political patronage, which led men to forfeit their political independence. In the city and the country they had set up women's groups to patrol polling places on election days.

Ultimately, the passage of women's suffrage proved to be a hollow victory for feminists on the Left. In 1948, Chilean President Gonzalez Videla outlawed the Communist Party in response to Cold War tensions and pressure from the United States. Women's organizations followed suit by expelling Communists from their ranks. When Gonzalez Videla signed the law granting full voting rights to women on January 14, 1949, leading activists in the movement did not even attend the ceremony (Rosemblatt 2000: 248).

The fact that women won the right to vote in several stages in Chile has shaped the political salience of gender in significant and surprising ways. In accord with women's limited voting rights during the 1934 election, the government set up separate polling places for women to prevent them from voting in all the races. Largely for the sake of convenience, men and women continued to vote in separate places even after women won full suffrage rights. Women and men still vote at separate polls today.[1] This practice has reinforced the extent to which people perceive politics as a gendered activity and has contributed to the establishment of women as an important electoral constituency. Chile is one of the few countries in the world where voting data is disaggregated by sex. In addition, a gender gap – a difference between the voting behavior of men and women – has been evident in Chile since 1952 (Figure 2.1). Politicians tend to view women as a crucial group of swing voters and pay particular attention to women in their efforts to get elected. Women's groups and female politicians have sought to capitalize on the gender gap by using it to lobby politicians on behalf of women's issues, both before and after electoral campaigns. Politicians' concern for reelection does not necessarily mean

---

[1] In 1997, a bill to eliminate separate polling places was introduced in the Senate, but was never voted out of committee.

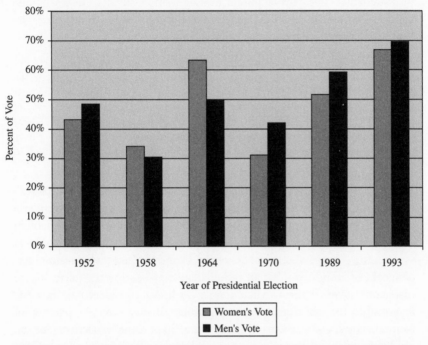

Figure 2.1. Gender Gap in Chilean Presidential Elections (Percent of Female and Male Support for Winning Candidate).

that they will forward women's agenda once in office, however. Chilean women frequently complain that they are "fished" (*pescado*) by politicians at election time – to use the Chilean vernacular – but ignored once the campaign is over.

María de la Cruz: The Chilean Evita?

Women's organizations mobilized to put the vote to work for them in the 1952 presidential elections. The Chilean Women's Party joined with eight other women's organizations to endorse General Carlos Ibañez del Campo the military dictator who had served as president from 1927–31. In endorsing Ibañez, officially an "independent" candidate, the Women's Party sought to enhance its political clout while maintaining an ideological commitment to autonomy from the parties. This position proved to be unsustainable. The party's public message emphasized women's unique approach to politics. In 1951 a declaration published in *El Mercurio*, the leading conservative newspaper, read as follows:

The Chilean Women's Party is made up of independent women who have not wanted to limit themselves by joining the ranks of the parties on the Left and the Right. The party defines itself in terms of a humanitarian ethos (*mística*) that rests upon the interests of women and the Nation, which it seeks to realize by way of politics. Distant from personalism, free from limitations, conscious of the disasters that have resulted from more than a century of partisan politics ... we have decided to support the candidacy of Señor Carlos Ibáñez del Campo (quoted in Klimpel 1962: 137).

Women's Party leader de la Cruz dedicated herself fanatically to Ibáñez's campaign. She made numerous trips up and down the entire country and gave speeches that became known for their "incendiary, passionate, violent and emotional" support for the candidate (Klimpel 1962: 137). De la Cruz's efforts infuriated members of the Women's Party, who accused her of speaking on her own behalf rather than representing the party. These suspicions proved true – when Ibáñez won, he considered de la Cruz responsible for his victory among women. Ibáñez won 43 percent of women's votes, compared to 32 percent and 20 percent respectively for the candidates who finished in second and third place (Figure 2.2). De la Cruz capitalized on Ibáñez's strong showing among women by running for the senate seat vacated by the new president. She also won with an absolute majority, 51 percent of the votes cast.[2]

In endorsing Ibáñez, Chilean women's organizations believed they were advocating a neutral, "antipolitical" candidate. Ibáñez portrayed himself as being independent from the established political parties and removed from the horse trading, politicking, and compromises associated with the party system. Yet many Chileans did not see Ibáñez this way. Many elites feared that Ibáñez was the Chilean version of Juan D. Perón, the populist leader who came to power in Argentina in 1946 with the support of the "the shirt-less ones," as the lower and working classes were called. Just like Perón, Ibáñez was a military leader whose popular support threatened the interests of the oligarchy. Many Chileans viewed María de la Cruz as the

---

[2] Seven months into her term in the Senate, de la Cruz would be subjected to a *declaración de inhabilidad* accusing her of accepting a bribe from a watch manufacturer. The accusation, which appears to have been a pretense for discrediting the senator for her enthusiastic support of the Peronist regime in Argentina, was found to be without merit (Klimpel 1962, 144–7).

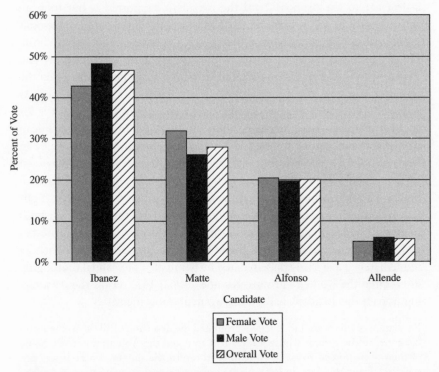

Figure 2.2. Results of 1952 Presidential Election.

Chilean Evita, Perón's powerful and unpredictable wife. As a senator with close ties to Ibañez, de la Cruz threatened conventional gender norms as well as standard practices in the economic and political realms. Thus many Chileans were predisposed to be skeptical about the new government's claims to be "above politics."

Women's groups would soon discover the limits of these claims. Having been handmaidens to Ibañez's victory, women's groups sought to convert their electoral capital into policy outcomes. They pressured the new president to implement their agenda. Yet the requirements of political engagement conflicted with women's claims to approach politics from a moral high ground and ultimately caused the women's movement to collapse. One of the women involved in these efforts was Felicitas Klimpel, a historian and a former leader of the Chilean Women's Party. Klimpel had proposed the creation of an autonomous organization that would include all the women's groups that had supported Ibañez. Women's groups turned a deaf ear to the proposal, and the president supported it but took no action. Early in 1953, however, Ibañez began to take women's proposals more seriously, apparently prompted by his Argentine counterpart Perón. He organized a meeting between Chilean women's organizations and Perón, who was then visiting Chile. At the meeting, Perón discussed the importance of the Argentine Women's Party, which Eva Perón headed. As Klimpel (1962: 147) recalled, Perón "spoke about how important it is for a government to have women solidly unified and invited the Chilean women's organizations to learn more about the great Women's Party in Argentina." After the meeting with Perón, two Argentine congresswomen invited seven leaders of Chilean women's groups (including Klimpel) to lunch. The Argentines presented the Chilean women with a check, a gift that was to remain secret – ostensibly a bribe to get the women's groups to give up their independence and formally join Ibañez. Klimpel protested and left the meeting in disgust. News of this exchange reached the media immediately, most likely disseminated by Klimpel. The scandal thoroughly discredited the women's groups. Klimpel (1962: 147) recalls the devastating impact this incident had on the women's movement:

Revelation of this event immediately prompted the desertion of all the women who belonged to the groups whose leaders had accepted the Argentine money. Some of them were forced to go to Argentina to return the money, where it was not accepted. From this date, in 1953, all the organizations that had participated in the Ibañez campaign disbanded completely. The women understood that they lacked the political maturity to engage in politics, and if divisions and conflicts were common among the country's political parties, the women were not disposed to participate in the same way.

Thus, within a year after the first Presidential election in which women could vote, women's organizations had demobilized in response to public humiliation. These charges of corruption came at a fragile moment, when the public was watching closely to see how women's participation in the political arena would unfold. Women's first venture into national electoral politics left them badly burned. Corruption was probably not uncommon among male politicians in Chile during this era. But women's claims to eschew the "dirty business" of politics made them vulnerable to public scrutiny on these grounds. Women's missteps, however small they may have been in comparison to men's, forced the autonomous women's organizations to disband. Their demobilization provided an opportunity for the political parties to build support among women. As Klimpel (1962: 147) observes:

The government and the masculine parties gained considerable advantage from women's sad experience. The government, in no longer having to promote opportunities for women, and the parties, in criticizing women's organizations and swelling their ranks with women who now totally doubted their capacity to organize themselves independently.

The parties would monopolize women's mobilization for the next two decades, until the next major realignment in 1971.

In supporting Ibañez, women's groups made strange bedfellows. They ended up being caught *in flagrante delicto*, engaging in the very kinds of political acts that they had condemned, in fact, upon which they had staked their legitimacy. To a certain extent, the alliances women's organizations made with General Ibañez foreshadow the links that would emerge between women and General Pinochet after the 1973 coup. Both Ibañez and Pinochet identified themselves as political outsiders and justified their ascent to power as an effort to undo the putative damage inflicted by civilian politicians and political parties. Both sought to "eliminate" the corrupting influence of party politicking, a phenomenon that Loveman and Davies (1997) refer to as "the politics of antipolitics." Moreover, both men sought to incorporate women as allies in their project, capitalizing on women's identity as political outsiders. Despite the setback that women faced in 1953, radical changes were brewing that would revive women's efforts to claim an autonomous political voice.

Women's participation in the parties has been channeled through gender-specific mechanisms. In the 1930s, parties established separate divisions for women, *departamentos femeninos*, in an effort to court women's votes. In the 1960s, the Christian Democratic Party (PDc), for example, had a women's division as well as separate divisions for labor, peasants, the poor, and youth. These departments sought to enhance the strength of the party among these constituencies by means of gifts and patronage. The parties depended on the divisions for mass mobilization in support of policy and during electoral campaigns, yet they also functioned as pressure groups within the party. Variation in the degree of influence that the divisions enjoyed reflected the party's priorities, the level of competition with other parties for voters within that particular sector, and the ability of division leaders to mobilize adherents and press for demands (Yocelevsky 1987: 280).

The women's divisions have proved advantageous to women in certain respects, but have also limited women's ability to attain central decision-making posts within the parties. Male party leaders often assume that their

31

female counterparts belong in the women's divisions, rather than on the political committees of the parties, where key decisions about policy are made (Frei 1994). Women's ability to rise to leadership positions has depended largely on their ability to mobilize women through the women's divisions and to use them as interest groups to bargain within the parties. As a result, women have stood to gain less by conforming to party discipline than men. Female party leaders face institutional incentives to adopt an "outsider" strategy of mobilizing women as nonpartisans. This strategy consistently allows women a voice in political decisions that they would not otherwise have. However, male party leaders still wield control over candidate nominations and advancement within the party. If female party leaders stray too far from the wishes of the party leadership, they can be punished. Party leaders typically use their ability to control the future careers of their more active members "in order to control the more extreme factions within the party," for example (Yocelevsky 1987: 282 n. 3).

Female candidates for political office have shown themselves to be quite resilient in using the women's divisions for their own purposes, in ways that the men who created them may not have envisioned. The separate units have provided female candidates with an opportunity to galvanize women's votes in ways less readily available to men. While male party leaders have viewed the women's divisions primarily as a way to mobilize female voters at election time, female party leaders relied upon them as a source of leverage to develop personal constituencies, promote women's issues, and advance their own careers within the party. Women who aspired to run for office found in these divisions a natural base of support.

The Cuban Revolution and Women in the Sixties

The dramatic changes that occurred in Chile during the 1960s swept through every arena of society, spurring both revolution and reaction in the political system; the Catholic Church; schools and universities; and families. Women responded to these changes in diverse ways. Many middle- and upper-class housewives opposed leftist politics on the grounds that it threatened the family and the church, two of the main institutions of Chilean society and the two that most directly affected women's lives. Women in the younger generation, especially students, embraced the climate of radicalism and became active participants in leftist politics. Women's involvement in the anti-Allende and anti-Pinochet movements can be traced to the way in which women were affected by a series of events that took place in the 1960s, particularly the Cuban Revolution, Vatican II, the rise of the centrist PDC, and the student protests.[3]

In Chile, as in much of Latin America, the sixties really began on January 1, 1959, as Fidel Castro marched into Havana with his revolutionary army. The Cuban Revolution sent shockwaves around the world and fundamentally reconfigured the global political landscape. The success of an indigenous revolutionary regime prompted Castro's supporters and opponents throughout the region to reevaluate the potential for revolution and shift their strategies accordingly. Although Marxism had been an active political force in Latin America since well before the Russian Revolution, the Cuban Revolution ushered in a new political era. For the revolutionary left, this era was one of hope; for the anticommunist right, it was one of fear. Castro's success provided concrete evidence that the leftist goals of a socialized economy and autonomy from the United States were attainable in Latin America, but also strengthened the view that the Left need not pursue an electoral route to socialism (Boeninger 1998: 133). This gave a new lease on life to leftist advocates of revolutionary violence (Halperin 1965). As scholar Jorge Castañeda (1993: 68) observes, "Before Fidel entered Havana, the left in Latin America was reformist, gradualist, or resignedly pessimistic about the prospects for revolution. For the three decades that followed, revolution was at the top of its agenda." Those on the Center and the Right, as well as the U.S. government, sought to prevent revolution while the Left sought to foment it. Although the Cuban Revolution did not, in the end, set off a wave of Latin American revolutions, it drew women into the political arena in new ways and in unprecedented numbers, both for and against radical change.

The U.S. government responded swiftly to the threat of revolution in the region with the Alliance for Progress, a program that sought to promote democracy by spurring economic growth, boosting education, and redistributing income. Chile, with its "long history of democracy and a tradition of social reform going back to the 1920s," was to be the "showcase" for Kennedy's new program (Sigmund 1993: 15). The Alliance for Progress failed to achieve its objectives, but the U.S. government sustained its commitment to Cold War politics by providing massive funding to reformist elements in the Chilean government – $720 million between 1961 and 1970 (Collier and Sater 1996: 310). These transfers funded the

---

[3] See Katherine Hite (2000) for a captivating biographical analysis of the revolutionary generation that emerged in Chile in the 1960s.

development of new programs, electoral campaigns, and a score of miscellaneous covert operations. U.S. aid provided a substantial boost to the efforts of reformers and anti-Marxist forces in Chile, efforts that they would direct partly toward building a base of support among women (Power 1996).

The Catholic Church and Vatican II

The Catholic Church responded to the radicalized climate in Latin America by shifting its attention from the wealthy elites to the poor and working classes in the third world (but see Gill 1998). Chilean Church officials toed the Vatican line and espoused a consistently anticommunist position up until the mid-1960s. In 1962, for example, the Chilean bishops issued a series of pastoral letters that called for major structural reforms, but condemned Marxism in unequivocal terms. The church highlighted the threat that Marxism posed to the family and especially to women's role within the family. As one of the pastoral letters read: "Communism deprives man of his liberty, suppresses all dignity and morality of the human person; it denies to the individual all natural rights ... [and] destroys any bond between mother and child" (cited in Smith 1982: 111). The church's focus on women reflected women's involvement in decades of struggle against anticlerical forces.

By the mid-1960s, however, the official church hierarchy had become more committed to progressive social change and more tolerant of Marxism, largely because of a series of reforms in church doctrine agreed upon by the Second Vatican Council between 1962 and 1965. Vatican II had a tremendous impact in Latin America because of the extreme economic inequalities there relative to other regions of the world (Mainwaring and Wilde 1989). In Chile, Vatican II prompted the PDC to embrace progressive ideas about political and economic development and to extend its base of support among poor and working-class people (Levine 1980: 23).

Many Chileans became involved in Catholic Action, a Vatican-sponsored organization of laymen and laywomen dedicated to promoting Catholic social doctrine. The focus of Catholic Action groups "included spiritual guidance, discussion of strategies for economic and social reform, and service work in factories, coal mines, and rural and urban working-class areas" (Smith 1982: 115). Many of the women who participated in women's movements, both against Allende and against Pinochet, had been members of Catholic Action. Coty Silva, who in 1980 would become a leader of a working-class feminist organization, began her career in public service in Catholic Action. Fanny Pollarolo, a feminist leader and leftist party activist, had a similar background. As a teenager in the early 1960s, she served as president of her local Catholic Action chapter. In her case, however, Catholic Action was affiliated with a conservative parish. "The priest [in our parish] dissolved Catholic Action because we were proposing social change activities (like visiting old people). This unleashed the beginning of a process within me, because it made me identify with a Left that I didn't yet really know anything about. When I entered medical school, I quickly identified with the Left as my principal reference group," Pollarolo recalled (quoted in Hola and Pischedda 1993: 198). In the early 1960s, Catholic Action closely allied with the PDC. When President Frei was elected, he recruited hundreds of its members to work in his administration. In the late 1960s, Catholic Action split into two factions over disputes regarding implementation of the Vatican II reforms.

While the official church softened its opposition to communism, reactionary movements within the church retrenched anti-Marxist views. Anticommunist rhetoric found expression in conservative Catholic groups such as Tradition, Family and Property, and Fiducia (Smith 1982: 146). These groups viewed the church's progressive turn "as a betrayal of the religion they were brought up to honor, revere and defend. . . . The most notable aspect of their social doctrine is a belief in the absolute sanctity of private property, combined with a healthy appreciation for the virtues of social inequality" (Levine 1980: 32). Members of these groups would become foot soldiers in the internal war against Allende in the early 1970s.

The Fear Campaign and the 1964 Presidential Election

The presidential election of 1964 brought the battle between the revolutionary possibilities of the leftist parties and the worst fears of the Right to a head, while paving the way for the victory of the centrist Christian Democratic candidate, Eduardo Frei. Salvador Allende ran as the leftist candidate under the banner of the Popular Action Front (FRAP), a coalition that included the Socialist Party, the Communist Party, and the National Democratic Party. FRAP promoted a revolutionary agenda at the same time that it sought to play down its admiration for the Cuban model, in light of popular disaffection with the increasingly totalitarian path along which the revolution had progressed. As Halperin (1965: 215) affirms,

"The press reports of economic failure and political oppression [in Cuba] found more and more credence with the Chilean public, and by 1964 Cuba no longer served as a shining example but had actually become a source of embarrassment for the FRAP propagandists." Radical Party candidate Julio Durán promoted economic liberalism and represented the right end of the spectrum. His candidacy was largely a token gesture; most rightist voters supported Frei in the hope of defeating Allende. The centrist Christian Democrats espoused a more moderate version of the Left's progressive agenda, free from the taint of Marxism. Dismissing FRAP's attempts to distance itself from Castro, the center-right parties launched a media campaign known as the fear campaign (*campaña del terror*) that hammered home negative images of Cuba and the Soviet Union. During the fear campaign, these two parties

deluged [the country] with posters, pamphlets, newspaper articles, and radio programs warning the Chilean people that an Allende victory would mean the end of democracy, the installation of a dictatorship, and the reduction of Chile to the status of a Soviet satellite (Halperin 1965: 217).

The conservative media, political parties, the Catholic Church, and the U.S. government all contributed to the effort to discredit the revolutionary left. Women formed a new organization called Women's Action of Chile specifically to organize women against the Left. As historian Margaret Power (1996: 46) affirms, "it is no coincidence that the vice president of Acción Nacional de Mujeres, Elena Larraín, later founded Feminine Power (El Poder Femenino), the women's organization that spearheaded female opposition to Allende." With generous funding from the U.S. Central Intelligence Agency (CIA), these groups broadcast radio broadcasts – as many as one every twenty seconds – and television spots and distributed thousands of posters *per day* throughout the country (Power 1996). Later, during the 1970 presidential election, the Chilean House of Deputies held a hearing to examine charges of electoral impropriety on behalf of Women's Action.

The campaign graphically portrayed the threat that communism posed to family life, especially to women and children. In one of the most widely remembered maneuvers staged to drive home this point, Fidel Castro's sister, Juana, visited Chile to alert people to the harm that communist rule had brought to Cuba. In a radio broadcast aired illegally the night before the elections, she warned, "Chilean mother, I know you will not allow your children to be taken from you and sent to the Communist Bloc, like they

36

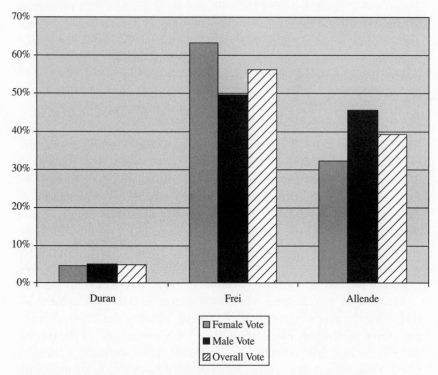

Figure 2.3. Results of 1964 Presidential Election.

do in Cuba" (quoted in Sigmund 1977: 35).[4] The tone of the fear campaign was shrill, insistent, even hysterical. The organizers of the fear campaign drew upon the experiences of the women who mobilized against President João Goulart in Brazil in the early 1960s (Hall 1964; Dulles 1970).

The fear campaign served the Christian Democrats well. They swept the election, winning 55.7 percent of the vote. Allende came in second with 38.6 percent and Durán garnered a mere 5 percent. The results were even more dramatic among women: 63.1 percent of women voted for Frei (compared with 49.6 percent of men) and 32 percent of women voted for Allende (compared with 45.1 percent of men). Even in poor and working-class districts, a majority of women voted for Frei (Power 1996: 69) (Figure 2.3). The results of the congressional elections, held a few months later in

---

[4] Campaigning during the two days prior to an election is illegal in Chile.

March 1965, confirmed the PDC's victory: the party won 42.3 percent of the vote which translated into 82 of the 147 seats in the House of Deputies and 21 seats in the Senate. These vote shares represented a significant increase from the previous congressional elections in 1961 – although the party did not control a majority in either house.

President Frei and the Revolution in Liberty

The Frei government (1964–70) embraced progressive reform in an effort to stem the tide of Marxism. The PDC had long envisioned a "third way" of development between capitalism and socialism. President Frei's platform included three main planks toward this goal: partial nationalization of industry; the mobilization of rural peasants and urban migrants; and agrarian reform. These policies affected men and women differently and promoted the widespread mobilization of women, both intentionally and indirectly. The networks that women formed during this period would later feed directly into women's protests both for and against Allende.

Frei sought to enhance Chile's control over its own development by increasing the role of the state in the copper industry, the country's leading source of revenue. Frei supported the "Chileanization" of the copper industry rather than complete and outright nationalization of foreign firms. The idea was to increase Chile's share of revenues while limiting its responsibility for production costs. The Chilean government purchased a 51 percent share of the North American–owned copper mines. The Braden and Kennecott companies welcomed Frei's proposal. They continued to manage the mines but profited handsomely from the additional investment provided by the Chilean government (Klubock 1998: 277). Ironically, this arrangement had the unintended consequence of radicalizing many of the men and women in many of Chile's mining communities, who joined the Left in demanding complete nationalization of the mines. Copper workers struck frequently throughout the 1960s and became the strongest sector of the labor movement (Klubock 1998: 277). The strikes in turn fueled militant resistance among the miners' wives: "women organized *ollas comunes* [soup kitchens], formed women's committees, attended union meetings, marched with their husbands from the mine to Rancagua and Santiago during strikes, and voted for the Left" (Klubock 1998: 277, 280). Yet women's role in these struggles did little to erode the patriarchal culture of life in the mining communities; on the contrary, union militancy reinforced conventional patterns of gender relations (Klubock 1998: 281). When Allende became president, patterns of gender relations within mining households would prove stable, but miners' allegiance to the Left would not. A strike organized by miners and their wives in 1973 would pose a formidable threat to the socialist government.

President Frei also sought to mobilize women directly. The government created programs to enhance the political participation of previously disenfranchised groups such as women, peasants, and youth, known as "Popular Promotion." Through Popular Promotion, the government mobilized hundreds of thousands of people who had never before participated in politics and formed thousands of grass roots community organizations, particularly the mothers' centers (*centros de madres*) and the neighborhood committees (*juntas de vecinos*). Looking back on the achievements of this program in his 1970 address to Congress, President Frei claimed to have created 20,000 organizations, including "3,000 neighborhood committees, 6,000 mothers' centers and 6,000 sporting clubs" as well as community leadership training courses for 7,000 people (Faúndez 1988: 152). An estimated 450,000 women participated in the mothers' centers, where they learned basic domestic skills such as sewing, crafts, and home management (Valdés and Weinstein 1989). This figure represents well over half the number of women who had voted for Frei in 1964 – 756,117. A policy of forwarding credits to the mothers' centers allowed them to purchase 70,000 sewing machines. Frei's efforts to make Popular Promotion a permanent feature of government met with strong opposition in Congress. The government's opponents on the Right and the Left viewed the program as a huge political machine and refused to support it (Sigmund 1977: 69). Nonetheless, Frei used discretionary funds to build it anyway.

Popular Promotion targeted those in rural areas as well as the hundreds of thousands of people who had migrated to Santiago and now lived in shantytowns that ringed the capital city. Initially, people called these communities *callampas* because they sprang up like mushrooms; they later became known as *poblaciones*. The Christian Democratic government sought to mobilize poor people within the communities where they lived rather than in the workplace. The party's focus on neighborhoods and households contributed to the party's success in mobilizing women. One Christian Democratic leader, interviewed in 1973, described the logic behind this strategy:

The very same workers who behave one way in the union, are forced to act differently in the *población* and their political consciousness in the union is weakened in the residential context (quoted in Bello 1975: 312).

This strategy also allowed the party to capitalize on women's central role in shantytown life. As the PDC leader further observed:

The presence of the female [in the *población*] is fundamental. She is the one who stays the whole day in the *población* and definitely is the one who sways the man in the joint decisions they make (quoted in Bello 1975: 312).

Popular Promotion focused on the domestic realm, and on the specific role that women occupied within that realm. While women's participation in this program tended to reinforce traditional gender roles, it also enabled women to develop leadership skills and to learn how to organize at the grass roots level. Many of the women who would become active in the opposition to Allende got their start in these organizations. Under Frei, the women's division of the PDC developed strong ties with the mothers' centers, especially in poor and rural areas, and funneled generous financial support from the government to them (Yocelevsky 1987). These organizations also formed in well-off areas in Santiago. The mothers' centers and the neighborhood committees in Las Condes, one of the wealthiest districts in the city, became the unofficial headquarters of the anti-Allende movement in the early 1970s.

Similar to the Popular Promotion program, agrarian reform indirectly fostered the mobilization of women in ways that mitigated against women's economic self-sufficiency. The program of agrarian reform initiated by President Frei aimed to increase agricultural productivity and to reduce disparities of wealth between large landowners and landless peasants. Frei sought to carve out a "third way" of development with this reform as with others:

While carefully praising the entrepreneurial initiative of some large growers, Frei condemned the under-utilization of agricultural property and warned Chile's land-owning elite that only efficient producers would be protected from expropriation measures. Increased productivity and an expanded sector of small and medium sized farms were to be the means by which Chile became agriculturally self-sufficient and by which the rural majority were lifted out of poverty (Tinsman 1996: 158).

By breaking up large farms and redistributing them among rural peasants, Frei hoped to create 100,000 new proprietors (Faúndez 1988). Congress did not pass the Agrarian Reform Act until 1967, several years after Frei took office, due to discrepancies among legislators over the extent and timing of the reforms. The new law stipulated that all holdings of more than 80 basic irrigated hectares (about 200 acres) would be divided up. The original landowners could reserve eighty hectares for their own use. The government sought to support the reform by fostering unionization among agricultural workers. Prior to Frei's election in 1964, fewer than 2,000 farmworkers belonged to unions; by 1970, this figure had risen to 114,000, or 30 percent of all agricultural workers (Faúndez 1988). By the end of Frei's term in office, nearly 15 percent of all agricultural land had been expropriated, creating approximately 30,000 new landowners, but the small size of the parcels earned this policy the moniker of "the flower pot reform" (*reforma de los maceteros*) (Kaufman 1972; Loveman 1976; Oppenheim 1999).

By giving property to those who had none, agrarian reform intended to restructure the balance of power between the lower and upper sectors of society, thus contributing to social stability and stemming the potential for revolution. But it actually had the opposite effect: many peasants took land reform into their own hands by seizing plots, which created a climate of violence in the countryside. Moreover, agrarian reform restructured the balance of power within the households of the rural poor and weakened the position of women, something that few people recognized or acknowledged at the time. Before the reform, many women had earned salaries as domestic employees and workers on the haciendas. Not only did agrarian reform put the deeds to rural land in the hands of male heads of households, but it reduced women's work to the status of "unpaid household help" within rural households in the lower sectors (Tinsman 1996). Agrarian reform thus exacerbated gender stratification within the households of the program's beneficiaries (Valdés, Rebolledo et al. 1995).

In the end, Frei's economic and social policies worked against one another. In the economic arena, the government reduced poverty in real terms and increased economic growth (e.g., copper production doubled), but these increases proved insufficient to satisfy the demands of newly enfranchised groups. Moderate successes provoked urgent demands from the lower sectors of society and put the upper classes into a defensive posture. As historian Brian Loveman (1988: 288) writes, "More than any other government program, official encouragement and other subsidization of the formation of thousands of organizations among Chile's urban and rural poor . . . upset the equilibrium of Chilean society." Instead of moderating demands for social change, Frei's policies exacerbated conflicts

41

between the Left, who viewed the pace of reform as too shallow and too slow, and the Right, who condemned the reforms as being too much too fast. Conflicts within the PDC hardened, and three factions became apparent: the *oficialistas* or *freistas* supported the government's program, the *rebeldes* wanted to increase the scope of reforms and the *terceristas* sought a compromise between the other two factions (Collier and Sater 1996: 312). The party leadership struggled to appease these different constituencies and hold the party together, which resulted in inconsistent policies. "The government sometimes did and sometimes did not call in police to squelch illegal rural conflicts, strikes . . . or land occupations," for example (Loveman 1988: 288). In 1967, the two progressive factions won control of the party leadership, but their ascendence to power was not enough to prevent the youth division of the party from defecting. Christian Democratic youth formed their own party the Movement (MAPU) for United Popular Action, in response to the massacre of eight squatters at the hands of Chilean police in Puerto Montt (Collier and Sater 1996: 325).

Meanwhile, support for the Left continued to grow. In 1965, a new party formed on the extreme left – the Movement of the Revolutionary Left (MIR). Unlike the other leftist parties, the MIR was a Guevarist party that embraced insurrection and eschewed elections. Between 1968 and 1970, the MIR staged numerous bombings, bank robberies, and airplane hijackings (Collier and Sater 1996: 324). These violent actions, combined with hundreds of strikes and land seizures each year, created a climate of instability that proved intolerable to the upper classes. Many on the Right developed a deep antipathy for the Christian Democrats and for democracy in general as a result of the Frei government's efforts to mobilize the peasantry and of its tolerance of illegal land seizures (Boeninger 1998: 139). The Liberal and Conservative parties responded by merging to form the National Party in 1966.

The Student Movement and Youth Culture

Young Chileans experienced the radical changes of the late 1960s along with their peers in the rest of the world as hippie culture began to percolate throughout Chile. Teenagers broke with the generation before them to an unprecedented degree, redefining themselves in terms of dress, music, and attitude and challenging the mores of traditional Catholic families. The generational divide that opened up cut across class boundaries and political affiliations. Chilean teenagers discovered marijuana and listened to Bob Dylan, Jimi Hendrix, and the Beatles, but they also embraced folk music based on traditions from the Andean region. The "New Song" movement, known as *Nueva Canción*, represented an indigenous response to Western rock and roll. The artists included Victor Jara, Violeta Parra, Quilapayún, and Inti-Illimani. People believed that revolution, the complete transformation of society, and the end of all forms of inequality and oppression, were imminent. As Sergio Martínez, a leader in the Communist Youth, recalled:

We were true believers, that history was really marching toward a luminous future ... We believed in a future in which, like it said in *The Internationale*, the earth would be a paradise (Martínez 1996: 13).

Parents viewed these changes with deep concern. Many equated the new youth culture with the depredations of Marxism and the destruction of the family.

Being a university student in the late 1960s proved an intensely politicizing experience for many, regardless of one's political views. Adriana Muñoz, a leader in the Socialist Party and feminist activist, described what it was like to be involved in leftist politics at that time:

It was part of the environment in which we lived. [The University of Chile was] "the school of Revolutionary Sociology." We had great professors: Clodomiro Almeyda, [Andre] Gunder Frank, Theotonio Dos Santos, all the Latin American social science intellectuals who had come to Chile to escape military coups elsewhere. . . . It was the time of Allende, of social movement, of Cuba (quoted in Hola and Pischedda 1993: 173).

Soledad Larraín, another activist and Socialist leader, entered the Catholic University to study psychology in 1966. "At the Catholic University, during the time of the University Reforms, in the school of psychology, everybody was a leftist," she recalled (quoted in Hola and Pischedda 1993: 159). Even Soledad Alvear, a lawyer and leader of the PDC who would become a prominent government minister in the 1990s, describes her student days in similar terms: "I entered the University [of Chile] at a moment of terrific student effervescence, because of the university reform and the extremist movements" (quoted in Hola and Pischedda 1993: 136).

The reforms Alvear describes took place in September 1967, when students at the University of Chile took over the campus (Jaksic 1989: 143). They demanded socially conscious courses, financial support for working-class students, and greater student and faculty input in university affairs

43

(Martínez 1996: 64). The students readily won concessions: the dean resigned and academic departments held representative elections. Within a few days, students at the Catholic University followed suit (Smith 1982: 138). The student takeovers fueled the mobilization of students on the Left *and* the Right. Jaime Guzmán, a law student at the Catholic University, started a movement that sought to eliminate the influence of political parties over university affairs. The movement called for parties to be replaced by corporatist guilds (*gremios*) organized according to occupation that would pursue the common good defined by the state. The student movements of the late 1960s were seminal in the formation of today's political leaders on all points in the spectrum: Left, Right, and Center.

The women who entered college in the late 1960s represented a new generation, the first generation of women who expected to pursue careers as a matter of course, in addition to (not in lieu of) getting married and raising families. This entailed a fundamental break with traditional conceptions of women's roles in society (Mattelart and Mattelart 1968). However, women were still perceived in traditional ways despite these changes. In college, for example, women joined revolutionary movements that promised an end to all forms of inequality, but they participated alongside university traditions that celebrated women as beauty queens. Campus newspapers heralded annual elections for the *reina mechona* of the university with prominently placed photographs of attractive young women. As yet, however, men and women experienced these transformations with little awareness of the significance of gender differences. Only later would the contradictions between the revolutionary rhetoric and patriarchal practices of the Left fuel the formation of feminist consciousness.

Conclusion

Chilean feminist scholar Julieta Kirkwood (1986) characterizes the period from 1953 to 1970 as one of "feminist silence" characterized by the dissolution of women's organizations and partisan control of women's issues. Once Chilean women got the vote, women's organizations retreated from politics. I account for the rise and fall of activism among women in terms of changes in the opportunities afforded to women's organizations by a transformation of the issues represented within the party system. The inception of a cross-partisan women's movement in Chile coincided with a period of realignment that shifted the primary cleavage among the political parties from religion to class. The strength of women's organizations derived from their claims to represent a new way of doing politics, one that juxtaposed women's ability to unite against men's proclivity to bicker over narrow partisan interests. Women's organizations capitalized on the climate of cross-partisan cooperation that characterized the Popular Front era in the 1930s and 1940s. Their ability to influence elites and mobilize grass roots support weakened once they became associated with a particular political tendency. This occurred in 1941 with the death of Popular Front President Aguirre Cerda and again in 1953 when women's organizations became discredited for their shady involvement in the Ibañez administration. As a result, leaders of women's organizations abandoned their efforts to organize autonomously and the movement declined. These events seemed to confirm a widely held view that women were not ready to engage in politics.

The events of the 1960s set the stage for the reemergence of women's mobilization in the 1970s and 1980s. The Cuban Revolution polarized Chilean society and drew women into political life. On the one hand, women became a key target audience for anticommunist rhetoric, which portrayed communism as threatening children, educational freedom, and the safety of church and home, issues commonly recognized as women's domain. Gender became a critical component of the way in which the Cold War was fought (Enloe 1993). Framing the war against communism in terms of women's concerns presaged the role that women would play in mobilizing against Allende, and, later, in supporting the military dictatorship. On the other hand, the revolutionary happenings of the sixties prompted many women to join the Left. They embraced the climate of protest sweeping university campuses and Catholic parishes. From this community of radical women would come the leaders of the feminist movement in the late 1970s.

PART ONE

Women Against Allende

3

The Revolution Hits Home

WOMEN ORGANIZE
AGAINST ALLENDE

The status of women in Chile during the 1960s resembled that of women around the world in terms of the degree to which women became involved in politics. But in 1970, women's activism in Chile diverged dramatically from what was happening elsewhere. Women began to mobilize in Chile that year, but not along feminist lines. In Chile, conservative women mobilized on the basis of their gender identity well before their counterparts on the Left. Immediately after Salvador Allende won the presidential election in 1970, a small group of women from conservative political parties organized a series of protests aimed at mobilizing female opposition to Allende. They believed that Allende's victory had precipitated the formation of an alliance among the opposition parties and saw the moment as a propitious one for women's mobilization. However, their perceptions about the possibility of a realignment among the parties proved to be wrong. As a result, their efforts failed to ignite popular support and had little political impact.

While the opposition parties did not form a unified coalition against Allende during this initial period, their positions gradually converged over the course of Allende's first year in office. The centrist Christian Democrats and the right-wing National Party moved closer together, largely in reaction to the new government's success in implementing socialist reforms and consolidating popular support. Opposition groups began to mobilize in response to changing conditions and increasing threats from the Allende regime. By the fall of 1971, the opposition had shifted to the right and the main opposition parties – the Christian Democrats and the National Party – were poised to form a new coalition with one another. These conditions would prompt female opposition leaders to make another attempt at galvanizing a mass movement.

The 1970 Presidential Election

Three candidates competed for the presidency in the 1970 election. Salvador Allende, a member of the Socialist Party, ran as the candidate of a coalition of six leftist parties known as the Popular Unity (Unidad Popular [UP]): the Socialist Party, the Communist Party, the Radical Party, the Movement for United Popular Action (MAPU), the Independent Popular Action Party, and the Social Democratic Party. Allende campaigned on the promise of pursuing a "peaceful road to socialism." His agenda included the creation of a unicameral legislature, radical redistribution of income, expansion of state services, greater nationalization of private industry, and intensification of agrarian reform, as well as the mass participation of workers and peasants in the policy-making process. Radomiro Tomic represented the centrist Christian Democratic Party (PDC) and forwarded a platform virtually identical to Allende's. Tomic hoped to capitalize on popular demands for progressive reform under the more moderate identity of the Christian Democrats. National Party candidate Jorge Alessandri represented the conservative end of the political spectrum. His constituents – landowners, businessmen, and middle-class bourgeoisie – advocated maintaining a capitalist economic system (Oppenheim 1999: 36).

Alessandri's campaign echoed the 1964 fear campaign to the extent that it focused on the dangers of communism and the threats that communism posed to women and children. Women's Action of Chile, the same group responsible for the fear campaign during the 1964 presidential election, took out a series of ads warning women not to vote for Allende. One ad in *El Mercurio* (August 1, 1970) read "Where is Daddy?" in bold headlines, above a photograph of a mother and her young son. It continued:

In many communist countries, this question has no answer. Hundreds of men have been seized from their homes and are in jail, concentration camps or disappeared for having criticized the government.

Leaders of Women's Action frequently framed anticommunist rhetoric in terms of opposition to party politicking. In radio spots the group "called on women to elect 'an independent government' and say 'No! to systems that destroy liberty. No! to petty politics that lead us to disaster'" (quoted in Sigmund 1977: 103). However, the Alessandri campaign did not rely exclusively on anticommunism in order to appeal to female voters. The candidate also promised to incorporate women into positions of power within his government. *El Mercurio* (August 1, 1970) published a campaign speech in which Alessandri asserted, "Women will be the base of my administration." Alessandri's female supporters issued an immediate response to this statement. The next day, the women's division of the Alessandri campaign published an ad in *El Mercurio* that sought to hold the candidate accountable to his promises:

> Jorge Alessandri has promised that women will have better opportunities to par-
> ticipate in his government and better security. We [women] demand a place
> working to direct great events in the public interest. Women have a different scale
> of values, different understanding of the priority of public issues and our own cri-
> teria about the importance of events. . . . The words with which Jorge Alessandri
> has encouraged women will not be a vain illusion in his government, because we
> will have a place at the table where decisions are made.

In this statement, rightist women did not portray themselves in conven-
tionally feminine terms, as mothers or denizens of the household sphere.
They explicitly demanded access to political power. They saw the female
vote as a way to exert pressure on Alessandri to permit women to participate in government and to shape the political agenda. They justified their
demands for representation on the grounds that women's substantive
interests differed from those of men.

The UP also courted women's votes. As a final campaign event, on
August 29, 1970, the Allende campaign staged a giant outdoor tea party.
Women gathered in hundreds of locations throughout the country and
sipped tea as Allende addressed them through a national radio broadcast.
The Left also engaged in more aggressive ways of limiting women's
support for the Right. While the 1970 campaign was under way, the
Chilean Congress held hearings to investigate the 1964 fear campaign.
Congress targeted two organizations – Women's Action and Youth Action
– for investigation on the suspicion that they had engaged in political activities that violated their charters as not-for-profit *social* organizations.
Members of Congress alleged that these organizations had received funds
from the U.S. Central Intelligence Agency (CIA), the Anaconda Copper
Company, and well-heeled interests in Chile, charges that would later
prove to be true (United States, Congress 1975). On August 14, 1970,
inspectors from the Ministry of Justice raided the headquarters of
Women's Action in search of evidence of these violations. Articles on the
congressional hearings appeared in the Communist Party paper *El Siglo*

on a daily basis throughout the month before the campaign, often on the front page – despite an apparent lack of new information uncovered in the investigations. The prominence of these hearings in the leftist media affirm that political elites were keenly aware of the stakes involved in courting female voters.

On September 5, 1970, Chile became the first country in the world to elect a Marxist government by democratic means. The presidency was not yet secure, however. Allende had won, but he faced a double minority – among the Chilean people and in Congress. He was elected with only 36.9 percent of the popular vote and his coalition controlled less than 23 percent of the seats in Congress (45 out of 200 in the Chamber of Deputies and the Senate combined). According to the Constitution of 1925, when no candidate receives an absolute majority of votes, Congress must select one of the two top candidates in a runoff within fifty days of the election. The date for the runoff was set for October 24, 1970. Precedent dictated that Congress would confirm Allende as the first-place finisher, but significant opposition threw his ratification into question. Allende's ability to pass muster in the runoff would require him to persuade his opponents to support him. Given the vehemently anti-Marxist stance of the National Party deputies and of some of the Christian Democratic deputies, this would not prove an easy task.

Allende fared worse among female voters than he did among men, confirming the conventional wisdom that women tend to vote more conservatively than men (Sigmund 1977; Kyle and Francis 1978; Chaney 1979). In this election, Allende received only 30 percent of the vote among women overall, compared to 41.6 percent of men's votes (Figure 3.1). Yet women's support for Allende in 1970 represents a 26 percent increase over the percentage of women who voted for Allende in 1952 (Figure 3.2). Allende's support among men rose 36 percent during the same period. Among working-class women, however, his support was substantially higher (Power 1996). The UP went on to increase its support among women during its first six months in office (Kyle and Francis 1978). These data make it difficult to affirm the conventional wisdom that women were the natural constituency of the Right; if this were true, then we should not expect to see women supporting the Left at all, let alone in greater numbers over time.

Among the general public, the outcome of the election prompted three kinds of responses: enthusiasm, ambivalence, and alarm. Leftists everywhere greeted the outcome triumphantly. The election culminated

The Revolution Hits Home

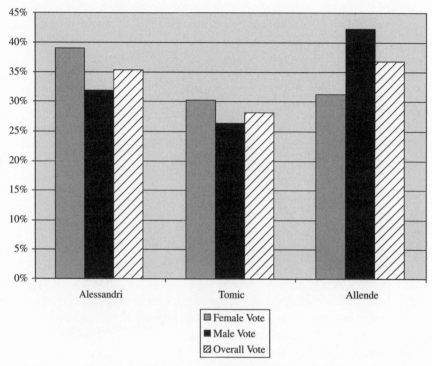

Figure 3.1. Results of 1970 Presidential Election.

Allende's three previous attempts to win control of the executive branch (in 1952, 1958, and 1964). The possibility of implementing a Socialist system without resorting to armed struggle sparked the hopes of those who had become disenchanted with the Left after the death of Che Guevara in 1967 and the Soviet Union's invasion of Czechoslovakia in 1968 (Martínez 1996). Leftist demonstrations grew in size and frequency after the election as followers of the new government confirmed their support.

Others responded to Allende's election with equanimity. Many moderates doubted that Allende's election would significantly disrupt the status quo. Allende was, after all, a career politician who had run for president four times. He was seen as someone who knew how to play by the rules of the political game. As historian Peter Winn (1986: 73) notes, "like LBJ [Lyndon Baines Johnson], Allende enjoyed a reputation as a master political manipulator; even his opponents proclaimed him '*la mejor muñeca que hay*'" ("the best wheeler-dealer there is"). Allende was a member of Chile's

53

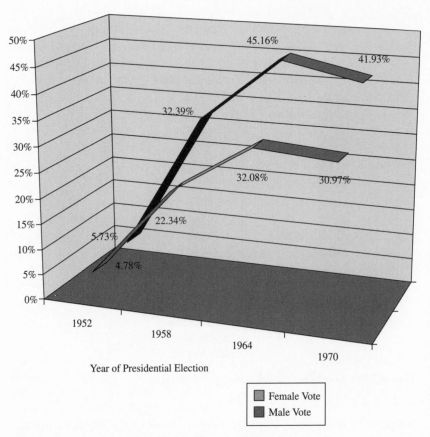

50% ────────────────────────────── 45.16% ─────────────
                                                           41.93%
45% ──
40% ──────────────────────────────────
35% ──────────── 32.39% ──────────
30% ──────────────────────────
25% ──────────────── 32.08%   30.97%
20% ──────────────
15% ────── 22.34%
        5.73%
10% ──
5% ── 4.78%
0%

        1952
                1958
                        1964
                                1970
        Year of Presidential Election

■ Female Vote
■ Male Vote

Figure 3.2.   Support for Salvador Allende, 1952–1970.

privileged elite and his taste for good liquor and fine clothes was well
known. From this perspective, many believed that Allende was unlikely to
foment radical change and predicted that the new government would represent the continuation of politics as usual. As Christian Democratic com-
mentarist Patricio Dooner (1985: 17) recalled, "Manifestations of doubt
and extremism [in the wake of Allende's election] were in the minority.
What dominated was the joy of the UP supporters, the hope of some of
the progressive sectors and a serene but vigilant calm of the majority, who
viewed the Marxist triumph with skepticism."

    For those on the right, however, Allende's election set off a panic.
Many conservatives had already begun to lose faith in the democratic

system in the 1960s, as they watched the Christian Democratic government chip away at property rights and fail in its efforts to curb leftist insurgency. Now democracy had allowed a Marxist take control of the
government. For the upper classes, the seven weeks following the election
were filled with uncertainty and apprehension (Oppenheim 1999: 54).
Several hundred people immediately left the country. Agustín Edwards,
editor of the conservative *El Mercurio* took refuge in New York as the
guest of the chairman of the Pepsi-Cola Corporation (Horne 1972;
Sigmund 1977).

Worries about property rights and potential violence were not the only
factors that motivated those on the Right, however. Allende's election
presented a profound threat to the social status of the upper classes, many
of whom saw in Allende's victory the end of class privilege. It meant
putting power in the hands of the *rotos*, to use the vernacular for the lower
classes.[1] One woman I interviewed revealed that the election of Allende
had a devastating impact on her sense of identity as a member of the upper
class. "If Allende had won, it would have been but really catastrophic, for
all that we represented and all that we wanted in life and had established
in life as principles of the right," she recalled:

One of the most vivid memories I have of [the Allende years] is that the lower
classes, who were like your domestic employees, who had always been submissive
and respectful toward their *patrón*, of all a sudden became insolent and no longer
submissive. They began to try to be your equal. One just wasn't accustomed to
this. These were things that, being very young and a newlywed, twenty-something
years old, made a very big impression on me (L. Silva 1994).

Fear gripped many of Santiago's elite families. Those who lived in the
wealthier neighborhoods of Santiago became convinced that "Marxist
hordes" planned to assault their homes, rob them, and seize their property on behalf of the government. As one woman related:

On two occasions they informed us that the hordes were coming up Providencia
[one of Santiago's main avenues]. On one of these nights I was alone with my son
and the maid . . . Around 11 p.m. I received a call from [a woman] who lived nearby,
inviting me to take refuge in her house. We spent the whole night there, leaving
our house alone. Later we learned that the groups had been dispersed by the police.
In any case, the fear was tremendous (Maturana 1993).

[1] The term *rotos* literally means the broken ones. In the parlance of the privileged, the term
is intensely derogatory. In working-class culture, however, the term has been resignified as
a point of pride.

55

Residents of these neighborhoods patrolled the streets and organized "defense committees" to protect against attack (*Qué Pasa* 1972). Women organized karate classes to prepare themselves in case of personal assault (Correa 1974: 92).

The fear campaign may not have prevented Allende from being elected, but it did provoke considerable anxiety among those who bought into the rhetoric. Both private citizens and the incoming government took numerous measures to allay the alarm set off by Allende's election, especially among women. On September 13, 1970, *El Siglo* reported that a group of women from well-to-do neighborhoods formed a crosspartisan group called the Feminine Unity Committee (Comité Femenino de Unidad) "to establish serenity and calm the spirits of all women, regardless of whom they voted for in the presidential election." The leaders of the organization set up a hotline and published their phone numbers in *El Siglo*. In September, they sponsored meetings at the University of Chile in which women could learn more about the new government's agenda. Leaders of the UP took measures to reassure women that their families would be "safe and protected" under the Allende administration. On September 23, under the headline "the Popular Government represents stability and security for women and children," *El Siglo* published a detailed outline of the government's policies for women, including the text of proposed legislation creating the Ministry of the Family and authorizing the creation of more mothers' centers. Two actresses developed a television show "to inform women what the new society will bring." The title of the show, "De Esto Se Habla" ("this is what we talk about") referred to "Así Se Habla" ("this is what they say"), a prominent feature of anti-Allende campaign propaganda that purported to reveal the Left's agenda of revolutionary violence. Thus, in the very first days after Allende's election, the media focused a considerable amount of attention on women. These measures heightened the political salience of women's concerns about Allende even more than the fear campaign.

As an effort to calm people's fears about the new government, however, these measures had little effect. The Right moved decisively to prevent Allende from taking office. Leaders of the National Party proposed a deal to the PDC in which the two parties would join forces against Allende in the upcoming runoff election. The plan was for the two parties to support Alessandri, the second-place finisher, over Allende. Alessandri would then step down and call for new elections in which former President Eduardo Frei would run on a center-right ticket that both parties would endorse.

Alessandri's brief tenure in office would have satisfied the constitutional prohibition against a president serving two terms. The possibility of an alliance between the Nationals and the Christian Democrats – a potential realignment – presented itself as an opportunity to women.

Women Respond to Allende's Election

The day after the election, a small group of women from the National Party and the PDC decided they had to "do something" to prevent Allende from taking office. They approached the leaders of their respective parties to request permission to hold a protest, but their pleas fell on deaf ears. Male party leaders rejected the idea of a demonstration by women and refused to support them. Anti-Allende activist María. Correa describes this meeting in *Guerra de las Mujeres* (*War of the Women*), her 1974 account of the movement. Approximately thirty women from the Alessandri campaign met with National Party leader Arturo Matte. Correa (1974: 10) recalls the dismissive way that Matte responded to women's concerns about Allende:

The men don't want to learn their lesson. They continue to leave no place for women at the table where decisions are made . . . And look what is happening! There were confused and polite explanations [from the National Party leaders], but they would not change their views, we knew it. What right do they have to hold back the intellectual and spiritual wealth of the Nation, the distinct and complementary contributions of women?

Correa depicts this meeting as symptomatic of women's exclusion from political power. Her views reflect her experiences as a woman with decades of experience in political parties. Correa joined the Liberal Party in 1946, three years before women obtained the right to vote. She helped to form the women's department of the party and served as secretary and later president. In 1957, she was elected to the House of Deputies, where she represented the first district of Santiago. She served one term.[2] When the Liberal and Conservative parties merged to form the National Party in

---

[2] Historian Felicitas Klimpel (1962) notes (somewhat scornfully) that frequent trips abroad punctuated Mrs. Correa's term in Congress: "She participated very little as a parliamentarian because of her marriage to the then Chilean Ambassador to Mexico, Mr. Smitman." Her only recorded activity in the House of Deputies was an amendment to the Commerce Code that allowed female merchants to participate in "collective societies" without their husband's permission.

1966, Correa was a founding member. She served two years on the party's Executive Committee, the first woman to hold such a position in Chile. Her recollections challenge the view of the anti-Allende women as a "ladies' auxiliary" to the opposition. In this instance – and in many more that activists in this movement would describe – women espoused different goals from the men in their party, pursued different strategies, and resented the lack of the support they received from men.

The women decided to protest despite official disapproval. On September 8, approximately thirty women gathered in front of La Moneda, the presidential palace in downtown Santiago. They dressed in black to mourn the death of democracy. "Our mourning was no fiction," Correa (1974: 12) recalls in her book, "it had a profound significance. It was the pain that filled the depths of the national soul." The women sang the national anthem and chanted slogans: "We want liberty," "Chile yes, Cuba no," and "Although we have a fatherland, we must preserve it." Police broke up the protest. Although *El Mercurio* attributed the demonstration to "supporters of the Alessandri campaign," several female leaders from the PDC also took part, including journalist Teresa Donoso. Donoso also wrote a book about the anti-Allende women's movement, *La Epopeya de las Ollas Vacias* (*The Epic of the Empty Pots*).

Two days later, on September 10, women organized a second march. This time they marched from the presidential palace toward the Congress a few blocks away. As the women marched, youth groups from the UP parties attacked them, throwing things and yelling obscenities. As *El Mercurio* reported on September 11, 1970:

About 100 Communist youth accosted and insulted a group of women who carried a Chilean flag and sang the national anthem as they passed through downtown streets after parading in front of the presidential palace. This shameful spectacle unfolded without anyone intervening on behalf of the women. Nonetheless, the women continued their march, although they were subjected to shoving and other rude behavior.

Donoso (1974b: 50) recalls the incident indignantly in her book: "That afternoon marked the first time that ordinary Chilean women were called prostitutes." Scuffles between the women and pro-Allende counterprotesters continued all the way to the doors of the National Congress. Despite these attacks, the women's protests did not provoke public outcry and did not engender a response from the political parties of the opposition. Another demonstration took place that same night: a group of men and women marched toward President Frei's house "to ask that he save Chile from Communism." Police broke up that protest with tear gas. On September 18, approximately 3,000 women gathered to watch the annual military parade, waving little black flags (Correa 1974: 14). The demonstrations continued for several weeks and took on the pattern of a ritual: "the processions continued: silence, national anthem, silence, waving white handkerchiefs, knocking on the heart of the presidential palace" (Donoso 1974b: 49). The women also collected an estimated 20,000 signatures for a petition asking President Frei "not to deliver the country to Communism" (Correa 1974: 17).

Women I interviewed claimed to have initiated these marches on their own. According to their story, they sought party support but did not receive it, so they decided to act alone. They criticized men's behavior. The absence of men in the marches reinforced their beliefs that men were not doing enough to prevent Allende from taking office. "The men are feeling the same thing [we are], but they are too proud to beg as we are doing. Nor can they use resources like [mourning clothes]. They don't have the courage to do the audacious things we are doing now. It's not their way of doing things," Correa writes (1974: 7).

Nonetheless, the women would not remain autonomous from men's organizations for long. They soon joined with the Fatherland and Liberty Civic Movement (Movimiento Cívico Patria y Libertad), a group headed by Pablo Rodríguez Grez, a young lawyer. Rodriguez garnered national attention the night of the presidential election when he expressed his antipathy for Allende on a panel discussion televised by Channel 13, the Catholic University station. A few days later, Rodríguez announced the formation of Fatherland and Liberty, whose goal was to generate popular support for the Alessandri proposal, the alliance of the Christian Democratic and National parliamentarians against Allende in the upcoming runoff. In a speech reported by *El Mercurio* (October 1, 1970) the group maintained that "the Congress . . . must give the people a second election to choose a government with majority support." Their efforts targeted the Christian Democrats. As Rodríguez declared at a rally on October 6: "In name of the 70% [of people who did not vote for Allende], I say to the Christian Democrats . . . you cannot deliver us to totalitarianism. . . . Christian Democrats, know that we are with you." The female protesters joined Fatherland and Liberty for a demonstration called "The Great March of Silence." Media coverage of these events highlighted women's involvement. The newspaper *La Segunda* published an announcement for

59

one of the marches that read, "Chilean woman: if you want to defend liberty, join us in the Great March of Silence." *El Mercurio* portrayed the women as representing national, politically neutral interests over the divisive and violent tactics of the Left. As with previous demonstrations, the march ended with fighting between agitators on the Left and the Right. As one article from October 6, suggestively titled "Women Ratify Their Democratic Vocation," states, "the parade . . . was subject to counter-demonstrations by extremist elements who tried to silence the libertarian voices of the women."

In response to these demonstrations, the incoming government supplanted its previous efforts to calm women's fears with denunciations against the "sedition" of the bourgeoisie. Pro-Allende editorials in *El Siglo* during September and October poked fun at "the widows" and caricatured them as rich housewives with nothing better to do. The government youth division of the UP organized "to protest against the terrorist actions of the ultraright, bullying by the *momias* who refuse to admit that the people (*el pueblo*) triumphed fair and square." Leftists referred to the upper classes as momias, or mummies: relics of the past who are dead to the need for change. Even the National Women's Front of the Popular Unity organized demonstrations "to stop the sedition and demand jail for the right-wing terrorists." Conservative media accounts also ridiculed women's efforts. One editorial cartoon published in *La Segunda* (October 7, 1970) featured a photograph of several men sitting in a living room, each holding a baby on his lap. One of them says, "I sure am getting tired of these women's marches that Pablo Rodríguez has been organizing." The cartoon pokes fun at the reversal of gender roles entailed by men having to stay home while their wives took to the streets in protest, led by the handsome young Rodríguez.

Women protested in the hopes of preventing Allende from being confirmed as president, but their efforts failed to forge a women's movement. Their expectations of success were not unreasonable, given that a majority of women had voted against Allende and that women's concerns were at the forefront of popular consciousness during and after the presidential campaign. Their inability to inspire support can be explained in terms of relations among the opposition parties at the time. The National Party ardently sought to unite the opposition against Allende, but the Christian Democrats remained divided. The conservative faction of the Christian Democrats would have preferred to return Frei to power, but the leftist faction controlled the party leadership and steered the party toward cooperation with Allende. Not surprisingly, the media associated with the National Party publicized women's mobilization far more aggressively than the media controlled by the Christian Democrats. The Nationals highlighted women's efforts in the hopes of generating support for the alliance, but the Christian Democrats did not. Many of the female protesters were members of the PDC, but they represented the conservative factions. My perusal of newspapers from the period confirms this hypothesis. Articles promoting the women's demonstrations figured prominently in *El Mercurio*, the newspaper owned by Alessandri, the presidential candidate of the Nationalist Party. The headlines of these articles hyperbolized women's actions and described them as representing national interests over the partisan concerns: "Women Reclaim Their Democratic Vocation" and "Women Ask For Liberty." *La Prensa*, the Christian Democratic paper, contained no coverage of these marches at all, supporting the view that the party did not wish to enter an alliance with the Right.

While the women marched and Chilean parliamentarians debated Allende's confirmation in Congress, the U.S. government weighed the possibilities of ousting Allende by extralegal means. United States opposition to Allende was already well known by this point. The Nixon administration considered two strategies aimed at preventing Allende's inauguration. Track I involved funding for an anti-Marxist media campaign and persuading Christian Democratic parliamentarians to accept the Alessandri proposal, basically by buying their votes. Track II proposed convincing retired Army General Roberto Viaux to orchestrate a coup. President Nixon ended up favoring covert financial aid to the opposition media and political parties over a coup, but he famously promised to "make the [Chilean] economy scream" by exerting financial pressure on the country.

Although the Nixon administration rejected Track II, the Chileans with whom U.S. government officials had been in contact decided to go ahead with the plan. Two days before Congress voted on Allende's confirmation, when it was apparent that Allende would be confirmed with Christian Democratic support, a group of military officers (including Viaux) and right-wing civilians set out to stage a coup. They had intended to kidnap General René Schneider, then Commander-in-Chief of the Chilean Army, and take him to Argentina, where they would "demand that [President] Frei resign, leave the country and dissolve Congress" (Sigmund 1993: 53). They had hoped to make people think that the kidnapping was the work

61

of leftist terrorists, thus discrediting Allende and prompting the military to intervene (Sigmund 1977; Loveman 1988). Their efforts backfired when Schneider was accidentally killed in the attempt. General Schneider had enjoyed considerable popular support and his assassination enraged public opinion. Schneider had been appointed by President Frei in 1969 in order to restore discipline within the army, in response to an uprising in the Tacna regiment in Santiago (known as the *tacnazo*). The general's commitment to constitutionalism distinguished him from prointerventionist factions within the armed forces. The assassination of General Schneider dealt a debilitating blow to the Right, and kept extremist forces from venturing too far into the public arena for more than a year. It effectively eliminated public support for a "military solution" among all but the most virulent hawks and prevented the formation of an alliance between the Right and the military for nearly two years (Tomic 1979: 232). As a result, public support for Allende rose, paving the way for his Senate confirmation. The Alessandri plan failed despite women's efforts. The Christian Democratic deputies cast their votes for Allende once leftist parliamentarians signed a statement that obligated them to abide by the constitution. This agreement, known as the Statute of Democratic Guarantees, ensured "the free functioning of political parties, trade unions, private education and the mass media and the independence of the armed forces from political control" (Sigmund 1993: 49).

Allende's First Year in Office

During Allende's first year in office, the government successfully implemented a series of dramatic reforms (Sigmund 1977; Valenzuela 1978; Loveman 1988; Collier and Sater 1996; Oppenheim 1999). The gross domestic product rose 8.6 percent, unemployment fell and, by 1971, the UP government had successfully completed two of its main political objectives: "massive redistribution of wealth and increased public support for its program" (Boeninger 1998: 173). The nationalization of North American–owned copper mines enjoyed widespread support because it was framed in terms of national sovereignty. Even the rightist National Party "didn't want or didn't dare" to oppose the government's expropriation of the Kennecott and Anaconda mines "in order to avoid being seen as defending North American interests against a legal national right to control the country's basic resources" (Boeninger 1998: 174). The results of the April 1971 municipal elections confirmed public support for the government's policies. Progovernment candidates won 50 percent of the vote, representing a significant increase over their share of the popular vote in the presidential election. The rationale behind the Left's economic program was to gain control of production and redistribute the profits among the lower and working classes.

By the end of Allende's first year, however, numerous indications of trouble had arisen. Inflation rose precipitously. By December 1971, inflation had been at 119 percent for over a year. It rose to 138 percent during the following year, and 314 percent the year after that (Oppenheim 1999). Slow rates of growth, strikes, shortages, and capital flight created a climate of economic chaos. The nationalization of domestic firms prompted fierce and immediate resistance from the opposition. Nationalizing foreign firms was one thing, but private companies owned by Chileans proved quite another. Formal mechanisms for nationalization stipulated congressional approval and required compensation for the owners. Yet the government applied these terms to very few of the 500 firms nationalized between 1971 and 1973. In all but eight cases, the government simply seized private companies and justified its actions in terms of a defunct 1932 statute that permitted the state to requisition industries in times of national emergency. These seizures came to symbolize the victory of the working class over the bourgeiosie. As Christian Democratic leader Edgardo Boeninger (1998: 179) recalls, "each factory takeover . . . was celebrated by government employees and the parties of the Popular Unity, and sympathetic communications media, as the triumph of the people in the struggle for the conquest of power and socialism." The revolutionary zeal of Allende's supporters enraged the upper classes. Lucía Maturana, a leader of one of the more prominent groups in the anti-Allende movement, recalled what happened when the government took over her husband's electronics business:

They took everything, TVs, radios, tape recorders and occupied the premises. They didn't let the managers enter the building and took over their personal checking accounts. Production fell to an absolute minimum and they couldn't pay the salaries. They had to borrow money from CORFO [Chilean National Development Corporation, a state-run lending organization], which meant that the business went into debt (Maturana 1993).

Maturana's experiences were typical among the leaders of the anti-Allende women's organizations.

Agrarian Reform

The scope and tenor of agrarian reform intensified dramatically under Allende. He sought to implement agrarian reform more fully than his predecessor Eduardo Frei, and he succeeded in doing so. By the end of 1971, the government had expropriated more than 3,000 estates, one-fifth of the country's productive land (Tinsman 1996: 370). A year later, by the end of 1972, the government had expropriated nearly half of Chile's farms and distributed more than nine million hectares to landless peasants (Tinsman 1996: 115; Oppenheim 1999: 58). Membership in rural unions doubled in the same period and the new unions played a more active role in the reform process. While the government initiated most of the expropriations, peasant organizations increasingly organized land seizures on their own and submitted them for government approval afterward. The threat to the agricultural elite could not have been more severe: "In sharp contrast to the emphasis of the past Christian Democratic agrarian reform on increasing productivity and creating a new class of private farmers, the UP called for the eradication of *all* latifundia, efficient or not, and for more collective forms of ownership" (Tinsman 1996: 370). These changes provoked confusion and violence in the countryside, between landowners and peasants, between the government and sympathetic but unofficial peasant organizations, between peasants who had already received plots of land under the Frei government and new beneficiaries, and between those who supported collectivization and those who preferred private holdings. Increasingly widespread rural resistance to agrarian reform found a symbol in Eliana Quezada Moreno, a woman who rode from her farm in the south of Chile to Santiago on horseback to protest the situation. *Tribuna* (January 8, 1972) reported that she wore only a bathing suit to highlight the economically deprived conditions then beginning to eclipse the countryside.

Rural agitation deeply troubled conservative political leaders, landowners for whom small farmers constituted an important base of electoral support. Three of the women who led the movement against Allende owned land that was expropriated under Frei and Allende. Decades later, María Correa remained bitter about the seizure of her family's farm. In an interview I had with her in 1993, Mrs. Correa fumed: "The [Frei government] robbed us. They robbed us and paid us with bonds that were worth nothing" (Correa 1993). Carmen Saenz, another anti-Allende leader, recalled that the expropriation of her father's wheat farm in the south of Chile caused a severe drop in production (Saenz 1993). Saenz came from a long-time political family. Her father was a Radical Party senator during the Popular Front era. She and her husband, Patricio Phillips, started the National Party and she served as president of the National Women and vice-president of the National Party during the UP. In 1970, Mrs. Saenz inherited a farm of her own from her grandfather. The small size of the plot – less than 100 hectares – legally precluded this land from being taken over, but the Allende government expropriated it nonetheless. "The moment arrived when the Allende government expropriated [my land], but I never signed anything. I was not going to be the agent of my own plundering. When the military regime took over [in 1973], I demanded the right to regain my land, and I got it back," Saenz declared during a 1993 interview. María Olivia Gazmuri, leader of the women's front for Fatherland and Liberty, described similar experiences:

The UP in the case of my family meant a complete dismembering. They took our land away from us, which was a well-worked farm, and not a farm that merited agrarian reform. My family split up, some left for the U.S., my father, mother and two younger brothers to the U.S. (Gazmuri 1994).

Although these women did not mention it, many landowners transferred land titles to women in their families in an effort to prevent it from being seized by the government. Because women had no independent legal standing, transferring the land to women was one way to avoid seizure. The plots of land that María Correa and Carmen Saenz inherited are relatively small, but for women with little economic power relative to men, this land may well have been a significant asset.

The Shortages

Ask any woman of mature age who lives in one of Santiago's well-to-do neighborhoods what she remembers about the UP and she will say "*las colas*," the long lines people waited in to buy food and basic supplies. As one woman put it, "There were no chickens, there was no toilet paper, no detergent, that is to say there was nothing" (SOL Leaders 1994). For the most part middle- and upper-class women could buy food on the black market. In July 1971, the Allende government acknowledged the problem of food shortages and created a network of distribution centers to resolve it. These centers became known as the food and price committees (*juntas de abastecimiento y precios* [JAPs]). Those opposed to Allende claimed that membership in pro-UP political parties was required to obtain food from the JAPs. Women who did not participate in the JAPs had no choice but to rely on the black market and waiting in lines to buy food. Even if they otherwise might have been sympathetic to the UP, the barriers to participation that women faced (lack of child care, lack of access to birth control, relatively few opportunities to join the formal workforce or participate in labor unions) prevented them from reaping the benefits of participating in those organizations – food from the JAPS or a daily half-liter of milk for their children, one of the centerpieces of UP policy for women. Others claimed that corruption was rampant in the JAPs. One woman, the president of a mothers' center, formed a JAP in her neighborhood. She claimed, however, that in order to receive food she was forced to bribe JAP officials, who distributed the supplies unevenly among families, regardless of the number of children they had, and often sold JAP food on the black market for huge profits (Sota 1994).

Women argued that they suffered the consequences of the food shortages more acutely and more directly than men. They emphasized the ways that the UP government made it impossible for women to fulfill their maternal duties and responsibilities. As Sara Navas, a leader in women's opposition to Allende, recounted (1993):

Women have to provide food for their children . . . and when women began to realize that basic food supplies were lacking, that there was neither medicine nor means of transportation, and she had to go to work and there were gas shortages, and that so many professionals had left the country and there were no doctors left and more than anything food shortages, and a feeling of insecurity because you couldn't walk in the streets. . . . *for the mother trying to defend her children it was impossible to be a responsible mother* [emphasis added].

Women's focus on concrete, everyday, private concerns challenged discussions about the abstract political implications of the world-famous "Chilean experiment with socialism" that predominated at the time. Women's opposition emerged as a "logical reaction to protect first their home, their children and to defend or support their men who had been persecuted or waylaid on ideological terrain," noted a reporter in *Eva*, a conservative women's magazine (*Eva* 1972a).

The Opposition Organizes

The political environment in Chile became increasingly polarized during the second half of 1971. As Luis Maira, a Socialist Party leader, recalled, "practically all the social organizations in Chile – unions, neighborhood councils, mothers' centers, student federations, professional bodies – became active centers of confrontation. Elections for leadership of these groups were defined in directly political terms – [you were either] for or against the government" (Maira 1979: 259). Key labor unions and professional associations (*gremios*) turned against Allende and organized strikes. Their actions threatened to impair the legitimacy of the "workers' government." Strikes organizes by the truckers and copper miners created particularly difficult problems for Allende, because they brought the most powerful industries in the country to a standstill at a time of severe economic crisis. Increasing levels of mobilization reflected a conscious strategy on behalf of opposition leaders. In June 1971, National Party leader Sergio Onofre Jarpa initiated efforts to mobilize social and economic organizations in the service of the political goals of the opposition. The imperative that Jarpa placed on political mobilization is evident in a speech he gave in December 1971:

In spite of the harsh lesson they got in September 1970, there are still some Chileans who think they have the luxury of thinking that "politics is only for politicians." Those who refuse to comply with the need to participate in political decisions and the activities of gremial and community organizations, cannot demand constitutional rights, or demand that others do what they are incapable of doing for themselves, because of fear, egoism or comfort (Jarpa 1973: 156).

Jarpa sought to mobilize people in part to destabilize the government, but his efforts also reflect the National Party's desire to regain the popular support it had lost to the Christian Democrats in the 1960s (Faúndez 1988: 185). Political instability resulted not only in response to conflicts between the government and the opposition, but as a function of a struggle for dominance among the opposition parties.

After half a year of dormancy, Fatherland and Liberty reappeared on the public scene. When it first formed in September 1970, the organization advocated a nonviolent, constitutionally sanctioned way to prevent Allende from taking office – the Alessandri plan. In March 1971, the group shed its identity as a civic movement and renamed itself the Fatherland and Liberty National Front. The new version openly espoused aggressive tactics and sought to build popular opposition to Allende by creating a climate of chaos that would undermine people's tolerance for Allende. As Manuel Fuentes, a former member of the group, states, "Fatherland and Liberty was created as an instrument of provocation and political destabilization" (Fuentes 1999). At its height, the group enjoyed a membership of approximately 1,200 people organized within five divisions: the Men's Front, the Women's Front, the Youth Front, the Invisible Front, and the Operations Front. Its members included supporters of Jorge Alessandri's presidential campaign, intellectuals affiliated with the Catholic University, well-heeled business leaders and right-wing politicians. Fatherland and Liberty openly supported a military coup relatively early on during the Allende administration. In April 1971, the Youth Front dispatched its members to paint the slogan "Armed Forces = Fatherland, Armed Forces = Liberty" around the city of Santiago (Fuentes 1999: 86). The group became recognizable for its swastika-like black symbol, which members wore on white armbands and helmets.

The Women's Front of Fatherland and Liberty included approximately 300 women. María Olivia Gazmuri, described previously as one of the women adversely affected by agrarian reform, served as president of the Women's Front. In a 1994 interview, Gazmuri claimed that most of the women in the group were poor, a view that diverges from most scholarly accounts of the organization. She reported that Fatherland and Liberty included "a lot of people from *poblaciones* (shantytowns), who understood that [the Allende government] meant that their children could lose their freedom, this is what most affected the women . . . In our head-quarters, it was rare to see a car, the majority of people who went there did not own a car" (Gazmuri 1994). Gazmuri claimed that few women from the upper classes joined Fatherland and Liberty because they feared the consequences of publicly supporting the opposition. "Many people said to us 'you are crazy' because we would go out on weekends to sell our magazine on the streets," she recalled (Gazmuri 1994).[3] Gazmuri also insisted that the group was nonviolent:

For many people it was a guerrilla organization, but that wasn't completely true. There was a group inside Fatherland and Liberty that you could have said was extremist, but that wasn't really the case. I would tell you the armaments that they had were five or six sticks and some helmets, no more than that. There was a small group that I never knew, because the leaders were always concerned with keeping things totally separate, that could have been involved in destroying a power plant, I know there were some people that they say were implicated in the death of someone in Concepción [a city south of Santiago], but I believe if this happened, it was pure lack of knowledge that I had (Gazmuri 1994).

[3] The name of the magazine was *Pueblo Libre*.

It "was a pacifist way to make revolution, absolutely peaceful . . . it was the only group very decidedly against the [Popular Unity], because we were convinced that it was really a bad government from every point of view" (Gazmuri 1994). Given the existence of separate divisions within the organization, Gazmuri might indeed have known little about the activities of the other front. Rodríguez may have encouraged women's participation in Fatherland and Liberty in order to put a pacifist face on an otherwise violent organization. Women's place in this organization echoes that of women in the Ku Klux Klan in the United States during the 1920s. In *Women of the Klan*, Kathleen Blee (1991: 2) writes, "[Klanswomen] insist that there were no victims, that to suggest otherwise is to fall prey to lies spread by enemies outside the Klan. Most deny that hatred of racial and religious 'outsiders' fueled the Klan in the 1920s."

Many new opposition organizations formed in 1971. One of these was Solidarity, Order and Liberty (SOL), a group started by a small group of married couples in June 1971. They decided to create a formal organization after several months of meeting informally to study Marxism – not to become Marxists but to understand the enemy better. The organization still existed in the 1990s. When I interviewed members of SOL in 1993, they referred to the group as a "civic family movement" that included men and women, but media accounts from the 1970s identify it as a women's organization (*Qué Pasa* 1972). Regardless, women comprised the bulk of the membership. The structure of this organization constituted one of its primary distinguishing features. SOL's members were organized in an anonymous, pyramidal hierarchy, which sources within the group claimed they copied from the Communist Party. Each group of five women formed a cell, which was headed by a "letter mother" (*letra madre*). Each of the five "daughters" then chose her own group of five, who were known as "granddaughters." Each pyramid consisted of a "letter mother," her five daughters and twenty-five granddaughters. Activists in SOL relied on a telephone chain to coordinate their activities, with the "letter mother" being responsible for contacting her five daughters, and so on. SOL members considered this communications network to have been critical in mobilizing the opposition. As one woman recalled:

[We were able] to organize the city of Santiago in such a way that . . . I could communicate with you and you with her and in half an hour, an hour or two, all of Santiago would be mobilized. We organized a neighborhood structure that was very useful (SOL Leaders 1994).

Estimates of the size of SOL given by SOL members range from 10,000 to 40,000. Despite members' claims that SOL represented women of all social classes, the current membership is decidedly wealthy. One clue to the nature of the membership is the group's insistence that the "letter mothers" select as members only those whom they knew and in whom they had "absolute trust," which suggests that they did not cast their recruiting nets too widely. However, members claimed that contact was made to people who lacked telephones (i.e., those in the lower classes) using domestic servants or other workers who traversed the *barrio alto*, the upper-class neighborhoods of Santiago, from the "periphery neighborhoods" in more modest sectors of the city (SOL Leaders 1994).

Anti-Allende activists tended to be involved in many organizations at once, forming overlapping networks that reinforced the opposition. Most of the women I interviewed participated in political parties, their local neighborhood committees (*juntas de vecinos*), mothers' centers, and independent organizations like SOL. SOL collaborated closely with Fatherland and Liberty. "We the women of SOL and [the women of] Fatherland and Liberty had almost the same orders, to defend supermarkets and radio stations from being taken over by the government," remarked one SOL member (SOL Leaders 1994). Lucia Maturana, a former president of SOL, claimed to have had "double militancy" in both organizations (Maturana 1993). Female leaders in the PDC participated in both SOL and Fatherland and Liberty (Christian Democratic Leaders 1994).

Women in the Opposition Media

Female journalists served as political entrepreneurs for the opposition during the Allende era. Four well-known female journalists played particularly prominent roles in the opposition's media campaign. These women – Patricia Guzmán, María Eugenia Oyarzún, Carmen Puelma, and Silvia Pinto – had cut their journalistic teeth in the fear campaign of 1964. Silvia Pinto wrote a weekly column in *El Mercurio*. Oyarzún wrote for numerous publications and broadcast her own radio show twice a week. Carmen Puelma and Patricia Guzmán served as directors of Radio Cooperativa, one of two main opposition radio stations, and Puelma went on to be editor-in-chief of *Eva*, a women's magazine (Pinto 1972: 148). Together all four women started a television program called "Women Improvise Too" ("Las mujeres tambien improvisan") that had wide appeal. Self-consciously abandoning all pretense of journalistic objectivity, these women referred to themselves as "trench journalists" (*periodistas de trinchera*) to suggest they were on the front lines in the war against Allende. In newspaper editorials and radio programs, they portrayed the UP as an acute political and social crisis, reported ceaselessly on government abuses, and exhorted people to participate in antigovernment activities.

This team of journalists was not unique in its political activism. The Chilean media maintained no pretensions of neutrality during the Allende era. The battle between the government and the opposition raged on the radio, in newspaper headlines, and television shows, as well as in Congress and in the streets.[4] While political forces on all sides used the media to whip up public support and amplify their claims, reporters maintained a degree of autonomy from their official patrons in the political parties. As Arturo Valenzuela (1978: 80) observed, "Leaders of the Popular Unity government and of the Christian Democrats both expressed their despair at the excesses of their respective media organizations, some . . . going so far as to say that the media was now the tail wagging the national dog." On several occasions, members of Congress denounced the false claims that had been made about them in the papers (República de Chile 1971: 1840). The disputes that sometimes arose between journalists and their patrons in the political parties no doubt reflects the ample financial assistance that journalists received from the U.S. government through the CIA. *El Mercurio* alone received $1.5 million dollars beginning in September 1971. Other opposition groups received a total of $6 million between 1970 and 1973 (Sigmund 1977: 285). The infusion of resources from the United States not only gave Chilean journalists free rein to attack Allende, but probably made them less accountable to their party sponsors.

When Carmen Puelma became editor of *Eva*, she transformed it from a conventional women's magazine to a vehicle of propaganda for the opposition. She added political commentary, interviews with leaders of women's opposition groups and detailed instructions for political mobilization to

---

[4] Five progovernment papers enjoyed national readership. *El Clarín* was the largest with 110,000 readers. There were also five opposition papers. The prominent Edwards family owned three of these along with a nationwide network of provincial papers. *El Mercurio*, the largest of the three, enjoyed a circulation of 140,000 readers. *La Prensa*, which represented the views of the Christian Democratic Party, was the second-largest opposition paper, with a circulation of approximately 30,000 (Horne 1972: 143). Other influential right-wing publications included *Tribuna*, which National Party leader Sergio Onofre Jarpa started in 1971, as well as *PEC*, *Sepa*, and *Qué Pasa*. When Allende came to power in 1970, half a million households had television sets, but radio commanded a far wider audience (Sigmund 1977: 102).

Eva's standard fare of recipes and beauty tips (McGee Deutsch 1991). "The heroic activities that the women of Chile undertook to recover the liberty of their country, looked to *Eva* as a guide, the voice of the vanguard," wrote Eudocio Ravines in *The Rescue of Chile*, an account of the anti-Allende forces. Recalling the efforts of Patricia Guzmán as director for Radio Cooperativa, Ravines (1974: 204) wrote: "She was from the same lineage of those who went out to the streets to sound, with worldwide resonance, the empty pots . . . When the Marxist government took power . . . [She] immediately changed her task from merely providing information to a dedicated struggle, valiant and unstoppable against the advance of Marxism."

Several of the people I interviewed for this book identified this group of journalists as being "the first voices to speak out" against the UP. Hermógenes Perez de Arce, an extremely conservative journalist and former politician, described them as the vanguard of the opposition:

At that time people were very afraid, so the first thing they had to do was over-come that fear. Everyone just wanted to take care of their own situation the best they could and leave the country, so nobody wanted to have any problems with the government. People wanted to sell what they had and didn't want government tax inspectors to come and take away their fortunes . . . Radio Agricultura [and Radio Cooperativa] in this sense risked everything, criticized everything and sought out people [like myself and the women journalists] who would say what they wanted to say (Pérez de Arce 1994).

In her account of the women's movement, Teresa Donoso, the Christian Democratic journalist who participated in the "mourning" marches against Allende, glorified the journalists' role in the opposition in flowery prose:

There was no doubt. The most revolutionary actors that modern-day Chile pro-duced were the women. And journalism produced the most illustrious part of the feminine revolution. And all women, the watchtowers of Chile along its entire lethargic geography, knew themselves to be represented by these four voices that were growing in intensity – by the end they were "word kamikazes." They were making the climate ripe for opposition, a battalion of female journalists [who] picked up the nation and shook it from north to south, showing it the path to its own sovereignty (Donoso 1974b: 55).

This group of women played a particularly significant role in mobilizing women among the middle and upper classes, encouraging them to become activists. The conservative media engaged in an aggressive campaign to discredit every government program and hyperbolize every problem in order to convey a climate of increasing social disorder and economic chaos.

As a result, the equanimity that characterized public opinion after Allende's election gradually dissipated over the course of his first year in office.

Toward a Unified Opposition

Allende also faced significant pressures within his own coalition. Party competition within the UP coalition became increasingly problematic for the government as the struggle for power among the parties clouded a more strategic focus on the overall revolutionary project (Tapia 1979). The coalition began to polarize into moderate and radical factions. The moderates, led by the Communist Party, "felt it necessary to adhere to the law" in order to implement government policy, "even if it meant going slowly to achieve the UP program" (Oppenheim 1999: 62). They sought to build alliances with the middle class and the Christian Democrats in order to win elections and control the legislature. The Socialist Party dominated the radical faction, for whom speed was of the essence. The radicals devoted their energies toward organizing at the grass roots level and intensifying revolutionary demands among the masses rather than negotiating or winning elections. As political scientist Kenneth Roberts (1998: 93) states, "the contrasting approaches of the two parties were perhaps best summarized in their respective slogans: whereas the Socialists pledged to 'advance without compromise,' the Communists preferred to 'compromise in order to advance.'" Over time, Allende's ability to mediate conflicts among his own coalition partners waned, contributing to a climate of instability and ungovernability.

Tensions between the right and left factions of the PDC became more pronounced during the first year of the UP government as well. Radomiro Tomic, the party's candidate in the 1970 presidential election, led the progressive faction. He continued to advocate collaboration with Allende. Recall that Tomic's platform for the 1970 election had looked quite similar to Allende's. However, the Allende government consistently refused opportunities to cooperate with the Christian Democrats, which diminished the power of the leftist faction within the party and hardened the party's opposition to the government. Former President Frei gradually reasserted control of the party and squeezed the more progressive factions out of the leadership. In June 1971, a small progressive group split off from the Christian Democrats to form a new party, the Movement of the Christian Left (Movimiento de Izquierda Cristiana [MIC]). When the MIC joined the UP coalition, the PDC lost six of its fifty-five deputies in

73

the lower house of Congress, which meant they were no longer the majority party in the House of Deputies.

The desire to recapture these lost seats provided an additional incentive for the Christian Democrats to ally with the right (Garcés 1976: 203). This fact was not lost on the Right, which hoped to persuade the Christian Democrats to join them. Ironically, the radical Left welcomed the MIC into the UP coalition for the same reason: it anticipated that doing so would prompt the opposition parties to ally with one another. By forcing the Christian Democrats into a coalition with the National Party, the Left hoped to exacerbate the divisions between the conservative and progressive factions within the PDC and prompt more of the latter to join the Left. Fostering these divisions was one way to chip away at the dominance of the opposition within Congress.

A series of other incidents in 1971 pushed the party further to the Right. On May 23, a leftist group called the People's Organized Vanguard (VOP) assaulted a supermarket, killed the policeman on guard, and stole his submachine gun. On June 8, VOP assassinated Christian Democratic leader Edmundo Pérez Zujovic – using the same submachine gun. The Perez assassination marked the "point of no return" in the widening gap between the government and the opposition (Maira 1979: 258). In October and November, students at the University of Chile organized a series of strikes, demonstrations, mass meetings, and violent protests, both for and against the government, events that added to the sense that things were spinning out of control.

Conclusion

When Allende won the presidency in September 1970, a small group of conservative women responded by organizing autonomously to prevent him from taking office. They framed their efforts in opposition to men. Rebuffed by male party leaders who expressly denied them a voice in determining party policy, they organized protests in the hopes of generating widespread popular opposition to Allende. They justified their efforts in response to their frustration with male politicians, whom they criticized for dismissing women's ideas and failing to take bolder measures to address what they considered to be a major political crisis. Women's actions reflected a measure of frustration with the democratic process, foreshadowing their eventual support for a military takeover. Women portrayed themselves as defenders of the nation and defenders of democracy against

Marxist totalitarianism, claims that must be considered disingenuous in the context of their efforts to subvert the democratic process by which Allende had been elected.

The women framed their actions in a way that had prompted women's organizations to coalesce around common goals in the past – but the timing in this instance proved to be unfavorable. They anticipated the formation of a new coalition between the National Party and the Christian Democrats, but the realignment did not occur. The PDC rejected the Right's overtures and voted to support Allende in the congressional runoff. The women based their expectations of success on the results of the presidential election, in which a large majority of Chileans – and an even larger majority of women – did not vote for Allende. But women overestimated the intensity of people's feelings about the Allende victory; at the time, only a small minority shared their view that Allende's election portended "the death of democracy." Thus, women's mobilization in September and October 1970 failed to trigger a mass response. Just a year later, however, conditions had changed significantly. The PDC leadership had shifted decidedly to the Right in response to growing economic and political instability under Allende and the party appeared ready to form a coalition with the rightist National Party against the government. Women's mobilization in the March of the Empty Pots set off a series of events that changed the political landscape.

4

Catapulting Men to Action

THE MARCH OF THE
EMPTY POTS

Nearly every one of the scores of books written about the Popular Unity (UP) period mentions the March of the Empty Pots, but few devote more than one or two sentences to it.[1] Yet this event played a pivotal role in shaping the future course of the Allende government. The March of the Empty Pots demonstrated a significant lack of middle-class support for Allende's peaceful revolution and sent a signal of domestic discontent to observers around the world. Women organized the protest at a moment when the opposition parties were poised to take definitive action against the government, in the face of a growing climate of crisis and instability. They timed the march to coincide with the end of Fidel Castro's three-and-a-half week visit to Chile. The march set off a series of events that changed the fate of both the opposition and the government in significant ways. The outbreak of violence during the protest prompted President Allende to declare a state of emergency in Santiago and united the opposition parties in an effort to impeach one of Allende's top cabinet ministers. Male party leaders framed their cooperation as a response to women's actions throughout the remainder of the Allende era. They would continue to invoke women's participation as a way to sustain unity within this new coalition. The impact of the March of the Empty Pots stemmed from the fact that it occurred at a moment when these parties were primed to ally with one another. Had the parties, and particularly the centrist Christian Democrats, not been prepared to cooperate, this protest would

---

[1] The complex events that transpired during the years of the Popular Unity have been the subject of innumerable studies. As Paul Sigmund (1993: 215) has remarked, "There are probably a thousand books on the 1970 to 1973 period [in Chile], one for each day of the Allende government." I have found Oppenheim (1999) particularly useful.

indeed have been a footnote, and would merit the scant attention it has received in the literature.

Fidel Castro Visits Chile

On November 10, 1971, Fidel Castro arrived in Chile for an extended state tour. Hundreds of thousands of UP sympathizers greeted Castro with great enthusiasm, packing stadiums to hear his famous three-hour speeches and greeting him warmly at every stop. Not surprisingly his presence in Chile infuriated right-wing sympathizers. A discussion about Castro's visit on the floor of the House of Deputies turned into a brawl, as progovernment and opposition deputies argued about the extent of religious freedom and civil liberties that existed in Cuba (República de Chile 1971: 571). On the day that Castro arrived (November 10, 1971), *El Mercurio* published an editorial that warned that Castro would try hard to push Chile in a more revolutionary direction: "This visit cannot be compared with the visits of other heads of state in the past. What is at stake now is the material expression of a long-standing mutual alliance [between Chile and Cuba]." Alongside the editorial ran another piece called "The Brutal Work of Women" that cautioned women about the harsh conditions to which they would be subjected under communism, by now a familiar refrain. Toward the end of Castro's visit, two officials from the U.S. State Department (under the Nixon administration) arrived in Chile. The day of the march, these officials issued a cryptic statement that "Allende's days in power are numbered." Their actions fed rumors among government sympathizers, including Allende, that the U.S. Central Intelligence Agency (CIA) had organized and financed the women's march (Sigmund 1977: 162). Regardless, the presence of Castro and Nixon's aides in Chile at the same time insured that the March of the Empty Pots would receive maximum attention in the international press.

The March of the Empty Pots

On November 26, 1971, Silvia Alessandri paid a visit to the Intendencia of Santiago to get permission to hold a demonstration in downtown Santiago on the first of December. Alessandri was a National Party congress woman and the niece of Jorge Alessandri, the 1970 presidential candidate. As Alessandri recalled in an interview:

77

I spoke with the *Intendente*, Jaime Concha, a good-looking guy (*buen mozo*) about my age, a great dancer . . . and I said "look Jaime, we are in a real bind. We women are going to revolt, we are going to stage a demonstration, and we have no money. We have no money to pay [the fee to register the march] because no one believes us. Not even the leaders of the right-wing parties believe us" (Alessandri 1994).

Alessandri's frustration echoes the sentiments that María Correa expressed when party leaders refused to sponsor women's protests in September 1970. Nonetheless, she persuaded the Intendente to grant permission for the march. The route they agreed upon would take the marchers from the Plaza Italia – a traffic circle along the main avenue of the city – through the Parque Forestal and along backstreets back to the main avenue, ending with a series of speeches at a plaza on Avenida Bulnes. The starting point for this route, the Plaza Italia, constituted the lower boundary of the *barrio alto* – a fact that would prove significant in the days to come. At some point before the march was to occur (accounts vary), the Intendencia altered the route. According to the new plan, the march would end at the Plaza Vicuña Mackenna next to the National Library, several blocks before the original destination. The Intendencia also authorized a progovernment demonstration that would take place *at the same time*. The second march would start one block away from the terminus of the women's march and head right toward it. The Intendente thus authorized two opposing demonstrations that were destined to crash right into one another. The abrupt change of plans gave the women little time to get the word out, adding to the potential for confusion. The authorization of the second march would become a central issue in the opposition's efforts to chastise the government for the chaos that ensued.

Around 6:30 in the evening on December 1, 1971 thousands of women converged at the Plaza Italia and began to march down the central avenue of the city toward the presidential palace. They banged on empty pots and pans (*cacerolas vacías*) as they marched, creating a tremendous clamor. Estimates of the number of women who participated in the march vary widely. The *New York Times* (December 2, 1971) reported that "at least 5,000" women marched. This is probably the most reliable figure, as it comes from the source with the least interest in inflating the numbers. Opposition newspapers in Chile reported anywhere from 50,000 and 200,000 demonstrators. Well-dressed upper-class women arrived in cars, while working-class women and members of *pobladora* and peasant organizations came in buses. Women from the three main opposition political parties participated – the rightist National Party, the centrist Christian Democrats, and the Radical Party – as well as "independent" women who claimed no affiliation to any party. Leaders of the march included representatives from the women's divisions of the National Party – Carmen Saenz, María Correa, and Silvia Alessandri – and the Christian Democratic Party (PDC), including Teresa Donoso and Teresa de la Maza.

A few blocks into the march, progovernment groups attacked the demonstrators. Construction workers perched on scaffolding high above the main avenue threw rocks and sticks at them. Some women threw rocks back. The opposition protesters soon met up with the progovernment protesters, who represented three youth groups – the Communist Ramona Parra Brigade, the Socialist Elmo Catalán Brigade, and the Movement of the Revolutionary Left (MIR) – who attacked the women with an assortment of "homemade weapons," including rocks, sticks, chains, and potatoes embedded with razor blades, known as *papas gillette*. The leftist protesters shouted "the most unheard-of insults" at the women, but many women insulted them right back. Police intervened shortly thereafter, throwing tear gas bombs to disperse the crowd. The women became trapped between the youth brigades and the police, all possible exits blocked. One of the protesters, Christian Democratic leader Pilar Lagarrigue, described this moment in testimony before Congress:

There was a huge flock of teargas bombs, really powerful bombs, about 10 or 20 of them . . . They closed us in . . . when we tried to retreat and behave like the patriots and Chileans, lovers of the Constitution that we are, they didn't let us. Armed members of the MIR came down Portugal Street, "Ramona Parra" came down Diagonal Paraguay [another street] and behind the police were more members of the MIR (quoted in Garcés 1972: 247).

Sixteen years later, in an interview in *El Mercurio* (March 22, 1987) Silvia Alessandri recalled how she felt at that moment: "When they beat us up, I felt morally defrauded, because they had given permission for us to march and stage a peaceful demonstration." Needless to say, the scheduled speeches did not take place. As a result of these events, 100 people were injured and sent to a nearby emergency clinic for treatment. One woman was permanently injured – she lost the ability to speak – as the result of the violence that broke out during the demonstration.

In the days that followed, opposition accounts of the march would denounce the brutal mistreatment of "defenseless" women. But many of the women came prepared to encounter violence. One woman carried a flag with a nail stuck in the pole, "so in case someone approached me I could hit them with the nail" (Puga 1994). Others had brought handkerchiefs, lemon, and salt in anticipation of being tear gassed. As María Correa recalled when I interviewed her in 1993:

When we were getting ready to go to the march, I thought, this isn't going to be so easy; this isn't going to be a story about pots and pans. So I took a pot, and I wore a very pretty, feminine dress, but I hid half a broom handle inside my shopping bag, so that I would be ready for the red brigades (Correa 1993).

Correa's admission reveals that at least some of the women knew that their demonstration could end in a riot. Anticipating the potential for conflict, the organizers invited men to accompany them, including members of Fatherland and Liberty and the youth brigades of the National Party and the Christian Democrats. María Correa claimed that the presence of the men prevented the march from becoming a massacre, but it is also possible that men's presence exacerbated the violence that occurred. Silvia Alessandri had a different take on the situation. In her 1987 *El Mercurio* interview, she maintained that the men came because "they did not believe we were capable; they came to watch to see if we were capable of organizing 'a hundred old broads' (*unas cien viejas*) as they put it. But it was a success!" Alessandri reiterated this theme when I interviewed her seven years later. She said men did not support the march because "we live in a macho country, machismo is so important [in understanding what happened]. But in spite of everything, we triumphed and showed what women were capable of doing" (Alessandri 1994).

The outbreak of violence during the march triggered a huge public outcry and prompted extensive media coverage. The march dominated the headlines of government and opposition newspapers for well over a week. In response to the chaos, Allende declared the city of Santiago a zone of emergency. *Puro Chile* (December 3, 1971) reported that he imposed a week-long curfew, banned street demonstrations, and prohibited the press from disseminating "alarmist news." The army controlled entrance and exit from the city. In an eerie foreshadowing of the future, Allende named General Augusto Pinochet, then chief of the Santiago military garrison, to oversee the emergency zone. Allende's decision to appoint Pinochet to this position demonstrates the level of trust that Allende had in Pinochet and in the military overall. Yet Pinochet's performance in this situation gave some indication of the military's capacity to use force against civilians. In a press conference announcing the state of emergency, a reporter asked General Pinochet whether he would call out the armed forces to maintain order. Pinochet replied that he preferred to leave the police in charge of the streets rather than the army. His explanation portended the coup that was still two years away: an article in *Tribuna* (December 3, 1971) quoted him as saying, "Because, gentlemen, this must be said, when the Army goes out to the streets, they go out to kill. Unfortunately, that's how it is. The Army is trained for war and doesn't possess, like the police, elements that allow them to dissolve street demonstrations." General Pinochet ominously added that soldiers carry weapons that dispense 180 rounds of ammunition per minute.

Pinochet issued a 24-hour suspension of *Tribuna* for violating the media ban. The previous day the paper had run the following headline in large, bold letters: "The blood of women has been spilled on the arrogance and incapacity of the Marxists." A photograph of a bleeding woman in the hospital accompanied the article. A few days later Pinochet suspended *Tribuna* a second time for printing an article that insulted the honor of the armed forces. The item in question, a poem entitled "March of the Women," appeared as a letter to the editor. The piece implied that the military had sold out to the Allende government. It read:

Our struggle began recently. The armed forces handed themselves over [to the Allende government] in exchange for a new car, a home and a salary increase. The police are afraid. Women of Chile, Chilean women, we will begin our march alone.

The government jumped to defend the armed forces. In response to the *Tribuna* poem, Allende issued a statement that appeared in the paper on December 5: "As president of the republic, I cannot allow the insolent affirmations made in today's edition of *Tribuna*, the newspaper of the National Party, to pass without raising my objection to them."

These incidents challenge the view that women were the military's "natural" allies. In suspending *Tribuna* on these grounds, Pinochet demonstrated no partiality to the women's cause. By no means did women and the military share common goals at this point, at the end of 1971. On the contrary, women constantly goaded the military in the hopes of inciting them to take action against Allende. Women sought to humiliate the military by hounding them relentlessly and accusing them of being Allende's pawns. After the coup, however, many of the women who protested in the March of the Empty Pots would emerge as some of Pinochet's most ardent supporters, and Pinochet would recast women as his one of his most loyal constituencies.

Despite the state of siege, the empty pot idea caught on like a prairie fire. Women organized marches throughout Chile. They began to bang on pots and pans from the privacy of their own homes; in Santiago, the *cacerolas* sounded nightly at 10 o'clock, creating a tremendous cacophony. The empty pot became an important symbol that appeared frequently in opposition activities over the next two years. Women brandished pots and pans at political rallies and politicians referred to them in speeches. Later, after the coup, the symbolic meaning of the empty pots would become inverted when people began to bang on them to voice their opposition to the military dictatorship.

For the time being, however, opposing political forces engaged in a battle to define the significance of the March of the Empty Pots and control its impact on the political situation. Progovernment forces emphatically denied women's agency in the event. They insisted that the march had been organized by right-wing extremist men who "hid beneath women's skirts." They accused the opposition of using gender to mask its "real" class interests. As a discursive strategy, subordinating gender identity to class interests would impede the ability of leftist women to raise gender-specific concerns. Within the opposition, however, both men and women alike highlighted women's participation in the March of the Empty Pots. Men in the opposition framed their own actions as a response to a gendered code of honor. Women within the opposition, on the other hand, viewed the March of the Empty Pots as an opportunity to assert their autonomy from the political parties and even to articulate an incipient vision of feminist identity.

The Government Reacts

Within hours of the March of the Empty Pots, women in the UP urged Allende to permit them to hold a counterdemonstration. Allende denied their request on the grounds that doing so would only incite further violence, or perhaps even provoke the military to intervene. He may very well have been right. Nonetheless, his decision had unfortunate consequences for the Left: the lack of a response by leftist women unintentionally served to perpetuate the notion that the Right, and not the Left, represented women's true interests. An organized response by women on behalf of the government, framed in gendered terms, might have defused the heresthetic power of the March of the Empty Pots and permitted the Left to regain some control over women as a con-

82

stituency. Joan Garcés (1976: 166) explains the logic behind Allende's decision:

The march of the women from the residential neighborhoods had just begun when various feminine leaders of the UP urgently requested a meeting with Allende. Leading them was Socialist Senator María Elena Carrera. The women informed him that in the working-class neighborhoods there were thousands of women gathered, ready to march downtown and show the bourgeoisie what "empty pots" meant to them. The president responded that what the right eagerly desired was, precisely, to provoke a confrontation among civilians, to legitimate their desire for the armed forces to intervene on their own and reestablish order, pitting [the military] against the government . . . so Allende prohibited sending out the women of the working class (*mujeres trabajadoras*).

The government did not authorize the women to march, but some women went ahead and organized a demonstration anyway – the same way that right-wing women responded to their male counterparts in 1970. María Mendoza, a labor activist at the time, laughed as she described what happened that day:

Our march was one of the most fun. When we heard about the March of the Empty Pots we, the women of the UP, decided to have our own march. We went out with empty pots, some women costumed in fur stoles, with images of the virgin, making fun of the other march. They started out for the Plaza Italia and we started at the Estación Central [on the opposite end of downtown]. We didn't get close enough to pull their hair, but there were two marches that day and they never talk about the other one (Mendoza 1994).

For several weeks afterward, the government engaged in strenuous efforts to discredit women's involvement in the March of the Empty Pots, unintentionally reinforcing its political significance. Progovernment forces insisted that the women who participated were merely pawns of other organized interests – the U.S. government, the upper classes, right-wing extremists. The progovernment media framed the march in terms that vilified the opposition and rendered women's participation insignificant. Their arguments proved very persuasive, especially on the Left; the belief that the anti-Allende women were just a bunch of rich old ladies from the *barrio alto* persists to this day.

The Opposition Unites

Three days after the march, on December 4, 1971, the PDC voted to initiate impeachment proceedings against José Tohá, Allende's Minister of the Interior. The vote within the party was close: ten in favor, eight against, and one abstention. The National Party joined the Christian Democrats as a cosponsor a few weeks later on December 22. They sought impeachment (*acusación constitucional*) on three grounds: the government's tolerance of illegal armed groups; freedom of assembly and freedom of the press; and interference in elections of the neighborhood councils. The first and second charges directly pertained to the women's march: the opposition charged that the government violated women's right to protest by failing to provide police protection and authorizing another march for the same time, and by failing to curb extremist violence. The opposition parties further charged that "the attack on defenseless women" violated the Statute of Constitutional Guarantees that Allende had signed upon taking office (Garcés 1972). It quickly became apparent that the hearings were not just about the March of the Empty Pots. Rather, they became "a political trial of the entire government and its program, in which [members of Congress] questioned all the activities of the Allende administration during its fifteen months in power" (Maira 1979: 20). The proceedings established a precedent of cooperation among the opposition parties and paved the way for a future electoral coalition among them. The opposition would initiate numerous impeachment motions against the government over the next two years, in a conscious effort to divert the energies of the Allende government away from substantive policy concerns.

The proceedings against Tohá represented the first occasion on which the opposition parties acted in concert with one another. The National Party had introduced impeachment proceedings against Allende's cabinet ministers on three previous occasions: against the Minister of Justice in January 1971, against the Minister of Work in March 1971, and against the Minister of the Economy in August 1971. Each of these motions had failed due to a lack of support from Christian Democratic deputies (Dooner 1985).

The hearings made frequent references to the role women had played in the march. The Socialist Party issued an official statement that condemned the proceedings:

[The hearings represent the] collusion of the *freistas* [the conservative faction of the Christian Democratic Party], Fatherland and Liberty and the National Party, with the blessing of Yankee imperialism. This anti-patriotic and right-wing cabal planned and executed the ridiculous march of the old ladies with the empty pots, with the assistance of armed bullies and the decadent youth of the plutocratic oligarchy of this country (cited in Garcés 1972: 85).

At one point during the debate, a deputy read from the list of women injured during the March to demonstrate the extent of their injuries and to show that not all the women who participated were from the upper-class neighborhoods. As he read the women's names, along with some biographical information about them, another parliamentarian interrupted him to ask what party the women were from. "What does it matter?" he responded, "They are only women!" (República de Chile 1975: 2816).

Communist deputy Volodia Teitelboim maintained that the U.S. government had organized the march. "The march was destined to show that [U.S.] presidential advisors Robert Finch and Herbert Klein were well informed of the internal and international plan to provoke a political crisis in Chile that would put an end to this legal and democratic government" (República de Chile 1975: 1719). Teitelboim made his case by pointing out the similarities between the March of the Empty Pots and the demonstrations women had organized in September 1970: "[The women] have returned to their ramblings a second time in order to get the outcome they didn't get the first time." He insisted that the opposition used women to mask its class interests: "They cannot appear as they really are, saying 'We have to salvage our privileges and maintain dominion. . . . They have to be sneaky (*trabajar con mano mora*), they have to make use of student groups and, this time, of women" (República de Chile 1975: 1719). In a farewell speech to Fidel Castro delivered the day after the march, Allende contended that the women who marched had never experienced hunger, cooked a meal, or washed a pot in their lives.

Whether or not working-class women participated in the March of the Empty Pots has long been a matter of dispute. Opposition newspapers went out of their way to show that women of all classes took part, while government papers insisted that only upper-class *momias* attended the march. An ad publicizing the march published in *El Mercurio* (November 29, 1971) featured interviews with female leaders from the shantytowns, including Otilia Contreras, a "national leader of pobladoras," Olga Salinas, a "peasant leader from Pomaire," and Dina Mendez, a housewife. *Tribuna* (December 3 and 10, 1971) reported that leftists had threatened *pobladoras* from outlying areas of Santiago, forcibly preventing them from attending the march. Coverage of the march in *La Prensa*, the Christian Democratic paper, also claimed that women from all classes participated. After the march, *La Prensa* (December 5, 1971) published a letter that had been sent to Allende by 150 women from Conchalí, a working-class area on the outskirts of Santiago. The women wrote to complain about the government's distorted account of what took place. During the congressional hearing, Christian Democratic deputy Andrés Aylwin quoted the testimony of a peasant woman (*campesina*) from Pudahuel, Señora Teresa Galvez: "I came to the march of the empty pots not because I was a person of means, no, I came because we really have nothing to eat, you can't find sugar, potatoes, rice, tea, etc. You can't find anything and if you do, they'll only sell you a half kilo of it. That's not enough for the 15 people who live in my house" (quoted in Garcés 1972: 249). A list of those injured during the March of the Empty Pots, published in *Tribuna* (December 3) and several other opposition newspapers, provides further evidence. The list contains the names of 100 people sent to emergency clinics during the march, along with brief biographical data. Thirty-eight of the 100 injured were women. Of these thirty-eight, fifteen were identified as either students or workers, eight were domestic servants (*empleadas*), two seamstresses, one shopkeeper, one journalist, and one nurse. The article identified the remaining ten only by name.

The motion to impeach Tohá, Allende's cabinet minister, passed narrowly. In and of itself, this particular motion did little to derail the government. The next day, Allende simply removed Tohá as the Minister of the Interior and renamed him Minister of Defense. But the opposition followed up by lobbing a volley of impeachment measures at government officials, introducing censure measures at a rate more than six times the historical average for this kind of legislation (Maira 1979). These measures severely impeded the government's ability to engage in the day-to-day business of governing. Luis Maira, a politician from the Socialist Party, describes this adverse impact in detail:

When the leaders of the National Party initiated their plan to effect multiple constitutional censures, they correctly anticipated that, even if unsuccessful, these would cause great difficulties for the government. If the petitions were successful, the various ministries would be denied stable leadership, and the government's efforts would be disorganized. The President would lose the aid of his best technical and political advisors, and those who enjoyed his greatest confidence. The time-consuming parliamentary procedure of censure would leave ministries without leadership for prolonged periods, with the result that the implementation of economic and social policies would lose consistency. The achievement of proposals would be delayed. *I insist that simply initiating these accusations was sufficient to provoke many of these effects* (Maira 1979: 255 [emphasis added]).

The issue on which the opposition parties united, the impeachment of Tohá, represented a significant change in strategy for the opposition and

Catapulting Men to Action

one that would have a devastating impact on the government's ability to implement its platform.

Feminine Power

In 1972, the organizers of the March of the Empty Pots formed a new group called Feminine Power (Poder Femenino), an umbrella organization for numerous groups of women who opposed the government. Feminine Power aimed to consolidate women's influence within the opposition. It was closely associated with the political parties yet not formally sponsored by them; to that extent it was an independent organization. On October 20, 1972, *Tribuna* reported that the coalition included the women's departments of the National Party, the PDC, and the Radical Democracy Party; women's trade associations; and various independent organizations, such as Fatherland and Liberty, Solidarity, Order and Liberty (SOL), and a group called Javiera Carrera. Although headquartered in Santiago, branches of Feminine Power sprang up throughout Chile. The group claimed to be independent, but individual members of Feminine Power remained deeply involved in conventional partisan political activities. The women who formed the leadership of the group, the Consejo Coordinador, for example, had ample experience as political party militants, getting the vote out and working at the polls during elections. Many came from prominent political families and were on a first-name basis with many of the opposition leaders (Correa 1974). Diverse groups of women formed Feminine Power in order to consolidate their leverage with regard to the parties. In terms of its organizational structure and its discursive strategies, Feminine Power emulated the Movement for the Emancipation of Chilean Women (MEMCh), the suffrage organization from the 1930s, and presaged the Coalition of Women for Democracy, a feminist umbrella group that would form in the 1980s.

The name *Feminine Power* self-consciously echoed the language of the liberation movements then sweeping the globe: *poder popular*, power to the people, youth power, and black power – the central slogans of the Left in the late 1960s.[2] When women in the group chose the name, they acknowledged that it would arouse controversy. "We will make a lot of enemies with that name; the men are going to regard it as a challenge," noted one of the women in Correa's account. "Fine, because that it is: a challenge,"

[2] I thank Karin Rosemblatt for this insight.

87

replied another. Correa's explanation for the choice suggests clear feminist sensibilities:

It seemed as if the name itself contained the magic interpretation of ancient hidden inhibitions, squelched for millennia, responsible for quieting our anxieties about taking action, of speaking, of showing our truth, of abandoning the audience and taking our place on the stage, to be heard. To deliver our different and complementary message, that continued to be absent when decisions were made. Immediately [by virtue of choosing this name] . . . in some way [we] succeeded in obtaining a legitimate right to participate in the struggle, which women had not yet found in the political parties, in the civic movements [SOL], which were less aggressive than this Feminine Power in action. Women began to ask, desperately, where they could sign up (Correa 1974: 57).

The formation of the group confirms the view that women identified themselves not only in opposition to Allende, but in opposition to their male counterparts. Participation in Feminine Power transformed women's views of themselves. "Women had begun to be aware of their importance and their abilities and they assumed responsibility. This made them look for better intellectual preparation to confront present and future events," notes Correa (ibid., 92). In response to this perceived need, Feminine Power offered classes in group dynamics, public speaking, and communications, aimed at "[making] up for the lack of political training in the majority of women" (ibid.). Correa also suggests that participation in the opposition required women to redefine the role of motherhood:

Once and for all, we must know that we, mothers, have to overcome the worry that we only had to provide our children with a nice home, nutritious food, warm clothing and a useful education. We have to give them much more. We have to create in them a conscience, to open the windows of knowledge for them so that the light shines through. . . . In the darkness, there is always the danger that anything can assault their virgin minds! But to do this, we must enrich our own knowledge and know how to project it. We have to find out the answers. We have to learn the valid arguments, to know what advice to give, what ideas to inculcate, what conduct to recommend, what influences to reject. We have before us an enormous task that requires profound preparation, a lot of time . . . and study and more study. We have to begin for ourselves! (ibid., 104).

Women talked about the movement in terms of a "feminine revolution" and as women's "awakening." Members of Feminine Power considered their movement to be the Chilean version of women's liberation. As Silvia Pinto explained, in an interview on the one-year anniversary of the March of the Empty Pots, they represented a kind of feminism that included men:

The awakening of the Chilean woman, in massive numbers, was announced with a march [the March of the Empty Pots]. It was a protest march, but against a very specific economic and political situation [i.e., not against men]. It was the first step of feminine activism that has been gaining force. We will never go back to the way things were before. . . . You are witnessing a true feminine revolution, democratic in all its forms. And what is most important is not to segregate ourselves from men but to integrate ourselves with them (*Eva* 1972a: 72).

Feminine Power ran an ad celebrating the anniversary of the march that pictured a woman waving a flag, her hair streaming behind her – an image of woman as proud, independent, and strong (Townsend 1993: 58).

The Battle for the Women

With the March of the Empty Pots, women coined a new discourse for the opposition. They legitimated the expression of sentiments that the Left had harangued as fascist sedition. The march revealed to the world that many Chileans ardently opposed the famed "Chilean experiment with socialism." On January 6, 1974, *Washington Post* reporter Marlise Simon wrote, in what would become a famous quote, "We knew Allende's days were numbered when the women took to the streets."

The mistreatment of women at the hands of police came to symbolize the threat that the Allende government posed to middle-class bourgeois life. The middle classes resented these attacks on their way of life, and resented even more being called fascists for defending the status quo. As one leftist leader recalled:

The truth is that the bourgeoisie as a whole felt itself profoundly attacked and threatened by the simple existence of the [UP] government. Very soon the bourgeoisie, relatively democratic in its traditional way of life, saw itself transformed into a fascist bourgeoisie, reacting spontaneously in a fascist manner, revealing a profound and instinctive class consciousness capable of being expressed with enormous power. (One of its first manifestations was the so-called March of the Empty Pots, led by women at the end of 1971) (Silva 1979: 323)

Joan Garcés, one of Allende's top advisors, describes the attack by police as a violation of the status of the middle and upper classes:

The *barrio alto* went wild with rage because the police had moved against their elegant women and their most impressive youth. Never in the history of the country had they seen anything like it . . . [the women] had always seen the police attack *los rotos* or communist agitators. The right was humiliated. Right-wing radios suspended their regular programming and replaced it with calls for mobilization (Garcés 1976: 166–7).

Yet at the same time, women's protests represented a reversal of conventional gender roles. Editorial cartoons in opposition newspapers portrayed the March of the Empty Pots as an attack on the masculinity of middle-class men. The cartoons drew the women who marched as well-fed amazons – more powerful, more courageous, and often physically larger than their husbands. They depicted men as smaller, weaker, and meekly compliant with their wives' demands. A call to join the protest published in *Tribuna* (December 1, 1971) jokes, "Leave your husband changing the baby and washing the diapers." A week later, on December 7, *La Tercera* published a photograph that showed two men talking. In the caption, one man says to the other, "Did your mother-in-law go to the march where they hit the women?" The second man, appearing beleaguered, responds, "No, unfortunately not!" The same edition of *La Tercera* also ran a cartoon that pictured two small, skinny men talking on the street, one of whom is accompanied by his stout-figured wife. He says to the other man, "you have to recognize that food distribution hasn't been very equitable," a reference to the food shortages against which the women were ostensibly protesting. *La Tercera* ran another cartoon on December 13 of two men walking down the street. One says, "I had a tremendous argument with my wife. She wanted to go to a protest and I wanted to go the movies." "How was the protest?" replies the other. Portrayals of men as submissive and women as demanding correspond to a comment I heard over and over again when I asked Chilean men to tell me about the March of the Empty Pots. "What you have to understand," they would say, "is that women are the brave ones in our country, women are the ones in control. We men just go along with what they say." As Hermógenes Perez de Arce, a conservative Chilean journalist and politician, remarked:

What happens is that the women in Chile show much more resolve than the men. They are more courageous and this manifests itself in politics. We men didn't dare to go out into the streets, for example, because the UP was greatly superior in this regard: they had armed groups, not heavily armed, but with chains, *laques* and helmets. They were very organized. Whatever demonstration we [men of the opposition] organized, they destroyed violently. This scared us and made it very difficult to organize large demonstrations of [opposition] men in the streets. Women on the other hand, were not afraid; they went out [to the streets] and got beaten up, the more fury [the women] had and they would go right back out again (Pérez de Arce 1994).

90

Some men viewed women's activism as a threat to their masculinity. The paper company union took out an ad that portrayed the March of the Empty Pots as a call to arms to the men of the opposition. The ad appeared in *Tribuna* on December 3, 1971:

The paper workers repudiate the cowardly attitude of the hordes made up of those who, calling themselves men, savagely attacked our women . . . Women of Chile, move forward with your efforts, *now that we are sure that your bravery will revive in men the virility that they brag about, but which in the majority of men remains dormant* (emphasis added).

While some accounts portrayed women's efforts as brave and heroic, others portrayed women as victims. The woman who lost the ability to speak during the March of the Empty Pots became something of a martyr. Opposition newspapers constantly referred to women who had been injured in street protests and to women who had fallen ill and even died from heart attacks or heat prostration while standing in lines. The media relied on depictions of violence against women in order to incite and mobilize the opposition, a point confirmed by Perez de Arce:

There was always a case like this on the front page of the newspaper, of abuse, of some violent act [against women] . . . so the women were very important because they would confront theses things head on. They would march in the streets, organize these marches, in the supermarkets they would protest with a certain amount of violence . . . Here [in Chile] this produced a great impact (Pérez de Arce 1994).

Opposition accounts thus portrayed women in two contradictory ways – as defenseless victims and as autonomous agents. These conceptions of gender roles make sense in opposition to new meanings of gender roles associated with the leftist government, particularly the "new man" (*hombre nuevo*) of the revolutionary left, personified by Che Guevara and Fidel Castro.

Women sought to spur men into action in other ways as well. They threw grain at soldiers during military parades and made fun of soldiers they encountered on the street. They sought to challenge soldiers to assume their roles as protectors. Lucia Maturana said that when she passed a soldier in her car, she would roll down the window and chant "The little chickens say pío, pío, pío!" a line from a popular children's song (Maturana 1993). María Correa reported that women sent chicken feathers to soldiers through the mail (Correa 1993). Carmen Saenz, one of the organizers of the March of the Empty Pots, summarized the overall intentions of women's actions. She maintained that the march was intended "to dare [men], to incite them. It was like lighting a flame, in which the women . . . woke up the men and said to them, 'Hey, listen, where are you guys?'" (Saenz 1993).

Mothers of the Nation

The women who organized the March of the Empty Pots claimed they were defending the nation. The opposition parties took this image a step further, by portraying women as representing or embodying the nation. A ceremony performed during a Christian Democratic rally on December 16, 1971, two weeks after the March of the Empty Pots, illustrates the symbolic equation of women with the nation. *La Segunda* (December 17, 1971) reported that four students representing different academic departments of the University of Chile marched into the stadium, each holding a corner of the Chilean flag. As they marched into the stadium, the loudspeaker announced: "The flag is the Chilean woman, for the Chilean woman is the country, she is the flag." Others in the opposition portrayed the essential problem that Chile faced during the UP era as a crisis of national identity, to which women had a unique responsibility to respond. One ad promoting the March of the Empty Pots, published in *Tribuna* (December 1, 1971) reads:

Our nationality is in crisis and national solidarity, which was the fundamental force in the construction of Chile, is being destroyed by the criminal divisions between class and enemy groups fabricated by communism to destroy the Chilean family. The Chilean women and mothers of the National Party cannot remain impassive before the anguished moment that Chile is facing. Conscious of our responsibility to the nation and our children we will lend our unconditional support to the march.

The National Party took out an advertisement in *El Mercurio* to elegize the march on December 5. It read:

The National Party expresses its total and enthusiastic adhesion, its admiration and sympathy, for the vibrant demonstration of hundreds of thousands of Chilean women, to defend the integrity of the fundamental values of the nation, nationality, legality, liberty and the right to a full life, without the limitations and privations witnessed by governmental incompetence.

The link between women's opposition to Allende and the appeal to national sovereignty reflected the nationalist origins of the right. These views intensified in response to the opposition's view that Allende was a pawn in the Soviet-controlled sweep of international communism, who had compromised Chile's national integrity. The right portrayed the UP as having sold Chile out to international socialism – even in the face of its own ties to the U.S. government and multinational corporations.

Anti-Allende women compared themselves to the "great women" of Chilean history who had helped found the Chilean nation. An ad publicizing the march in *La Prensa* on December 1, 1971 issued a dramatic appeal:

Chilean woman, don't fail, you are the light and the defense of your children, you have to defend this home, physical and spiritual liberty, remember that you are a descendant of Guacolda and Javiera Carrera, indomitable women who defended the integrity of Chile.

In her account of the women's opposition, Teresa Donoso (1974b: 16) compares the movement to the actions of Inés de Suarez, the companion of Pedro de Valdivia; to Judith (of the Old Testament); and to Fresia, the heroine of *La Araucana*, a Chilean epic poem:

[These] three women, who nearly lost their lives to danger. These three women demonstrated that catapulting men to action is not unique to a particular race or historical period. Rather, it appears to be women's eternal duty. These three proved that this impulse, baptized as "feminine power" in Chile, was born with the dawn of the world.

The organizing committee of the march took out an ad in *El Mercurio* on December 5 that summoned all of Chile's heroines to describe the event:

It was an event the likes of which have never been seen in the history of Chile. The spirit of the mothers of the nation guided us and inspired us: Fresia, Inés de Suarez, Javiera Carrera, Isabel Riquelme, Paula Jaraquemada, Irene Morales. Even the soul of the *cantineras* [canteen operators] of the War of the Pacific appeared in the streets to give a drink of water to those of us who were, for reasons of age or sickness, exhausted. No fear existed among us. What did we have to fear if we marched through the streets of the Nation waving the flag and singing the national anthem? (See also *Tribuna* [December 6 and 30, 1971]).

These references identified women with the nation and portrayed women as the brave ones, who boldly went out to the streets to protest even when violence was imminent. They risked their lives to defend the country against threats to its sovereignty. The physical and verbal attacks to which women were subjected – at the hands of UP counterprotesters and at the hands of the police – symbolized for the opposition the deplorable condition to which the country had descended. Acts of violence committed against women came to represent attacks on the nation.

The Catholic Church: A Missing Frame

Given the influence of the Catholic Church over politics in Chile, one might expect that women in the opposition would have incorporated religion into their arguments against the government. Yet appeals to Catholic imagery appeared only rarely. Only one organization made explicit references to religion: the Housewives' Front (FRENDUC), an organization that claimed a membership of more than 300 women. The Housewives' Front took out weekly ads in *Tribuna* throughout 1972 in which they publicized the *Rosario por la Patria*, a weekly prayer vigil held in churches throughout Santiago. None of the other opposition organizations made references to God or to the church in their demonstrations or activities and none claimed the church as an institutional ally. This is particularly intriguing given that most of the women I interviewed for this project claimed that they were practicing Catholics and supported Catholic positions on issues such as abortion and divorce, largely because, as they put it, "Chile is a Catholic country." President Allende noted the absence of references to the church in women's demonstration as an indication of the high degree of religious freedom in Chile, as reported in *El Siglo* (December 5, 1971).

Women who opposed Allende did not appeal to the church because Chilean church leaders did not oppose Allende. Under the leadership of Archbishop Raúl Silva Henriquez, church officials mediated between the government and the opposition during the UP years. Henriquez convened a meeting between Allende and Christian Democratic leader Patricio Aylwin in the last days before the coup in the hopes of negotiating a compromise, an act widely acknowledged to be the last opportunity to avoid a military solution to the brewing crisis.

The church's refusal to take sides enraged hardliners within the opposition. Many of the women in SOL and Feminine Power had little interest in forging compromises: they simply wanted Allende out of power. To this end, they viewed the church as an adversary that frustrated their attempts to garner support for military intervention. A meeting between Cardinal Silva Henriquez and Castro prompted María Correa to remark, "I'm ashamed of the Cardinal's attitude. He appears in the company of the communists so frequently, as though he has forgotten the cruel persecution done to the Catholic Church in the Marxist world" (Correa 1974: 29). Correa remarked that Feminine Power even staged a protest in front of the Cardinal's house to demonstrate their displeasure (p. 65).

Women Outside Male Politics

Women's groups within the opposition insisted on their nonpartisanship. In its propaganda, Feminine Power invoked the spirit of unity among women who represented various parties. The women in this organization "understand that the only salvation of Chile lies in the union of all the democratic sectors . . . Neither political affiliation nor membership in different parties or movements matters to them" (*Eva* 1972b: 41). Such comments were typical among women who participated in various groups within the opposition, and appear frequently in press accounts from the period. A leader of SOL, for example, claimed that although all the opposition parties were represented within the group, SOL itself "did not belong to a particular party" (Maturana 1993). Literature distributed by FRENDUC stressed nonpartisanship as well. As one of FRENDUC's ads in *Tribuna* (May 10, 1972) read: "Behind our organization, there is not, we repeat, NOT ONE POLITICAL PARTY. The housewives who belong to FRENDUC can belong to whatever party or sympathize with whatever democratic group." An article on Feminine Power published in *Eva*, the opposition women's magazine, begins with the following statement: "No one asks what political party the others belong to. In reality, no one is interested in this. But one thing is clear: they aren't Marxists" (*Eva* 1972b).

Claims to nonpartisanship had a gendered aspect. Women portrayed themselves as uniquely capable of transcending party conflict, while men were mired in turf battles that impeded the progress of the opposition as a whole. *La Tercera* (December 4, 1971) reported one activist as stating, "[Men] are always wrapped up in the quarrels of criollo politics or bound by political loyalties that create real walls between brothers." Women perceived their role as being able to cut through the political rhetoric of empty promises and the partisan loyalties that prevented men from accomplishing substantive goals. One sympathetic journalist *La Tercera* (December 5, 1971) claimed that, as a result of the March of the Empty Pots, "the opposition, at the level of masculine leadership, would have to draw the conclusion that the Chilean woman is not averse to uniting without respect for political differences, when there are more profound interests at stake, affecting the home, her husband, her children and Chile as a whole." Feminine Power engaged in a relentless campaign to convince opposition politicians to unify against the UP, in which women directly addressed electoral issues. Correa recalls a meeting between Feminine Power and party leaders in her book: "We women will not permit the party leaders to abandon the country this way. It is also our land and the land of our children, and we women outnumber the men. Either you achieve the unity that can save us from Marxism, or we will never vote for you again" (1974: 81). Feminine Power sought to encourage male party leaders to "imitate their example of unity." At one point the group advocated locking up all the male leaders of the various political parties in a room together until they reached an accord (*Eva* 1972b: 41).

Women participated in politics on the basis of being nonpartisan, but in so doing they engaged in a strategy practiced by many different groups throughout Chilean history. Although women portrayed themselves as above the fray of party politics, the very same women frequently were militants in political parties. Women used two contradictory strategies in mobilizing against Allende: they claimed to be nonpartisan in order to forge unity among the parties of the opposition, but they simultaneously mobilized voters on behalf of particular political parties. The ability of women to cross the boundaries between conventional partisan activity and mobilization on behalf of cross-partisan issues is particularly remarkable given that party affiliation has always functioned as a powerful source of collective identity in Chile.

Conclusion

The March of the Empty Pots signaled a pivotal change in the political environment. The combination between the way in which women framed their activities and the timing of their protests triggered the formation of a broad, cross-partisan movement of women against Allende. In turn, women's participation across party lines legitimated the union of the centrist Christian Democrats with the rightist Nationals against the Marxist government by providing a noneconomic rationale for their cooperation.

The account presented here takes issue with conventional wisdom that portrays women as pawns of the right. In 1974, Marlise Simon, the *Washington Post* reporter, maintained that women's mobilization against Allende "made it clear how far women could be used and pushed without their full knowledge to produce the desired results." Simon also claimed that Chilean women's groups received "money, arms and tactical advice" from their Brazilian counterparts in order "to make the women 'feel' that they were running the show" (quoted in Cusack 1977: 115–6). This chapter shows that men and women had different interests in mobilization; the parties used women to serve their purposes, but women also used the parties to pursue their own goals.

The intensity and breadth of press coverage of this event provides a key measure of its importance. The government and the opposition battled ferociously with one another to control the media framing of this event. Opposition papers denounced the way women had been treated during the march and heralded it as a wake-up call for men to take action. Progovernment papers framed the demonstration in class terms, insisting that the women who protested were upper-class members of the bourgeoisie who hid their real interests "beneath their skirts." The conservative opposition prevailed in its efforts to monopolize women as a constituency because its views of women resonated with widely held norms about the status of women. The salience of these norms trumped numerous efforts on behalf of the Left to reclaim women as a base of support. The March of the Empty Pots had a lasting impact. The opposition parties would invoke women's involvement at several points over the next two years in order to maintain and strengthen the new coalition, and the military government that took power in 1973 would appropriate the March of the Empty Pots as a symbol of women's support for anticommunism.

5

"Feminine Power" and the End of The Socialist Revolution

The breakdown of democracy in Chile has been explained in terms of class divisions (Stallings 1978), U.S. government intervention (Petras and Morley 1974), partisan conflict (Sigmund 1977; Valenzuela 1978; Valenzuela and Valenzuela 1986), and institutional design (Taagepera and Shugart 1989; Shugart and Carey 1992). None of these accounts has discussed the relevance of gender differences – yet many of Chile's political battles were fought in terms of gender. In the period that followed the March of the Empty Pots, politicians in the government and the opposition alike framed many important events in gendered terms. They competed with one another to claim "feminine power" on their behalf. They did so largely in anticipation of the 1973 congressional elections, which would be closely contested and in which women's votes would likely determine the outcome.

At the same time, female leaders both within and outside the parties sought to sustain women's mobilization and to consolidate their leverage over policy outcomes. Women took advantage of political instability to promote policies they cared about as well as to forward their own careers in the parties and in Congress. They succeeded in doing so to a then unprecedented degree: in 1973, female candidates won 14 of the 150 seats in the House of Deputies, or 9.3 percent. Unfortunately, the coup cut short women's opportunities to translate their electoral clout into policy change. Once in power, Pinochet took over the women's movement, retooling it to suit his own purposes. Women's mobilization left an important legacy for the anti-Allende opposition, for the Allende government, and for the military regime that seized power from Allende. For each of these distinct constituencies, "the valiant Chilean woman" who rose up to combat Marxism became an enduring symbol.

98

"Feminine Power" and the End of the Socialist Revolution

The Allende Government Responds to Feminine Power

In April 1971, Allende publicly referred to women as "second-class citizens" in response to the fact that a majority of women voted for opposition candidates in the municipal elections. A year and a half later, the government had changed its tune. On November 28, 1972, *Puro Chile* reported that Allende gave a speech in which he declared, "There is no revolution without the presence of the woman." This change came about partly in response to the March of the Empty Pots. The Allende government introduced a series of policy initiatives in response to the opposition's apparent monopoly of women's support, largely at the urging of female leaders on the Left. Nonetheless, the Left embraced women's issues in a half-hearted or perhaps merely inconsistent way: appeals framed in the Marxist language of class trumped appeals framed in terms of gender. As many scholars have observed, the Allende government's efforts to recruit and incorporate women reveal contradictory ideas about gender roles (Rosetti 1983; Kirkwood 1986; McGee Deutsch 1991). As Heidi Tinsman (1996: 384) observes, "The UP's emphasis on women as mothers existed in tension with its claim to promote women's equality." Contradictions regarding the status of women within Popular Unity (UP), both in rhetorical and real terms, prevented the Left from mobilizing women on a scale equivalent with the center right and would later fuel the emergence of feminist consciousness among many women on the Left.

To illustrate the government's discursive ambivalence about gender, I analyze the UP's proposal for the Obligatory Social Service (Servicio Social Obligatorio [SSO]), a program designed to enlist women as volunteers in state-run day-care centers and hospitals. The government proposed the SSO in July 1972. The program would have required young women between the ages of 16 and 21 to provide three months of volunteer service in day care centers, hospitals, and health clinics – the female equivalent of compulsory military service. Presidential candidate Jorge Alessandri had outlined a similar program in his 1970 campaign, so it is likely that Allende expected it to generate widespread support. This did not turn out to be the case. The program proved controversial and sparked vocal opposition. Government propaganda for the program illustrates the contradictions in the Left's views of gender ideology: some statements framed the program in terms of women's roles as mothers, some in terms of women's equality, and some combined both appeals.

99

To mobilize support for the measure, the government sent a four-page color flyer to women's organizations throughout the country; it appeared as an insert in *Puro Chile* (August 10, 1972). The flyer emphasized the role women would play in deciding whether the Servicio would be implemented. It read:

Young Chilean Woman: you have been given the honor of creating the law of obligatory social service for women. For the first time, we as young Chilean women, united with all women, can express our will regarding a law that will permit us to decide the commitment and the participation of young women in the new society. . . . Participate! The people must decide what they want, and not others.

On September 5, *La Nación*, the government newspaper, maintained that allowing women to decide for themselves whether this program would be implemented was a way of breaking with the "*machista* and paternalist schemas of the past." In this article a government spokeswoman framed the program in terms that promoted women's equality:

The attitude of the Workers' Government is completely different from that of the previous, traditional governments. While the Right and its mechanisms of propaganda tend toward easy flattery (*halago fácil*), to stimulate frivolity, to convert women into objects, to recognize women as subjects only in their capacity as consumers, etc., at the same time they condemn her to a situation of dependence and double-exploitation. Bourgeois laws sanctify the incapacity of married women and their humiliating dependence on their husbands.

In the July 20, 1972 issue of *Qué Pasa*, Carmen da Fonseca, a government lawyer, stated that the program would "end the passivity of woman, who has always been a spectator to great events in history." In another interview with *Puro Chile*, September 15, 1972, da Fonseca affirmed that "to educate the woman about all the things she does, will be to liberate her. For many years, she has been denied the right to know, particularly [women] in the working class." Da Fonseca and others within the UP portrayed the Servicio as helping women overcome subordination by providing them with training that would educate them and thus reduce their economic dependence on men.

Other government officials justified this program in terms of conventional conceptions of women's roles as mothers. Carmen Gloria Aguayo, one of the primary advocates of the program (who would later become an activist in the feminist movement), defended it in terms that centered on motherhood. As *Ercilla* reported on August 16, 1972:

"Feminine Power" and the End of the Socialist Revolution

One important aspect [of the SSO] is that the service will prepare the future mother by giving her practical instruction in maternal-infant problems. And before applying this knowledge with her own [children], she will share and communicate [her knowledge] with others.

In *Clarín* (November 28, 1972) Allende spoke about the Servicio in terms that appealed to a feminine spirit of sacrifice: "It is a high honor for every Chilean girl to give a few months of her life to care for children, the future and the most precious thing that our nation has." The government surveyed 160,000 women in 3,027 mothers' centers and youth groups about the program. On September 9 and 10, 1972, the government sponsored local congresses in *comunas* throughout Chile to solicit women's opinions about the proposal. The measure met with widespread approval: *La Tercera* (November 28, 1972) reported that 79 percent voted for it, 12 percent voted against, and 9 percent did not respond.

Opposition leaders blasted the program, condemning it as a vehicle for Marxist indoctrination (*concientización*), particularly reprehensible because it targeted vulnerable young women. Journalists in opposition newspapers drew attention to the text of the proposal, which was written in formal Marxist terminology. It discussed the need to develop "instruments of popular mobilization," for example. Opposition papers reported that the government had not distributed this document to the women who voted on the measure, thus hiding its real objectives (See *El Mercurio* and *La Tercera* [December 3, 1972]). *La Segunda* (September 8, 1972) insisted that the government had inflated its estimates of women's support. A 91 percent response rate is unusually high for any survey.

Antigovernment forces also opposed this policy on the grounds that it represented an attempt to penetrate family life and violate the private sphere. One extreme-right publication, *PEC* (December 1, 1972) called the proposed Servicio "another means of control on the way to Communist dictatorship" and claimed that women trained by the program would function as spies in people's homes. *PEC* warned that young women providing child care through the program would brainwash children with Marxist propaganda and use them to gather information about families opposed to the government, views echoed in less extremist publications as well. *La Prensa*, the Christian Democratic newspaper, reported the results of the survey on November 28, 1972 under the headline "Maneuver by the Government and by the JAPS: They Want to Make Women Into Spies." In another article on August 14, 1972, entitled "The Weaker Sex Won't Accept the Military Service," *La Prensa* interviewed university beauty queens, coffee shop hostesses, and beauty parlor attendants about the program. Each interviewee emphatically expressed her love for children but indicated that she opposed the program on the grounds that she had enough to do already. The brief article was accompanied by three prominently placed photographs of attractive women, one with the caption, "With her large eyes, long legs and long hair, Erika also says NO to the Servicio."

Submitting the SSO to women's organizations for approval involved considerable resources and time. This cumbersome process drew vocal conservative opposition, and thus exacted high political costs. The government could have chosen an easier way to staff day care centers. The decision to go the high-cost route suggests that the government had other goals in mind besides simply recruiting teachers. The effort to survey women's organizations reflected the UP's goal of enhancing popular participation, but it also served as a mechanism to build support among women's organizations. As with many programs the government introduced, however, the SSO inflamed the opposition and hardened its resolve against Allende.

The Opposition Sustains Women's Power

The spectacular and unexpected success of the March of the Empty Pots prompted the opposition to mobilize women in response to other issues and to frame them as women's concerns. One example of this lies in the opposition's efforts to defend Chile's private paper industry. In the wake of the impeachment of Allende's Minister of the Interior, the government stepped up its efforts to nationalize the Papelera, Chile's only privately held paper company. The company, owned by the Alessandri family, produced the newsprint on which most opposition newspapers were printed. The government already owned the one other paper factory in the country. The opposition viewed the campaign to nationalize the Papelera as an attack on freedom of the press, because it would give the state monopoly control over the production of newsprint.

Protecting freedom of the press constituted one of the central issues in the Statute of Democratic Guarantees that President Allende signed in 1970 in order to win Christian Democratic support in the congressional runoff. In general terms, the government kept its promise: the large number of opposition newspapers and the often inflammatory and libelous articles they published attest to weak or nonexistent censorship on behalf of the government. Nonetheless, the opposition remained constantly alert to the possible erosion of its right to self-expression and frequently denounced any effort by the government to chip away at that right. Respect for freedom of the press under Allende was as much a product of opposition vigilance as it was of Allende's magnanimity toward his opponents (Valenzuela and Valenzuela 1986). Allende claimed that nationalization of the Papelera would increase the firm's efficiency. He authorized the Chilean National Development Corporation (CORFO), the state-run lending organization, to buy up shares in the company from individual shareholders. At the same time, the government mandated price increases for the firm's raw materials and prohibited the company from increasing the cost of its finished product, a move that political scientist Paul Sigmund (1977: 157) identified as "a patent effort to bankrupt the company."

To prevent a government takeover, the opposition mobilized women in defense of the company in order to play down the partisan and class nature of the conflict. The wives of the paper workers formed a separate organization and, in the hopes of capitalizing on the success of the March of the Empty Pots, planned a demonstration called "The March of the Women" to take place on March 24, 1972. Opposition leaders also dedicated funds, some from the U.S. Central Intelligence Agency (CIA), to buying up stocks from shareholders and financing a propaganda campaign. They carried out this campaign, not surprisingly, in the opposition newspapers (United States 1975; Sigmund 1977).

The government canceled the "March of the Women" the day before it was to be held, unleashing a furious response within the opposition. The government claimed to have canceled the march on suspicions that the right-wing group Fatherland and Liberty planned to attack progovernment organizations during the march. On March 25, *Clarín* reported that police raided Fatherland and Liberty's headquarters and arrested thirteen of its members on charges of sedition. Police acted on the basis of inflammatory announcements about the march aired on opposition radio stations, which typically exaggerated what was at stake. Journalist Teresa Donoso recalls the text of one of these ads:

Women, the country is in danger. The nation is under attack. It calls you. Defend her. Defend your constitution. Defend the sacred rights that the fathers of the country left us as a legacy upon founding this Republic. Women, the fatherland calls you (quoted in Donoso 1974a: 165).

103

Headlines about the canceled march in opposition newspapers attacked the masculinity of government officials and portrayed the decision as weak and unmanly. "THE GOVERNMENT WAS AFRAID OF THE WOMEN!" read one headline in *Tribuna* (March 23, 1972). "MINISKIRTS PROVOKE PANIC AMONG MINI-MEN!" read another on March 24. The opposition-led House of Deputies called a hearing to investigate the cancellation of the march – a clear effort to draw parallels between this demonstration and the wildly successful March of the Empty Pots. Members of Congress questioned Hernán del Canto, Allende's Minister of the Interior, about the government's decision. During this hearing, Del Canto justified the government's actions in chivalric terms: he insisted that he had canceled the demonstration out of concern for the safety of the female protesters. In *El Mercurio*, March 24, he claimed that the march would have threatened public order and would have "repeat[ed] the disaster that occurred last December" when protesters attacked women in the March of the Empty Pots. Del Canto explicitly denied that the government was afraid of women: "On the contrary, we have a lot of affection for women. We love them very much," he maintained in *La Tercera* (March 23, 1972). Leftist deputies echoed Del Canto's assertions that the government canceled the march in order to protect women from "dangerous elements" who were trying to hide behind the women. In this instance, government officials gained the upper hand by claiming to protect women's interests. Their focus on women's safety represented a reversal of the government's position with regard to the March of the Empty Pots, in which leftists downplayed women's agency.

The October Strike

In October 1972, shopkeepers and small businessmen in Santiago organized an indefinite strike against government-mandated price increases and the ever-present threat of government intervention. This event, known as the "October Strike" (*paro de octubre*) was central in catalyzing Allende's downfall. On October 6, the opposition convened a mass demonstration in downtown Santiago. Jorge Fontaine, then president of Chile's most prestigious trade association, issued a statement in which he asked "men, and not just women and youth" to join the protest, a clear reference to the degree to which women and youth had dominated the opposition's previous demonstrations (Fontaine 1999: 145). Nonetheless, women still figured prominently in the protest. Patricia Guzmán, one of

104

the "trench journalists" described in the previous chapter, addressed the assembled crowd:

We women have come to this meeting, once again, to give testimony to our faith in democracy, to our courage and our decisive spirit of struggle . . . We don't want any more declarations. We have had enough complaining and analysis of the situation. Too many words have been employed in the service of denouncing the government. The moment for action in Chile has arrived (quoted in Donoso 1974a: 231).

The strike officially began on October 11 when truck drivers in the southern province of Aysén stopped work in protest of the provincial governor's threat to nationalize the trucking industry. The national trucking federation quickly joined them. Within a few days, nearly all of the professional trade associations in Chile had declared their allegiance to the indefinite strike, including the "engineers' association, bank employees, gas workers, lawyers, architects, taxi and bus drivers, doctors and dentists" and 100,000 peasants in cooperatives loyal to the Christian Democratic Party (PDC). At its height, the strike involved between 600,000 and 700,000 people (Sigmund 1977: 186). This strike was not organized by political parties per se, but the leaders of the organizations that were involved represented clearly identifiable party affiliations (Valenzuela 1978: 78).

The government responded aggressively to the October Strike by throwing strike leaders in jail, taking over radio stations, implementing a curfew, and requisitioning privately owned stores and shops. Progovernment organizations attempted to pick up the slack in production by increasing the scope of the food distribution networks in working-class neighborhoods and manning abandoned factories. Despite these efforts, the strike paralyzed the country. It was difficult to deny its effectiveness. As Paul Sigmund (1977: 186) notes, "The observer walking around downtown Santiago felt he was in a ghost town." The strike represented a new level of conflict between the forces of the government and the opposition. Women in the opposition actively supported the strike by participating in the boycott and harassing noncompliant shopowners.

Female leaders in the leftist parties used this opportunity to try to mobilize women on behalf of the government. They framed their appeals to women *in the same terms as their counterparts in the opposition*. One woman in particular, Socialist Party Senator María Elena Carrera, repeatedly tried to mobilize leftist women in the hopes of restoring harmony within the UP coalition. For the most part, her appeals failed to generate a groundswell of female support equivalent to that on the center right, but women's support for the Left did increase, as electoral data from congressional elections suggest. Nonetheless, the opposition continued to monopolize women's support throughout the UP period. Had the governing coalition fractured and a new alliance formed, the mobilization of women on the Left might have reached a more impressive level.

In a congressional debate about the October Strike, Senator María Elena Carrera appealed to women to diffuse the conflict. She warned that the strike could lead to a violent civil war "in which none of us will be spectators." She called upon women to transcend sectarian divisions and put an end to the climate of violence:

We call on all the patriotic women of our country, so that together with the authorities, we can put an end to the disaster that the fascists have brought about.... The women of the Popular Unity believe that [violent] confrontation must be avoided. For this reason, we call all the women to make their husbands exercise good judgement, all the men of the National Party, of Fatherland and Liberty and of the right wing of the Christian Democratic Party (República de Chile 1972b: 547).

Christian Democratic Senator Patricio Aylwin interrupted Carrera to demand that she "explain these dangers to us and be more precise about the nature of this threat." Aylwin maintained that the crisis had not been caused by men's poor judgment, but rather by women's lack of tolerance:

The truth is if Madam Senator were to tour the vast sectors of Chile, not the upper class, but the middle class, and even the poor, the proletariat, peasants, she would see that the women are the ones who exhibit the greatest indignation and spirit of resistance with regard to the arbitrary acts of the Popular Unity. It is us, the men, who should calm the women down (República de Chile 1972b: 548).

Thus challenged, Carrera quickly changed her tone, abandoning her appeal to women in favor of more conventional leftist rhetoric: "Hate has been disseminated by the [rightist] Reaction and the people who support them. And they are right to do so: that's how the class struggle is. They are our enemies and they have their reasons for doing what they're doing" (República de Chile 1972b: 549). The remainder of the debate centered on the truckers rather than on women. Opposition senators claimed the strike had been organized by "poor truckers" protesting against the economic situation, while progovernment legislators maintained that the truckers were "fascist pawns" being used to discredit and destabilize the government.

Carrera's statements reflect a fundamental tension in the Left's efforts to mobilize women. Leftist leaders tried to reclaim women away from the Right, but they failed because their reliance on the ideology of class conflict consistently took precedence over claims premised on gender. They did not generate a way to frame their appeals in terms that resonated with women while at the same time maintaining a class-based perspective.

Ultimately, Allende resolved the October Strike by incorporating members of the armed forces into his cabinet. He named Army Commander-in-Chief Carlos Prats as Minister of the Interior and Air Force Commander General César Ruiz as Minister of Transportation and Public Works, among others. At this point, both the government and the opposition viewed the military as a politically neutral force.

The 1973 Congressional Elections

Both the government and the opposition looked to the March 1973 congressional elections as a way to resolve the increasing deadlock between the government and the opposition. The results would determine who would control Congress for the remainder of Allende's time in office. Both sides sought to win a decisive majority that would empower them to end the climate of chaos and confusion. If the opposition controlled two-thirds of the seats in Congress, it could vote to impeach Allende. If the government controlled Congress, it could pass its reform agenda more smoothly. The opposition parties formalized their alliance, naming it the Democratic Confederation (Confederación Democrática [CODE]). Yet the connection between them was weak: "beneath the common slogan of 'beginning the reconstruction,' each party adopted different tactics and sought to emphasize its own individuality. Consequently, there was no common program, nor even a united campaign. Electoral interests predominated and limited the alliance's ability to mobilize support" (Tapia 1979: 54). The opposition parties did cooperate in their efforts to win women's votes, however. They sought to present a united front through constant references to the March of the Empty Pots during the campaign.

Female legislators kicked off the campaign season by introducing bills that promoted women's rights. On December 12, 1972, Socialist Senator Carrera introduced a bill that extended maternity leave from six to twelve weeks, a measure that aimed to build support among working women. Carrera characterized the bill as one of "the many things the UP has done

107

for the family in its two years in government" (República de Chile 1972c: 1840). As the "government of the workers," working women were a natural constituency of the UP. Overall, however, working women comprised a minority of Chilean women in the 1970s, and thus their support could only extend so far. The Senate approved Carrera's bill. Fifteen days later, on December 27, Christian Democrat Wilna Saavedra introduced different legislation for women in the House of Deputies. Saavedra's bill proposed reforming the civil code to extend legal status to women. Saavedra had first initiated this legislation in 1968 when, as she stated on the floor of Congress, "in [my] double responsibility as parliamentarian and as Chilean delegate to the Interamerican Commission on Women [of the Organization of American States]" she convinced then Minister of Justice William Thayer to convene a committee to study the civil code. She framed her sponsorship of the bill explicitly in terms of women's rights: "I pursued this honorable and just objective for the cause of women's rights and in an effort to recover women's deep aspirations for the conquest of their civil rights" (República de Chile 1972a: 1533). The House of Deputies passed Saavedra's bill. The smooth passage of these bills differentiated them from the vast majority of legislation that was held up on partisan lines. In both cases, however, the bills did not make it to the other chamber and were indefinitely tabled.

The opposition worked hard to convert the mobilization of women against Allende into electoral capital during the congressional campaign. Campaign literature featured the symbol of the *cacerola* and made frequent appeals to "the Chilean woman" as a key constituency. Both parties nominated leaders of the women's opposition groups as candidates for congressional office. The PDC nominated Wilna Saavedra and Carmen Frei for reelection in the House of Deputies. The National Party nominated Silvia Pinto, one of the "trench journalists," and Silvia Alessandri, the woman who had obtained the permission for the March of the Empty Pots. Pinto's candidacy capitalized on her status as a leader of the women's movement. As one of her campaign ads in *Tribuna* (March 1, 1973) read:

SILVIA PINTO along with Carmen Puelma, María Eugenia Oyarzún and Patricia Guzmán started the anti-Marxist resistance in Chile. Ever since September 5, 1970 . . . without tears, with courage, they alerted us to the dangers of Marxism and they continue combating its abuses. The liberation of this country from the shameless, the incapable and the immoral depends on your vote. Silvia Pinto: symbol of the valiant Chilean woman.

108

The congressional elections failed to provide a decisive mandate for either side. The UP candidates did better than expected, winning 43.7 percent of the vote. The opposition won a majority of votes – 54.7 percent – but far less than the two-thirds majority required to impeach Allende. Among women, 59.6 percent voted for the opposition and 38.8 percent voted for the government candidates. These results indicate that both the government and the opposition increased their support among women over time, but within different districts. Overall, however, the government simply failed to garner *enough* additional support among women to win control of the legislature. These indecisive results further exacerbated tensions between the two sides. As former presidential candidate Radomiro Tomic recounted, "From March on, but particularly between June and the day of the *coup*, the country was overwhelmed by illegal activities, violence, and terrorist attempts . . . The opposition sought – successfully – to show that the government had lost all control over public order" (Tomic 1979: 234).

Women and Educational Reform

The government did little to restore public trust in the wake of the election. In March 1973, the government introduced a plan to reform Chile's educational system, the National Unified School (ENU). The proposal struck right at the heart of the fears of the middle and upper classes because it threatened the existence of private schools, especially Catholic ones (Fischer 1979; Farrell 1986). The principal change this reform would have entailed was the introduction of a new curriculum based on "socialist-humanist" values. Announcement of the ENU proposal in February 1973 sparked a two-month campaign against it, led by student groups, parents' associations, and the Catholic Church (Fischer 1979: 114). Women condemned the ENU as a threat to their role in rearing and educating children. Sara Navas, the leader of the campaign against this proposal, described the implications of the proposed reforms on childrearing in a 1993 interview:

In order to have the right to an education, you would have had to register your newborn child within 40 days [of birth] . . . and from that date on, the state would practically take over the child's education: the child would have to attend the nursery imposed by the state, which would be day care in the first period in the life of the child, and then prekindergarden, then to kindergarten . . . and if you didn't register your child within 40 days, you wouldn't have the right to have milk,

109

or medical attention, because health was also going to be controlled by the state. *It was a way of taking newborn children away from their mothers* (emphasis added).

One article criticizing the ENU in *Tribuna* (April 7, 1973) featured a photo of a woman gazing adoringly at her son. It carried the following caption:

The always emotional mother-child link finds itself in grave danger. Between the tender bonds of [mother and child] the state imposes the official will to convert the woman into a simple reproducer and the child into just one more item off the production line.

Robbed of their maternal duties, women would become nothing more than a baby machine; as a result, children would lose their identity and individuality. On April 12, 1973, the Minister of Education announced that the government would postpone implementation of the ENU in order to facilitate a "full, democratic and constructive debate" (quoted in Fischer 1979: 116). Introduction of this proposal served only to further polarize existing political conflicts.

Wife Power: The Coppermine Strike

Shortly after the ENU debacle, Allende faced another crisis. In April the workers at one of Chile's largest coppermines, El Teniente, held a seventy-six-day strike to demand a wage increase. The strike froze the production of copper and brought an economy already on its knees down to a prostrate position. The strike cost Chile an estimated $1 million per day in lost copper revenues, revenues that were essential to financing the socialist project (Sigmund 1977; Klubock 1998). The actions of workers against the government-held mining company also dealt a blow to Allende's credibility as president of the "worker's government."

The wives of the miners played a prominent role in the strike. Miners' wives joined with female employees of the mining company to form the Feminine Miners' Command (Comando Femenino de Mineros) to support the strike. They organized some of the most impressive and well-coordinated protests that occurred during the UP. They blocked buses carrying strikebreakers to the mines and they took over several local radio stations, one of which they held for forty-one days.

Historian Thomas Klubock argues that the miners' wives drew upon "women's moral authority as wives and mothers, as well as decades-long traditions of women's mobilization in El Teniente" (Klubock 1998: 294). But they also capitalized on the discourse of "feminine power" associated with the anti-Allende groups and used that rhetoric to pursue their own goals. The opposition characterized the miners and their wives as part of their campaign of direct opposition to the Allende government, but the miners remained fiercely independent. They resisted efforts to become co-opted by the opposition. Voting data support the argument that the miners' wives cannot be considered part of the anti-Allende women's movement. More women than men voted for Allende in the mining regions, the only areas in Chile where this was true (Neuse 1978: 139).

Both the striking mineworkers and the women in the Feminine Command repeatedly insisted that the strike was "not political, but gremialist," or in other words, about labor issues rather than a protest against the government. They characterized the strike as an effort to force the government to pay mineworkers in accord with legislation already on the books. The mobilization of women and the use of the "feminine power" discourse complemented efforts to portray the strike as nonpolitical.

On June 14, the Feminine Command organized a march from the mine in Rancagua to Santiago (approximately sixty miles) in order to meet with Allende and negotiate an end to the strike. On June 26, Allende received the delegation of miners' wives and promised to resolve the situation in three days. This meeting provides strong proof of the autonomy of the miners' wives from the Feminine Power women's movement. The women in the anti-Allende opposition would never have advocated such a move: female leaders in the opposition would have viewed efforts to negotiate with Allende as treason to their cause.

The notion of "wife power" inspired the wives of other professional groups to protest. When transportation workers went on strike a month later, in August 1973, their wives staged a sit-in at the Congress building in downtown Santiago and took over radio stations throughout the country. In Rancagua, even doctors' wives organized, claiming that they too faced problems running their households and were deeply troubled by shortages in medical supplies. But the significance of women's mobilization changed dramatically when the wives of military officers became involved.

Wife Power: The Military Wives

In the final weeks of the UP, the wives of armed forces officials staged a series of protests to demonstrate their support for military intervention. On August 20, 1973, three weeks before the coup, several hundred women demonstrated in front of the Ministry of Defense to protest against the resignation of Air Force Commander General César Ruiz. When Ruiz sought to resign from his post in the cabinet, Allende requested his resignation as commander-in-chief of the air force as well. The president's request represented an unprecedented degree of civilian interference in the military chain of command. Infuriated, Ruiz called a meeting of 120 air force commanders and announced his resolve to resist Allende's decision. A coup became imminent at this moment: "Hawker Hunter jets had already taken off from Santiago for bases in Concepción, where the navy, like the air force, was on alert status" (Sigmund 1977: 231). The meeting came to a tense resolution in which Ruiz reluctantly agreed to step down as air force commander in response to pressure from army commander and Minister of Defense Carlos Prats. The women protested right outside the building as this meeting took place.

A bizarre incident occurred that same day that heightened the tensions that pervaded the country. A woman named Alejandra Cox was driving along a street in Las Condes, the well-to-do district in Santiago. From the window of her car she saw General Prats stopped in traffic in the car next to her. Cox expressed her antipathy for Prats by sticking her tongue out at him. Prats responded by drawing his gun on Cox. He fired one shot in the air and another at the door of Cox's car. Apparently he had thought she was a man because of her short hair. Both cars drove through the intersection and got out to inspect the damage. Prats apologized profusely when he discovered that Cox was a woman. According to one account, she accepted his regrets, and that afternoon they exchanged letters of apology (Fontaine 1999). Prats then drove to his office in the presidential palace and informed Allende what had happened. Allende responded by calling a state of emergency, construing the event as an assault on Prats and an indication of deeper trouble to come.

The next day 300 army officers' wives staged a protest in front of Prats' house to demand his resignation as commander-in-chief. Police arrived and dispersed the protest with tear gas, further enraging the hardliners in the armed forces. Prats offered his resignation the next day, and General Augusto Pinochet took his place. This change cleared the path for the coup to take place. Journalist Patricia Verdugo (1998: 14) argues that pro-coup military officers sent their wives to protest, as a signal of the uprising.

These demonstrations marked the first point that military wives participated in the opposition movement. In retrospect, it appears that they got involved only once a coup was inevitable. Prior to this point, they had not participated in any of the civilian women's organizations. Under ordinary circumstances, their protests would have been considered highly irregular given the strict discipline expected of military families, but Allende's decision to appoint military generals to his cabinet in 1973 changed this situation. Military wives played a small role in the anti-Allende women's movement and they joined the action relatively late, long after other constituencies of women had established a public presence. After the coup, however, military wives would become the single most important group of women in the government.

Women Call for Allende's Resignation

On September 4, 1973, the government sponsored a rally to commemorate the third anniversary of Allende's election. Estimates for the number of supporters who turned out range widely – from 20,000 to 1 million (Sigmund 1977: 238). In any case, hundreds of progovernment groups marched past the presidential palace in an impressive show of support. Opposition women responded the next day with a march to demand Allende's resignation. This demonstration took place on September 5, 1973 – just six days before the coup would take place. Estimates for the number of women who participated also range widely – from 15,000 to 300,000 (Sigmund 1977: 238). Women pointedly expressed their frustrations with Allende in *La Prensa*, the Christian Democratic newspaper, September 2, 1973:

Chilean woman: Mr. Allende does not deserve to be president of the Republic. Mr. Allende has led the country to disaster. We don't have medicine for the sick! We don't have bread for our children! We don't have clothes with which to cover ourselves! We don't have a roof over our heads! We have been insulted, humiliated, persecuted for defending our children, for showing solidarity for our husbands on strike, for taking to the streets to awaken the dormant conscience of so many men.

Allende's announcement that Chile had only enough bread to last three more days precipitated widespread panic and eroded confidence in the government. In their demands for Allende's resignation, Feminine Power took out an ad in *La Prensa* on September 4 that invoked a statement that Allende had made in a speech months earlier: "You said, Mr. Allende, 'I would not hesitate to resign if the workers, peasants, technicians and professionals of Chile demand or request this of me.'" Thousands of women

113

marched toward the center of the city, chanting *que se vaya* ("he must go!"). As with the March of the Empty Pots, this demonstration provoked violence between right and left groups and ended when police dispersed the crowd with tear gas. In this climate of chaos, the Christian Democratic newspaper *La Prensa* echoed the call for military intervention on September 7 – on the grounds that a coup was necessary to protect women. On page one, the paper printed a photograph of a pamphlet distributed by the Chilean Navy, which read as follows:

The mother is sacred. The nation is sacred. Both are in grave danger. Extremism doesn't even respect women. The best guarantee Chile has are its armed forces. They will protect you from the cowardly crimes that you are victim of, at the hands of professional agitators.

Feminine Power issued a statement in *La Prensa* that same day calling explicitly for the military to intervene. This organization petitioned the Congress to declare the President unfit (*declarar inhabilidad*), threatening that they would beg the military to intervene if Congress failed to act:

If inside of one week the Congress has not used the only legal mechanism that remains to the country, we will find it necessary to knock on the doors of the barracks of the armed forces to beg them to save the nation, restoring order and tranquility and peace for people and security for their possessions, as our Constitution warrants.

The military would later refer to this statement as proof of women's support for a military coup, which was carried out on September 11, 1973. On that day, Hawker Hunter jets bombed the presidential palace with Salvador Allende and many of his closest aides still inside. Allende committed suicide in response to the coup.

Women and the Military Government

When the military took power, it halted the trend toward progressive reform that had begun in the 1960s and put it into a quick reverse (On the dictatorship, see Valenzuela 1978; Valenzuela and Valenzuela 1986; Varas 1987; Arriagada 1988; Constable and Valenzuela 1991; Angell and Pollack 1993; Drake and Jaksic 1995; Oppenheim 1999). While some within the military envisioned their task as a short-term repair, the dominant powers within the armed forces believed otherwise and "saw their mission as breaking with the past and creating a new political, social, economic and military order" (Arriagada 1988: 32). The junta dissolved

Congress, declared a state of siege and replaced national and local government officials with military appointees. It banned Marxist political parties and suspended all others. It replaced university administrators with military personnel. It declared union elections illegal and mandated that union meetings could only be held in police stations (Arriagada 1988: 39). The military imposed strenuous neoliberal economic reforms and initiated an aggressive privatization campaign. The initial phase of the military's project of reconstructing Chile's economic and political terrain was aptly named the "shock treatment" (Oppenheim 1999: 128).

Many within the opposition celebrated the coup with enthusiasm. Some families put flags outside their homes to show their support. Most believed that the military would restore order quickly, convene new elections, and return to the barracks. People fully expected that the military would respect the rule of law. When the junta called leftist leaders in for questioning, they responded quickly and voluntarily, in a poignant demonstration of their faith in Chile's democratic tradition. Even workers who had taken over their factories believed that Pinochet would permit them to maintain control (Winn 1986). Few anticipated the terror and violence that the military had already begun to perpetrate against civilians. Yet the brutality of the coup, with the death of Allende and the bombing of the presidential palace, provided clear signals of what was to come.

The military quickly incorporated women into its project of "national reconstruction." In the weeks following the coup, the wives of the junta members and other military officials donated their jewels and valuables to the military government. Several donated their wedding rings, which they considered an act of supreme sacrifice. On September 21, *La Prensa* quoted one woman's declaration of support for the new regime:

To donate my wedding ring has a personal meaning more than material value. My husband has given his whole life to the Armed Forces and to Chile. Now it is as if I've given these thirty years of marriage to help the reconciliation of the Chilean people, all the Chilean people. . . . The only thing that we can say to all the women is do not let yourselves be enslaved for anything. As Chilean women have demonstrated their courage, so can other women. Life is very beautiful and to live it, you need complete liberty, without oppression.

Italian women who donated their wedding rings to Mussolini made similar statements about their commitment to *Il Duce* (De Grazia 1992: 77). These words would ring hollow as the military's human-rights abuses became evident.

115

General Pinochet understood women's power and sought to monopolize it to further his own interests and those of the military as an institution. He put women's traditionally nonpartisan status to use on his behalf. Although most of the opposition groups formally disbanded, Pinochet and his wife, Lucia Hiriart, kept the spirit of women's resistance to Allende alive. Throughout his sixteen years in power, Pinochet and his female supporters made constant references to the March of the Empty Pots. He appointed female opposition leaders to positions of power within the government and created a vast network of new women's organizations. This was the genius behind the programs that the military created for women: the voluntariat (*voluntariado*), an enormous voluntary social service corps of middle- and upper-class women created and led by Lucía Hiriart; CEMA-Chile, a network of mothers' centers loyal to the regime; and the National Women's Secretariat, a government agency created to oversee programs and policies for women (For feminist perspectives on the dictatorship, see Munizaga 1983; Chuchryk 1984; Lechner and Levy 1984; Valenzuela 1987; Bunster 1988; Munizaga 1988; Munizaga and Letelier 1988; Molina 1989; McGee Deutsch 1991; Boyle 1993; Chuchryk 1994; Valenzuela 1998).

Solidarity, Order and Liberty (SOL) was one of the few groups that remained active and established close ties with the new government. Most of the groups that participated in the opposition disbanded after the coup. Former SOL leader Lucía Maturana (1993) explained that the military permitted SOL to exist because it was "the only organization that could give the government guarantees that we had not been infiltrated by the Marxists," supposedly because of its impenetrable pyramidal structure. In 1975, at the invitation of the Ministry of the Interior, SOL organized a series of social service projects; the group took charge of some centers for underprivileged children and collaborated with the National Women's Secretariat in poverty-eradication programs. The Minister of the Interior thanked the leaders of SOL for their efforts in a special ceremony (SOL Leaders 1994). During the military government, SOL's membership dropped from 10,000 to about 3,000. By 1994, when I interviewed members of the organization, the size of the group had dwindled to about 200 to 300 women, who referred to themselves as "the old guard" (SOL Leaders 1994).

Many of the women who had led the female opposition movement accepted positions within the military government. Importantly, the only women whom Pinochet singled out for appointment were those who had served as leaders of organizations with no links to the political parties. Pinochet took women's claims to be nonpartisan more seriously than the women had. Carmen Grez, for example, a self-described housewife and president of a mothers' center in Providencia, was appointed as head of the Women's Secretariat and later Minister of the Family. Sara Navas, head of the group that opposed the ENU, was named as Chile's delegate to the InterAmerican Commission on the Status of Women of the Organization of American States. Pinochet appointed María Eugenia Oyarzún, one of the famed "trench journalists," first as Chile's ambassador to the Organization of American States and later as the mayor of Santiago. The regime incorporated only those women who were truly nonpartisan, excluding female party leaders who had mobilized *in the name* of nonpartisanship.

The regime shunned women from the Christian Democratic and National parties despite their initial support for the coup. One woman, a Christian Democrat who had been president of a mothers' center in Las Condes and an active member of SOL, described how surprised she was to find herself shut out by the military. She recalled attending a meeting of women convened by the military a few months after the coup, to gather volunteers for its national reconstruction projects:

> As I had some facility with the microphone, I spoke. Everyone knew me from my work in CODE [the Democratic Confederation, the opposition coalition]. . . . They asked me to talk about my work in the mothers' centers so I talked about how the mothers' centers had been used for political ends in the past two or three years, when they shouldn't be political at all. . . . Someone in the audience raised her hand and said, "That's Carmen Puga, she's a Christian Democrat and a party militant; that's why she's talking about mothers' centers that way. *We* have never used the mothers' centers for political reasons" (Puga 1994).

Thus identified as a party member, Puga became the target of hostility, despite her support for the cause at hand. Puga's willingness to participate in the regime was not unusual among Christian Democrats, at least in the period immediately following the coup. The party sustained its support for the military during the first few months after the coup, but withdrew it when it became evident that the Junta did not intend to relinquish power to civilians. The party first expressed opposition to the military government in November 1974, after the Junta exiled Renán Fuentalba, a prominent Christian Democratic leader (Guilladat and Mouterde 1998:

73). Soon after, the PDC initiated discussion with the leftist parties about the formation of an alliance against the regime.

The military capitalized on women's resistance to the UP and converted it into a permanent rallying cry against the threat of communism, glorifying the March of the Empty Pots in particular. Year after year, in speeches commemorating the anniversaries of the National Women's Secretariat and CEMA-Chile, Pinochet, his wife, and other regime officials referred to the "valiant Chilean woman who was the first to take up the struggle against Marxism." These efforts began immediately after the coup in 1973 and continued until the very end of the dictatorship in 1989. Pinochet continuously reaffirmed women's commitment to the cause of anticommunism. He frequently portrayed the military as having responded to women's demands to take power, invoking the letter in which they resolved to "knock on the doors of the barracks" unless Allende resigned. As Pinochet stated in *El Mercurio* on April 24, 1974, seven months after the coup:

They knew even then, the Chilean women, that the country was in danger and that, with the inefficiency of political action thus demonstrated, only in the Forces of Arms and of Order existed the salvation of Chile. Now that the path of our history has been rectified by the military *movimiento* of the 11th of September, it would not be right to forget the agreement we made with the women of our country. *Their voice was for us the voice of the country, that called upon us to save it* (emphasis added).

On the second anniversary of the coup, on September 11, 1975, Pinochet reaffirmed this point:

Chile commemorates today the recent achievement of its National Liberation. Barely two years ago, somber misgivings filled the air, and the general feeling of anguish knew no bounds. Chilean women instinctively sensed the destruction of their homes and realized the extent to which violence had undermined their children's most elemental safety (República de Chile 1975: 13).[1]

The March of the Empty Pots remained a salient point of reference throughout Pinochet's sixteen years in power. In 1977, Pinochet decreed December 2 "the Day of the Woman," in commemoration of the anniversary of the March of the Empty Pots. The day became known as National

---

[1] This source, *Chile Lights the Freedom Torch*, provides an amusingly poor translation of Pinochet's speech and a summary of the day's events. A description of the rally reads: "The crowd became enormous and incalculable. . . . Next, President Pinochet addressed to all the Chileans a brief harangue" (p. 7).

Women's Day, to distinguish it from International Women's Day (March 8), which the military saw as a communist holiday because it commemorated the struggle of workers.

Invocations of the "heroic efforts of the Chilean woman" resounded in speeches and the official press throughout the duration of the regime. In referring to the activities that women organized against Allende, military spokespersons called upon women to sustain the spirit of sacrifice for the good of the nation. The military's constant invocations of the anti-Allende women's movement must be viewed in light of the small role that military wives actually played in that movement, as I suggested previously. On the basis of their rhetoric alone, one would think that military wives had led the movement from its inception. In 1977, the director of the National Women's Secretariat gave a speech memorializing the March of the Empty Pots, reported in *El Mercurio* on March 29:

They asked us to bring empty pots and pans. We joined in the *Plaza Italia*, many with worry, many with doubt. A little while passed, more arrived, but we wondered, would this do anything? How many women will come? Will they listen to us, or only laugh at us? . . . Those were long hours, of struggle, of pain, humiliation, that remain recorded on the pages of history. Human beings who were wounded, some never to recover. That so-called government, on giving the order to attack the women, took a fatal step. The war had begun.

In 1980, in the wake of a plebiscite held to ratify the new constitution, the director of National Women's Secretariat again invoked women's opposition to Allende in *La Segunda* on September 12: "Remember how [the Chilean woman] struggled, how she sacrificed, how she passed those days asking herself if her children would return home safely from school . . . For this we went to the streets. We took to the streets with anguish in our hearts, for the future of Chile. Today, seven years later, the Chilean woman has not forgotten those days."

Progovernment newspapers continuously invoked the March of the Empty Pots in an effort to cement the regime's claims to represent women. A 1982 editorial in *La Nación*, the official government newspaper, marked the ninth anniversary of National Women's Secretariat on October 14:

The mere mention of the Chilean woman evokes in our memory her decisive participation in the ill-fated days of the Marxist government of the so-called Popular Unity. With the courage of a soldier she confronted extremist violence and imposed her voice and her will over the slogans of the moment. . . . Since then, and the arrival of the liberating eleventh of September, the Chilean woman has

119

devoted herself with decisiveness and pure patriotism to the great task of reconstruction. In every imaginable arena, the feminine presence has constituted an impressive contribution to the country (see also *La Nación* August 3, 1982 and October 15, 1982).

On December 4, in 1984, *La Nación* commemorated National Women's Day with an editorial:

The Chilean woman was the first to give the battle cry and the most decisive battle to put an end to the chaos and tyranny. . . . It was the Chilean woman who combated the Marxist government with force and demanded the intervention of the Forces of Arms and of Order to restore the liberty of Chile.

And again on the same date in 1986:

It is precisely the woman who will have to play a decisive role in the productive continuation of the work of progress and liberty that the government of President Pinochet has carried forward, not only because she was in the vanguard of the struggle to defend the liberty of Chile, taking the first step to combat Marxism, but also because during these years she has closed ranks in defending peace, tranquility, order and the family.

The March of the Empty Pots remained a constant point of reference and a rallying cry for the military throughout the dictatorship. The Pinochet government engaged in a permanent campaign to sustain the mobilization of women that had supported the coup. On the one hand, these quotes reflect Pinochet's efforts to maintain women's support for the regime, especially as women began to mobilize *against* the regime and Pinochet's hegemonic claim to represent women came under attack. Pinochet invoked the women's movement to keep the threat of Marxism alive and to justify the military's intervention. On the other hand, military officials addressed women's efforts only during events that pertained exclusively to women, such as celebrations of National Women's Day and anniversaries of the National Women's Secretariat. Relatively few of Pinochet's other speeches refer to women at all (República de Chile 1990). The military honored women in order to secure their loyalty to the regime and to build a base of popular support.

Conclusion

To a certain extent, the anti-Allende women's movement became more "real" after Pinochet took power. By constantly invoking the March of the

Empty Pots, he ensured it would have a permanent place in public memory, perhaps a larger space than it may have otherwise warranted. He breathed life into the movement at the same time that he co-opted it on his behalf. Women's recollections of this movement must be interpreted from this perspective. I often suspected this to be the case when I encountered what seemed like "canned" responses to questions about the UP during my interviews. In Chile in 1993, four years after the end of the dictatorship, I witnessed firsthand the fervent appeal that Pinochet still held for women. *Pobladoras* spoke fondly of *"mi general"* and voiced nostalgia for the days of order under military rule, while women in the *barrio alto* flocked to beauty parlors to get made up for the parades held on the anniversary of the coup (Sota 1994).[2] The 1998 arrest of General Pinochet in London rekindled their adoration.

Studies of women's movements lament the nearly universal tendency of women's movements to decline once a particular crisis has been resolved. In this case, however, women mobilized with the explicit intent of forcing men to take action. The short-term goal of provoking men, and the military in particular, into action constituted one of this movement's primary aims all along. Women's efforts to get Allende out of power bolstered the view, already prevalent, that women naturally supported conservative political causes and opposed radical change. The military further reinforced the connection between women and the desire for order by incorporating tens of thousands of women in programs created along these lines. Given the extent of repression that Pinochet exerted over Chile – no freedom of the press, no Congress, no demonstrations, no meetings, no opposition – women's quiescence seemed guaranteed. In this context, the emergence of a feminist movement was nothing short of amazing.

While women on the Left organized frequent demonstrations and protests during the Allende era, their efforts were stymied by the fact that the UP coalition remained intact. Increasingly deep divisions emerged between the radicals and the moderates within the coalition, prompting many to accuse Allende of being unable to control his own allies. Yet a climate of intense polarization between the *upelientes* on the one side and the *fascistas* on the other kept the coalition together, and conditions were not propitious for the mass mobilization of leftist women on the basis of

[2] I thank Cynthia Sanborn for the beauty parlor tip.

their gender identity. After the coup, as we shall see in the next chapter, very different groups of women mobilized against the military to demand that Chile return to democratic rule. Women opposed to the regime even reclaimed the *cacerola* as their own symbol, and banged on them to protest against Pinochet.

PART TWO

Women Against Pinochet

6

Gendered Networks and the Rebirth of Civil Society

Many Chileans welcomed the coup as a temporary means of reestablishing order. Yet it soon became clear that General Pinochet intended to alter the structure of Chilean politics and society in fundamental ways. The government shut down democratic institutions in order to weaken the influence of political parties, which had long been considered the "vertebral column" of civil society (Valenzuela and Valenzuela 1986; Garretón 1989). The military systematically annihilated the leaders of the Left through disappearance, torture, and murder. The figures are grim: "Within six months [the military] had arrested 80,000 persons, and 160,000 suffered politically motivated job dismissals. An estimated 200,000 persons, including political refugees and their family members, went into exile" (Roberts 1998: 94). José Tohá, the cabinet minister impeached in the wake of the March of the Empty Pots, was sent to a concentration camp on Dawson Island, an isolated spot in the south of Chile. He died there a year later (Bitar 1987). Hernán del Canto, the minister identified as saying "we love women very much" in Chapter Four, went into exile in Colombia and then East Germany after soldiers robbed his house. He did not return to Chile until 1988 (Hite 2000: 113). Carlos Prats, the former Commander-in-Chief of the Army, fled to Buenos Aires with his wife. Both were killed outside their apartment by an assassin in September 1974. The regime expelled some 30,000 students and replaced several thousand university faculty members with military personnel. It restructured the economy to reduce the role of the state, cutting social service budgets severely. And it imposed restrictions on civil liberties to prevent the expression of dissent. Pinochet clarified the long-term nature of the junta's plans in March 1974, when he issued the "Declaration of the Principles of the Government of Chile." As this document read:

The armed forces and the police do not set timetables for their management of the government, because the task of rebuilding the country morally, institutionally and economically requires prolonged and profound actions [that are] absolutely imperative to change the mentality of the Chileans (quoted in Lowden 1996: 29).

A climate of intense fear pervaded the country.

Given the deep conflicts that divided the various factions within the opposition, one of the most difficult problems would prove to be the formation of a united front against the military. The challenges included finding spaces within which to express their views and discovering ways to repair the divisions that had emerged between the Left and the Center during the Popular Unity (UP) period. Yet despite these extreme conditions, and in some cases because of them, opponents of the regime slowly rebuilt civil society and began to mobilize against the regime. The proscription of the political parties inadvertently provided an opportunity for new kinds of organizations to emerge within civil society. Women played an important role in this endeavor. Three overlapping networks of women's organizations formed in the first ten years after the coup, around the issues of human rights, feminism, and economic survival. During this period, opposition groups remained relatively isolated from one another, sometimes even unaware of each other's existence. Protest activity on behalf of the opposition occurred sporadically throughout these ten years and had little impact on the regime. Not until relations among the parties changed would organized mass protest among women emerge.

Three factors fostered the development of women's resistance during this period: support from the Catholic Church, assistance from the international community, and contradictions within the regime's own policies. The Catholic Church provided an institutional umbrella that sheltered the opposition from repression and lent moral and material support to victims of the regime and their family members – most of whom were women. The international community bolstered the formation of the resistance in many ways. Foreign governments accepted tens of thousands of exiles who fled from Chile to escape political persecution and economic recession. Chilean exiles formed an international solidarity movement against the regime. In response to pressure from their domestic constituents, these same governments pressured the military regime to reduce repression and address human-rights concerns. International organizations provided a forum for the opposition and funded Chilean organizations that supported a return to democracy.

Finally, contradictions within the regime's own policies fostered the development of the opposition and promoted women's participation within it. While the government proclaimed the importance of the family as the basic unit of society, many of the regime's policies adversely affected families. While the government heralded women as its natural allies, military police threw opposition women in jail and subjected them to torture and rape (Bunster 1993). The establishment of networks around these issues – against human-rights abuses, against the regime's treatment of women, and against economic crisis – set the stage for the emergence of a women's movement in the early 1980s.

Gendered Repression

The violence perpetrated by the Chilean military has been well documented in numerous sources (for a review, see Corradi, Fagen et al. 1992). Human-rights issues have become even more prominent on the political agenda since the arrest and detention of General Pinochet in London in October 1998. New information about human-rights abuses continues to be brought to light.[1] The gendered nature of repression helps explain the prominence of women in the organized opposition, particularly around the issue of human rights. The military highlighted traditional gender differences as one of the keys to restoring order. The regime's strategies ranged from the relatively benign to the perverse, beginning with efforts to force people to conform to conventional gender norms in terms of dress and appearance. As activist María Mendoza recalled:

On September 13, 1973, I was walking down the street [in downtown Santiago] and soldiers stopped me and beat me up for wearing pants and having long hair. I didn't realize we were in a dictatorship. After the coup, women had to be well-dressed, their hair done, makeup, dresses. I wasn't into being feminine then. With the men, they arrested you if you had a beard, because only Communists had beards. Such ridiculous things (Mendoza 1999).

The vast majority of those whom the military arrested and disappeared were men, but women felt the terror just as acutely. Socialist

---

[1] On March 29, 2000, Francisca Mendoza registered the disappearance of her husband, Nelson Poblete, before Investigations Police in the city of Concepción. He had disappeared in December 1973. "I was too scared to do this before," she said, but felt that it was finally possible that "after so many years his body will be found so that I can finally give him a dignified burial" (*Santiago Times* 2000).

127

Party leader Adriana Muñoz recalled her situation immediately following the coup:

The day of the coup, my father had a big barbecue and celebrated with all his friends. They put out the flag, they danced the *cueca*, they sang the national anthem. I was inside the house with my two-week old son, crying desperately because my husband had disappeared, and listening to the shots and the bombing of the presidential palace. I was contemplating all this and terrified that [the military] would come to look for me . . . My father was having this big party and meanwhile, my whole world fell down around me (Muñoz 1994).

In addition to instilling fear, repression profoundly affected people's gender identity – what it meant to be a man, or a woman – both on the level of the individual and for society as a whole. Those arrested and sent to concentration camps were subjected to violence intended to destroy them physically and mentally. Torturers inscribed punishment upon the bodies of their victims in sexualized ways with a repertoire of punishments that included rape, electric prods applied to the sexual organs, and a constant stream of sexually abusive insults (Bunster: 1993). The capriciousness of the violence used against political prisoners suggests that extracting information from people did not appear to be the primary goal of torture, although it certainly played a part. In an account of his experiences in a concentration camp in 1974, Chilean writer Hernán Valdés characterizes the regime's violence as an effort to decimate the culture and identity of the Left:

the examples of wanton, brutal hatred are not simply reflections of a certain "evilness" or "cruelty" on the part of those serving the new regime; they should be seen as expressions of cultural hatred: as the almost irrational resentment of beings dependent on a particular culture toward those who had tried to change it (Valdés 1975: 9).

Gender roles and sexuality figured prominently in the military's efforts to reconstruct the identity of their victims.

Torture reinforced conventional gender relations in unintended ways. In *Tejas Verdes*, the camp where Valdés was held, the soldiers subjected men to the constant threat of sexual assault. "The soldier scrutinizes us, one by one, trying to find some feminoid trait. We instinctively look serious and put on a hard, set expression. For an instant my sandals seem suspicious, but my feet are so filthy as to dispel the illusion" (ibid., 73). At the same time, Valdés describes the consternation that male prisoners felt over the intimate relationships that sometimes developed between soldiers and female prisoners in the camps. His account implies that the men held their *compañeras* accountable to a gendered code of honor. Men blamed the women who had sex with the soldiers for their moral weakness, failing to see how the soldiers used sex to emasculate the men, or how women might have used sex as a way to ensure their survival. He writes:

We couldn't figure the women's behavior out. Were they participating [by consorting with the soldiers] out of fear, sheer despair, cynicism or pleasure? . . . We [the men] were all outraged. Someone recalled how in the National Stadium the women prisoners had preferred to be shot rather than let the soldiers lay a finger on them. We couldn't explain this kind of collusion (ibid., 78).

Men's failure to validate the experiences of female prisoners would contribute to the emergence of feminist consciousness among some of the women who had been taken as prisoners during the regime.

Women's Defense of Human Rights

Women began to mobilize in defense of human rights immediately after the coup. The Association of Democratic Women formed just three weeks later, on October 1, 1973, to work with political prisoners and their families (Chuchryk 1994: 156). This group and others provided material and spiritual assistance to prisoners and their families, tracked human-rights abuses, protested against the regime, and petitioned international organizations for help (Orellana and Hutchison 1991). Women organized informal networks of support for their male relatives who were being held in prisons and detention centers around Santiago. They visited the prisons on a daily basis to distribute food and clothing and to gather information. Sometimes female relatives had to be very well organized in order to outwit the authorities. As María Mendoza recalled:

You never knew when someone was going to be released [from prison]. Sometimes they would let someone out at 7 p.m. They would simply put them out onto the street with no money and no way to get home. If they didn't get home before the 8 p.m. curfew, the police would arrest them again and take them right back to prison. So we organized the people with cars to be ready to pick up people at a moment's notice (Mendoza 1999).

Church leaders mobilized quickly in response to the situation. In October 1973, "Catholic, Lutheran, Baptist, Methodist, Methodist Pentecostal and Greek Orthodox Churches, and the Jewish community" joined to create the Pro-Peace Committee (Lowden 1996: 32). By March 1974, this organization employed 103 people and had received 1,300 petitions for legal aid from the relatives of people who had disappeared (ibid., 34). Other organizations emerged, defying the state of siege. In June 1974, repression became much more systematic after the creation of the Directorate of National Intelligence, known as the DINA. Its first task was to eliminate the Movement of the Revolutionary Left (MIR), then the Socialist Party, then the Communists (ibid.: 37). After the murder of 119 members of the MIR, a group of their relatives formed the Association of the Families of the Detained-Disappeared (AFDD), which would become one of the principal human-rights organizations in Chile. The military forced the Pro-Peace Committee to dissolve in 1975 after learning that it had provided assistance to people the regime considered to be terrorists (members of the MIR). Cardinal Raúl Silva Henriquez responded by establishing the Vicariate of Solidarity on January 1, 1976, a move that consolidated Catholic leadership within the human-rights community. The Vicariate would become the primary source of refuge and help for victims of human-rights abuses throughout the dictatorship. The Vicariate organized crafts workshops for women to make *arpilleras*, tapestries embroidered with scraps of recycled cloth. The *arpilleras* depicted the political struggles of human-rights activists, protests, and stories of the disappeared, as well as scenes from everyday life. The workshops provided therapy and a source of income for the relatives of the victims and for the Vicariate. The *arpilleras* became very popular, prompting the Vicariate to organize a system for their production:

The workshops fixed a date once a month for the finished *arpilleras* to be turned in. The elected treasurer of the group took them herself to the Vicariate, which bought them. The number bought each month varied according to money on hand and the number of *arpilleras* coming in, but the rule of thumb was that each woman made four *arpilleras* a month, one a week. Most of the material for the *arpilleras*, provided by the Vicariate, was collected by them through appeals within Chile and abroad (Agosín 1996: 21).

Each month all the women from *arpillera* workshops around Santiago would meet, as many as eighty or ninety at a time (ibid.: 25). The Vicariate continued to sponsor the workshops until 1992 (ibid.: 31).

The violence unleashed against Chilean people after the coup mobilized the international community as well. The nature of repression severely limited the possibilities for public expressions of resistance in Chile, but protesters in foreign countries staged demonstrations that kept the military regime in the public eye. In the United States, the actions of groups such as the Chile Solidarity Committee swayed public opinion about events in Chile and exerted pressure on American lawmakers to implement sanctions against Pinochet. Within five days of the coup, demonstrators in the United States staged protests demanding a Senate investigation of the role of the U.S. government in Chilean affairs. A week later, on September 23, protesters gathered outside the New York offices of International Telephone and Telegraph Company (ITT) to oppose the company's actions against Allende. Members of the Weather Underground allegedly bombed ITT's New York offices on September 29. Demonstrators in Spain marked the Chilean coup with protests against the Franco regime on September 23, prompting a fierce crackdown by the Spanish government. The Franco regime responded with a decree that forbade Spanish citizens from drawing comparisons between Chile and the Spanish Civil War. In Geneva, Switzerland, on June 9, 1974, twelve hundred people marched to oppose Chile's presence at the general assembly of the International Labor Organization. On June 29, 1976, protesters in the United States demonstrated against the appearance of the Chilean naval training vessel Esmeralda as part of "Operation Sail," the much-touted visit of the Tall Ships in commemoration of the U.S. Bicentennial. State and local officials joined protesters in their efforts, citing evidence that the Chilean military had used the Esmeralda as a torture ship for political prisoners.[2]

Within Chile, however, protests did not take place until several years after the coup. Even a severe economic recession in 1975 and 1976 did not spur people to mobilize. This can be explained in terms of the level of repression and fear, but also to the absence of organizational networks independent of the banned political parties. Initial demonstrations against the regime denounced human-rights violations and appealed directly to the international community to intervene on behalf of the regime's victims. The first protest took place on June 15, 1977, when a group of relatives of the disappeared occupied the Santiago offices of the United Nations' Economic Commission on Latin America (ECLA) and staged a ten-day hunger strike. The New York Times reported that the group, which included twenty-four women and two men, demanded an international investigation into human-rights abuses in Chile. They timed their protest

---

[2] All information in this paragraph came from news abstracts of articles in the New York Times, in Lexis-Nexis Academic Universe [database online] – available from the Washington University Libraries Web site at http://library.wustl.edu.

to coincide with a meeting of the General Assembly of the Organization of American States in Grenada. The protest spurred a series of articles in Chilean newspapers, the first public acknowledgment in Chile that disappearances had actually occurred. The sit-in prompted protesters in the United States and Sweden to follow suit by occupying ECLA's offices in Washington, D.C. and Stockholm. On March 25, 1977, the *Washington Post* reported that U.N. Secretary General Kurt Waldheim responded by negotiating a settlement with the Chilean government to release information on the whereabouts of the strikers' relatives.

International influences, especially changes in U.S. foreign policy, dramatically affected the level of repression in Chile and changed the nature of opportunities available for protest. With the election of Jimmy Carter to the presidency in 1976, the U.S. government formalized its insistence that foreign aid be linked to a country's record on human rights. This shift in policy clearly influenced the Chilean military's decision to dismantle its security apparatus, the DINA. In August 1977, Pinochet shut down the DINA and replaced it with the National Center for Information (Central Nacional de Informaciones [CNI]). Some worried that the CNI represented a merely cosmetic change in Chile's security apparatus, but the number of disappearances fell to zero after it was created (Sigmund 1993: 111).

The cessation in state violence opened a space in which more protests began to emerge within Chile. The period after 1977 might be characterized as a "political opportunity" for protest to occur. Nonetheless, this abatement in state terror did not foment *widespread* protest. Chileans organized fewer than ten protests per year in 1978 and 1979, and approximately twenty per year in 1980 and 1981 (Foweraker and Landman 1997: 122). The demonstrations that did occur were small, relatively isolated, and still subject to ferocious repression. They did not set off a reaction among the general public, although they did galvanize the resolve of protesters, strengthening their determination to fight against the regime.

The first mass protest to occur in Chile took place two months after the dissolution of the DINA, on November 17, 1977. Approximately 100 members of the AFDD staged a demonstration in the plaza outside the Foreign Ministry, with pictures of their loved ones pinned to their clothing. The protest coincided with the arrival of new U.S. Ambassador George W. Landau in Santiago. The *New York Times* reported that Chilean police arrested the group, charged them with disorderly conduct, and released them later that afternoon. On January 3, 1978, approximately 400

Chilean students staged a protest against the government on the eve of a plebiscite that had been called to show support for Pinochet. According to the *New York Times*, police dispersed this protest "with only minor skirmishes." Six months later, in June, the AFDD held a sixteen-day hunger strike to demand information about missing persons. Five hundred university students staged a protest to support them. According to the *Washington Post*, "police broke up the protest, briefly detaining several dozen." On September 5, 1978, 350 students protested outside the University of Chile law school, "singing the national anthem and shouting 'liberty and justice'" in defiance of the university administration's refusal to allow an assembly to show support for the Sandinista rebels in Nicaragua. In retaliation, soldiers "expelled students, arrested, beat and banished them to remote villages for 90 days" (Constable and Valenzuela 1991: 261). In 1978, the AFDD staged a series of dramatic public actions, chaining themselves to the iron fence surrounding the Congress in downtown Santiago and conducting hunger strikes. Several new human-rights groups formed, including the National Committee for the Rights of Youth, the Peace and Justice Service, the Chilean Commission of Human Rights, and the Commission for the Defense of the Rights of the People (Lowden 1996: 84).

In 1979, the discovery of a mass grave in Lonquen, an abandoned mine outside Santiago, marked a turning point in public sympathy for the issue of human-rights violations in Chile. Five of the fifteen bodies discovered had been reported as missing at the Vicariate, providing incontrovertible evidence that disappearances had occurred. Before Lonquen, many people had believed the government propaganda that insisted that Marxists had fabricated the disappearances. These revelations prompted a series of demonstrations, including one in which fifteen hundred people formed a human chain stretching from the center of the city to the entrance of the mine (Agosín 1987: 7). Thousands of people attended a funeral mass for the victims (Lowden 1996: 82).

Given that most of the victims of human-rights abuses were men, it is not surprising that most of the activists in human-rights organizations were women. Of the 2,279 disappeared persons identified in the government's official report on human rights violations, 126 were women – only 5.5 percent (República de Chile 1991). Nonetheless, female activists in human-rights organizations did not identify themselves in gendered terms and they did not frame human rights as a women's issue. Members of the AFDD, for example, did not emphasize their identity as mothers, as the

Argentine Mothers of the Plaza de Mayo, or the El Salvadoran CO-MADRES would just a few years later.[3] Few of them espoused a feminist orientation. In discussing her work as a participant-observer with the AFDD, writer Marjorie Agosín (1987: 9) confirms this point: "The term 'feminism' rarely entered into our conversations. The women do not see their actions as a form of liberation of their sex." María Elena Valenzuela (1995: 168) attributes this to the "close links of these groups to the proscribed political parties, out of whose ranks most of the victims of the repression came." Connections between human-rights activists and the parties prevented them from mobilizing separately as women. Despite the predominance of female activists in these organizations, only later would they identify themselves with the women's movement. Eventually, however, some of the women who participated in human-rights organizations began to extend the notion of human rights to include women's rights. Betty Walker (1994) worked with human-rights groups for the Vicariate in the south of Santiago. She soon learned the limits of working within the church: "I began to get involved with what is the core issue for women, sexuality, the body . . . things that prompted the Vicaría to ask me to resign." In 1979, a group of women in the Chilean Commission on Human Rights started the Committee for the Rights of Women; many of these women would later go on to participate in feminist organizations.

Feminism

The feminist movement began as middle-class women formed a series of small, informally organized discussion groups to talk about the social and political situation under the military regime. These gatherings, which feminists would later identify as consciousness-raising groups, provided an intimate forum in which women could reflect on their experiences living under dictatorship.

Small autonomous consciousness-raising groups (*grupos de autoconciencia*) provided many women opportunities to speak and to lead previously denied to them by the political parties on the left. . . . The organizations tended to be very volatile; groups appear and disappear continuously . . . [but] what has been of primary importance is the search for more democratic forms of organization that permit the full

---

[3] For more on the CO-MADRES, the Committee of Mothers and Relatives of the Political Prisoners, Disappeared, and Assassinated of El Salvador "Monseñor Romero," see Stephen 1997.

participation of women and prevent the bureaucratization of power (Astelarra 1986: 130–1).

These groups provided a space for women to get together during a period in which civil society had ceased to exist. "We were living in a period of complete atomization and total destruction of the social fabric, particularly on the psychological level. In these groups we began to reflect in a very loose manner, without any specific agenda, about our past and present situation as women," remarked activist and scholar María Elena Valenzuela (1993).

In 1978, a group of fourteen university-educated, professional women formed the Association for the Unity of Women, known as ASUMA. They had been active in leftist politics prior to the coup and they represented a new generation of women. Unlike their mothers, they expected to pursue their own careers outside the home as a matter of course and sought to break with women's traditional roles in society. As Valenzuela put it, "we were searching for our own identity. We were breaking with the model that [women] had always followed" (1993).

In 1979, ASUMA became affiliated with the Academy of Christian Humanism (AHC), a wing of the Santiago diocese created in 1975 "to promote research, development and communication of the social and humanistic sciences" (Puryear 1994: 44). Funded by the Ford Foundation, the Inter-American Foundation, and Catholic groups from abroad, the AHC came to serve as "an institutional umbrella for the many talented groups of social scientists forced out of the country's universities" during the dictatorship (ibid.: 36). As part of this project, the AHC organized a network of study groups intended to foster free-ranging discussion among professionals and intellectuals in the opposition. These study groups facilitated cooperation among the leaders of the socialist Left and the centrist Christian Democrats. The AHC's study group on economics, for example, struggled to develop an economic policy that was acceptable to all the various factions within the opposition as a viable alternative to the regime's policy.

These study groups established a space in which diverse groups within the opposition could bridge the deep conflicts that had developed among them during the Allende era. Participants developed strategies they could agree upon and formed close relationships with one another (Brunner and Barrios 1987; Lladser 1988; Puryear 1994).

When ASUMA joined the AHC, it became known as the Women's Study Circle. Women's association with the AHC provided feminist

135

intellectuals a safe place to meet and allowed them to organize public events with a measure of protection from military repression. It also legitimized women's issues and lent prestige to the group, which facilitated its efforts to reach out to more women. In May 1979, the circle drew upon this newfound legitimacy to hold a conference, which approximately 200 women attended (Ediciones ISIS 1986: 26).

Over time, the Women's Study Circle became increasingly committed to more explicitly feminist goals, which generated conflict both with women outside the circle (the group's potential base of support) and with its church-based sponsor, the AHC. Initially, for example, the members of the circle avoided using the term *feminist* in public:

We completed our third and fourth conferences, always taking care not to frighten the participants and not even daring to call ourselves feminists (Ediciones ISIS 1986: 27).

Feminists' experiences with the AHC formed the basis for creating a movement. Between 1979 and 1983, the Women's Study Circle and other similar organizations

began to unite more as a movement, with women who had leadership experience in the political parties. These women had already begun the process of individual self-awareness and wanted to direct their efforts outward, in a more collective manner, to try to generate impact. They worked with women who were returning from abroad, where they had been studying [feminist] issues (Valenzuela 1993).

At the same time, however, the church set clear limits on the issues women could address. While the church openly defied the military government on human-rights issues, its views on issues such as abortion and divorce closely matched those of the military regime.

Most of the women who became leaders in the feminist movement did so on the basis of their previous affiliations with other organizations. Their political stance was informed primarily by the highly politicized climate that characterized university campuses in the late 1960s, as well as by the Catholic Church as it wrestled to address social and political issues in the wake of Vatican II. Almost of all the women who joined the feminist movement had been active in leftist political parties.

Women's Organizing in the Shantytowns

The most explosive rates of mobilization among women occurred in the shantytowns (*poblaciones*) that ring the city of Santiago. Women comprised

136

the vast majority of participants in what became known as popular economic organizations, a category that included income-generating workshops (for handicrafts, clothing, and food); subsistence organizations (soup kitchens and shopping collectives); and community groups organized around housing, legal services, and self-help. Scholar Clarissa Hardy estimates that 120,000 *pobladores* were involved in popular organizations as of 1983 – and 80 percent of them were women (cited in Molina 1986: 35 n. 27). Amid the crisis, many men lost their jobs for political as well as economic reasons. The military fired public-sector workers who had affiliations with the Left. Private employers followed their example. The economic crisis created by the transition to neoliberal economic policies hit the poor and working class particularly hard. The recession thrust many working-class families below the poverty line and forced women to find alternative ways to provide for their families.

Soup kitchens (*ollas comunes*) became a mainstay of support for *pobladores* during the military regime. They were perhaps the most common kind of organization in the shantytowns. For many decades prior to the coup, Chileans had organized soup kitchens to feed people during protests, strikes, and land seizures. During the UP, for example, Allende's opponents formed soup kitchens during the truckers' strike and the miners' strike. During the dictatorship, however, soup kitchens became permanent fixtures in many poor communities, "organizations that lasted over time and were not set up to support other actions," as scholars Teresa Valdés and Marisa Weinstein (1993: 152) observe. Organizers of the kitchens tended to view them as political spaces from which to mobilize against the regime, in part because the soup kitchens required active participation in order to function. In order to eat in the *ollas comunes*, families paid a small fee each month, raised outside money, gathered wood for the cooking fires, took turns cooking, and elected leaders. In this respect, the *ollas comunes* differed from the popular dining halls (*comedores populares*) in churches where families ate meals that others had prepared for them (Valdés and Weinstein 1993). Despite the more participatory nature of the *ollas*, many people saw them solely as a means of sustenance and felt ashamed about having to eat in a soup kitchen.

Popular feminism refers to the struggle for women's rights among poor women, *pobladoras*. It joins the everyday, survival-oriented concerns of *pobladoras* with an awareness of the larger causes of problems specific to women. *Pobladora* feminists view the problems of Chile's poor, such as lack of housing, unemployment, high food prices, drug addiction, and

137

alcoholism, from a feminist perspective. Three groups in particular dedicated themselves to the concerns of *pobladoras* during the dictatorship: the Committee for the Defense of Women's Rights (CODEM), Women of Chile (MUDECHI), and the Movement of Shantytown Women (MOMUPO). CODEM and MUDECHI were large, nationwide federations of women's groups affiliated with political parties representing the radical Left. As a result, they addressed the problems faced by poor women from the perspective of their position as a subordinated class. A group of four women affiliated with the Communist Party started MUDECHI in 1982. They had participated in the Women's Department of the National Union Command (the CNS, a dissident union) but felt frustrated at the CNS' inattention to the concerns of poor women. The women used their contacts in the party to build support. Within a year the organization included 12 women; it eventually grew to 200 within Santiago; and finally to 8,000 women in 60 groups nationwide (Valdés and Weinstein 1993: 162). MUDECHI's agenda initially centered on social and political problems but soon evolved into income-generating activities.

MOMUPO, on the other hand, formed independently from the political parties. In 1980, eight women founded MOMUPO to mobilize working-class women from shantytowns in the north of Santiago. The women knew each other from participating in Catholic Action during the 1960s. They had served as party militants and government officials during the UP, and were married to workers from the same factory. Being working-class women, they brought a "strong sense of class identity" to women's issues. They shared religious, political, and work-related connections. They held meetings of 40 to 50 women from *poblaciones* around Santiago to discuss "unemployment, health, neurosis and the anxiety produced by tenuous living situations." They met in the Vicaría Norte, a local parish church. Each of the original eight women began to organize women in a different sector of the city. An innovative leadership structure contributed to the organization's success in building support; each of the local groups elected a delegate to the MOMUPO council, which then elected an executive committee of five. This format insured the continuous representation of new groups in the leadership and limited the power of the "old guard" (Valdés and Weinstein 1993: 169). By 1987, they had formed eighteen groups throughout Santiago.

While the leaders of MOMUPO had been actively involved in political parties prior to the dictatorship, they sought to establish links with women who had no previous history of participation in parties or other social organizations. "We seek to break the umbilical cord that links political parties with organizations in civil society," stated MOMUPO leader Coty Silva in 1984 interview (quoted in Molina 1989: 141). Initially, the group did not openly oppose the dictatorship, in an effort to avoid scaring off potential participants. Many of the women who came to MOMUPO events in the early years "were in favor of the *milicos* [slang term for the military], or that is to say, they were very ingenuous, they believed the stories the military told," Silva remarked (1994). MOMUPO differed from other organizations in the women's movement in this regard. Marina Valdés, another one of the group's founders, described how working-class housewives, with no prior political experience and little political awareness, perceived their situation during the dictatorship:

For the housewife, the ordinary woman, the only thing she knew was that she was suffering . . . that her family was splitting apart, her husband didn't have work, that she had to go to work, that her unemployed husband began to drink, that her children took drugs and that her husband, sitting at home, resented her going to work. This provoked all kinds of conflicts (Valdés 1994).

MOMUPO helped its members understand that their personal problems resulted not from individual failings but from the larger political system. MOMUPO helped women see that "the public penetrated the private," and to persuade *pobladoras* that "we had to concern ourselves with the public in order to keep our families together" (ibid. 1994). In other words, problems experienced in the private sphere of the home required a collective political response. MOMUPO tended to organize small, local-level protests, "concrete campaigns that responded to the demands felt the most strongly by *pobladoras*, activities in which you see a direct outcome," Silva noted (1994).

MOMUPO's insistence on working with women who were less politically aware irritated some of the more active female party militants within the organization. The *políticas* (women in political parties) advocated taking direct action against the military regime:

The more political women were hardline combatants; they wanted to fight [the battle against the dictatorship] on the front lines. It was very difficult for the women in the political parties . . . to understand that we wouldn't accomplish anything that way. The people who joined [MOMUPO] found that kind of confrontation the most frightening (Silva 1994).

For similar reasons, party militants within MOMUPO accepted a feminist viewpoint with great reluctance (Valdés 1994). Yet MOMUPO's success in

139

mobilizing women eventually convinced the *políticas* within the organization of the virtues of a nonconfrontational approach. When the political situation changed in 1983, the group did join the opposition movement.

International Dimensions of Chilean Feminism

The regime's policy of exiling its opponents unwittingly strengthened the women's movement in Chile. Many foreign countries willingly accepted Chilean exiles; in turn, those in exile established relationships with people and institutions in those countries, further publicizing Chile's plight. Although far from their homeland, many men and women stayed politically active by organizing the opposition from abroad, creating an worldwide network of Chilean solidarity groups. As Socialist Senator María Elena Carrera recalled,

It was a big job to organize the exiles . . . In all the countries where there were Socialists there was an organization of the party, and in all the countries where there were Chileans there was a Popular Unity organization. We had organizations in thirty-five countries, women of the UP . . . Chilean women are tremendous; you have to tie them down to keep them from organizing. So we began with just letters with our signatures giving the necessary authorization for the organization – letters that were passed around, photocopied, and sent to places where we knew that there were women (quoted in Wright and Oñate 1998: 159).

Many Chilean women learned about feminism while abroad, especially those exiled in Europe and North America. When they returned to Chile, they brought feminist ideas about women's roles with them.[4] As Adriana Muñoz recalled, "I was in exile [in Austria] for ten years. I dedicated myself to Austrian politics and social organizations; it was during this time that I became a feminist" (quoted in Hola and Pischedda 1993: 174). Even for those who were not politically active, exile proved to be a powerful consciousness-raising experience. No longer able to afford domestic servants, for example, many exiled women "were obligated to take on domestic roles and responsibilities and often, for the first time, were confronted with the contradictions of female roles," noted Patricia Chuchryk (1994: 161). These new ideas did not always translate well upon return to Chile. Some women developed feminist consciousness while abroad, but abandoned it once they returned to Chile (Kay 1987). Exiles did not always receive a warm welcome upon return to their homeland. Many of those who stayed

---

[4] For a review of books on the Chilean exile community, see Wright 1995.

in Chile resented the exiles for having been able to escape. The regime fostered these feelings of resentment by attempting "to discredit the exiles by concocting the image of a 'golden exile' – a comfortable, even luxurious existence that contrasted harshly with the economic hardship faced by many Chileans at home" (Wright and Oñate 1998: 9).

Antiauthoritarian opposition movements and international organizations established strong connections in all the Latin American countries that underwent transitions to democracy. International recognition legitimized opposition groups and helped them mobilize popular support for the return to democracy (Castañeda 1993). International agencies donated considerable amounts of financial assistance geared toward promoting grass roots opposition to the military government. Feminist non-governmental organizations relied on financial support from international organizations and foreign governments. International meetings and conferences, particularly the United Nations–sponsored women's conferences and Latin American feminist *encuentros* (meetings), fostered the development of feminism in Chile. The *encuentros*, regional gatherings of feminists held every three years, have provided quantitative (in terms of numbers of participants) and qualitative (in terms of issues) measures of the feminist movement both as a national and a regional phenomenon (Sternbach, Navarro-Aranguren et al. 1992). The regional *encuentros* have helped to counter "feelings of political isolation" that many feminists experience in their own countries.

Celebrations of International Women's Day (March 8) became a focal point for the incipient women's movement in Chile.[5] According to legend, International Women's Day commemorates a spontaneous demonstration organized by women garment and textile workers in New York City on March 8, 1857. The workers protested against low wages, a twelve-hour work day, and heavy workloads. Police brutally repressed the demonstration (Zophy and Kavenik 1990: 287). Supposedly, the holiday was established fifty years later to commemorate their efforts. The date has been celebrated worldwide throughout the twentieth century – despite the fact that neither the original protest nor the anniversary march actually took place, as historian Temma Kaplan convincingly maintains (1985). Chilean women have commemorated the date with ceremonies, cultural events, conferences, and street demonstrations nearly every year since 1945. "One of the most permanent occasions for staging public acts [for women] has

---

[5] Sonia Alvarez (1990: 103) describes a similar phenomenon in Brazil.

been International Women's Day . . . Each year this celebration has taken on a different character in accord with what is happening in the country or in the world at large," note Gaviola et al. (1986: 51) in their history of the Chilean women's movement. These annual celebrations took on particular significance during the dictatorship because it provided an opportunity for women to coordinate their activities.

The eighth of March was, for many years, the initial kickoff of social mobilization, since feminine organizations of the opposition year after year, especially after 1983, achieved – on the basis of constant work – unified accords to celebrate International Women's Day, converting it into a day of denunciation and expression of discontent (*Análisis* 1988: 22).

March 8 galvanized the women's movement and kicked off the start of the new political year (Frohmann and Valdés 1995). During January and February, all Chileans who can afford it go on extended vacation; Santiago empties out and many businesses and government offices shut down. In the Chilean calendar, March marks the end of summer vacation and the beginning of a new year. The size of the demonstrations and degree of organization that could be pulled off, particularly at that time of year, provided an important indicator of the strength of the women's movement (Silva 1994). International Women's Day activities provided important information to supporters and opponents alike; "it demonstrated to them the degree of accord, consensus or force achieved by the opposition to initiate action after the customary summer recess" (*Análisis* 1988: 22).

Not everyone viewed international support for Chilean feminism in such a positive light. The celebration of International Women's Day presented a significant problem for the military government, for example. The military repudiated the event because of its socialist connotations, but at the same time it could not afford to ignore a holiday that commemorated women because the government claimed to represent the interests of Chilean women. Initially, the regime attempted to appropriate International Women's Day for its own purposes and reshape it to fit the military's gender agenda. The Pinochet government first tried to "nationalize" International Women's Day. When the United Nations declared 1975 the Year of the Woman, First Lady Lucía Hiriart responded by renaming it the "*National* Year of the Woman." Mrs. Hiriart responded to the slogan for the Year of the Woman – "Equality, Development and Peace" – by declaring, "We want to add to our year the concept of

GENEROSITY, which is what Chilean women have heaped upon this country, with even greater intensity since the eleventh of September 1973" (Poblete 1987: 66). Two years later, in 1977, the government created its own alternative to International Women's Day. Pinochet decreed December 2, the anniversary of the March of the Empty Pots, National Women's Day. As I discussed in the previous chapter, the regime observed National Women's Day with speeches commemorating the struggle of women against Allende, ceremonies recognizing officials in the National Women's Secretariat, and the announcement of new policies and programs for women.

Each year, the events that the opposition organized to celebrate International Women's Day revolved around bolder and bolder critiques of the military. At first women easily obtained official permission to hold events. Women's organizations escaped censure and repression by disguising the political character of the events they organized. In 1976 and 1977, for example, celebrations that involved women from political parties, human-rights groups, labor unions, and social organizations were convened in the name of the Union of Domestic Workers (Poblete 1987). Later on, the regime resorted to outright repression. In 1979, the women's divisions of the dissident unions obtained permission to hold a rally at the Santa Laura stadium in Santiago. *El Mercurio* (March 8, 1979) reported that police revoked the permit the day before the rally. The government issued a statement condemning International Women's Day as a celebration of "Soviet imperialism." The same scenario unfolded the following year: *El Mercurio* (March 8, 1980) reported that police initially granted the right to hold an event to celebrate International Women's Day but then revoked it, and the government denounced the holiday as "serving the interests of international communism." Despite these efforts, annual celebrations of March 8 became bigger and more widespread – and met with more and more repression. The military and the police dispersed the marches with tear gas and water cannons and detained hundreds of women.

Celebrations of International Women's Day provided a sense of historical continuity and legitimacy to the women's movement. The events often included speeches that reflected upon the history of women's involvement in society and politics. Feminist historians looked to the early women's movement for clues about how to construct unity within the contemporary movement. As scholars Alicia Frohmann and Teresa Valdés (1995) declared:

This search [for women's history] can lend new meaning to a women's movement that, although fragmented, fights from different perspectives for the democratic reconstruction of the country and for the presence of those who have established themselves as social actors in this process.

Attention to women's history proved particularly important to feminists seeking to forge a Chilean feminist identity and to build a movement.

Institutionalization of the Regime

The political climate in Chile changed again in 1980 as the government stepped up repression in response to increasing demands to restore democracy. The military sent protesters into internal exile, banishing them to remote villages. At the same time, however, the size of protests increased dramatically, as Chileans prepared to vote in a plebiscite on a new constitution. The Constitution of 1980 institutionalized Pinochet's vision of government and stipulated a series of mechanisms designed to protect the military's interests and enhance Pinochet's ability to remain in power. Voters approved the new constitution in a referendum held on September 11, 1980. The clause that would become most relevant to the possibility of a return to civilian rule was one that called for a plebiscite to be held in 1988, in which voters would choose whether to approve a presidential candidate selected by the commanders-in-chief of the armed forces. Pinochet was sworn in as president on March 11, 1981, for an eight-year term. He then moved his headquarters into La Moneda, the presidential palace that the armed forces had bombed in 1973 (Constable and Valenzuela 1991: 73). The chances for the restoration of civilian rule seemed more remote than ever.

Conclusion

Throughout the twentieth century, political parties had always provided the framework for mobilization in Chile. When the military came to power in 1973, it banned the parties and destroyed the infrastructure upon which political and civil society had been built. The vacuum created by the ban on parties allowed party activists to form new organizations and facilitated the participation of people who had never been engaged in political activity. Hundreds of women joined new organizations. However, these groups did not yet constitute a movement. Those involved in organizations did so clandestinely and sought little publicity. Women's groups

144

lacked an overarching frame that united their efforts against the regime: women in human-rights groups focused on obtaining information on their disappeared relatives, feminists sought to articulate a gendered perspective on the crisis, and women in the shantytowns organized to provide basic human needs.

Some protests occurred during the ten years from 1973 to 1983, but they failed to provoke a wave of dissent or shifts in the balance of power between the government and the opposition. The relative absence of protest during this period stands in marked contrast to the high levels of mobilization in Chile during the previous decades. Protest did not emerge in response to the recession that occurred in 1975 and 1976, challenging structural theories that suggest that movements are likely to emerge under conditions of economic inequality or relative deprivation. Nor did an alleviation of repression after 1977 lead to the emergence of widespread anti-regime protest, although it did facilitate the expression of some dissent. Nonetheless, the formation of organizational networks along these lines set the stage for the emergence of widespread protest and coalition building among women's groups in 1983. A change in the nature of political opportunities – a realignment among the opposition parties – set off a cascade of protest actions and triggered the formation of a mass movement among Chilean women.

7

Women Defend Life

MASS PROTESTS AND THE
WOMEN'S MOVEMENT

Chileans tend to associate the March of the Empty Pots with the women who mobilized against Allende. During the dictatorship, however, those who *opposed* the regime, men as well as women, banged on empty pots and pans to demonstrate against Pinochet. The empty pot became a powerful symbol of opposition to the military, just as it had signified opposition to Allende during the Popular Unity (UP) years. The *cacerolas* sounded again during the Days of National Protest, a series of mass demonstrations against the military regime that took place every month between 1983 and 1986. During these protests, a wide array of organizations representing labor, students, the poor, white-collar professionals, and women took the streets to denounce the regime. The center-left opposition parties embraced mass mobilization as a conscious strategy to overthrow Pinochet. Initially, the fall of the regime seemed imminent, but within a few months, the military had regained control and showed no signs of collapse. Moderate middle-class sectors withdrew their support for the protests as violence escalated in the shantytowns, and divisions within the opposition parties reemerged.

The reappearance of political parties in the public arena marked an important moment in the possibility for democratization. The opposition political parties formed two competing coalitions, the Democratic Alliance (AD) and the Popular Democratic Movement (MDP). The formation of these alliances constituted a moment of political realignment. Yet conflicts between the two coalitions threatened to derail return to civilian rule. In late 1983, the moment at which people believed the prospects for overthrowing Pinochet were high, debates over strategy plagued the opposition parties and prevented them from forming a united front against the dictatorship.

During this same period, women's organizations within the opposition formed a series of coalitions aimed at supporting the transition to democracy and advancing women's interests. The movement coalesced when women framed their mobilization in terms of their status outside the political arena. In this case, the frame that proved most resonant embraced the idea that women's style of political engagement differs fundamentally from men's style. The timing and framing of women's protest allowed diverse organizations across the entire spectrum of the opposition to converge: human rights, the poor, and feminists, as well as movement activists and female party leaders. Given the conflicts that divided the opposition, women worked hard to sustain the movement, as well as to develop a list of demands to be incorporated onto the opposition platform. Ultimately, this alliance among women would allow them to exercise an unprecedented level of political clout in setting the political agenda.

The Return of the Empty Pots

Many have credited Pinochet with creating an economic miracle in Chile, but periods of economic boom during the dictatorship alternated with severe recessions. In 1982 the Chilean economy took a hard hit from the international debt crisis. The banking system failed in the second half of the year; nearly all of Chile's banks had declared bankruptcy by the beginning of 1983. This downturn prompted a deep recession in which unemployment rose to more than 30 percent and the gross domestic product fell by 21.3 percent. The failure of the military's neoliberal economic model, upon which it had staked its success, damaged the regime's political credibility and inflicted significant financial harm upon many of the groups that had considered themselves allies of the military (Puryear 1994; Silva 1996). Furthermore, Pinochet resisted domestic pressure to take measures to alleviate the impact of the recession, which turned many of his erstwhile supporters in the business community against him (Silva 1996). Even Pablo Rodríguez, the leader of Fatherland and Liberty, abandoned Pinochet and "began calling for the creation of a Popular Front to rescue Chile from economic ruin" (Schneider 1995: 155).[1]

The extent of the economic crisis and the government's ineffectual response to it prompted the opposition to mobilize against the regime. On

[1] Pablo Rodríguez would represent Pinochet in the high-profile lawsuits against him in 1998.

May 11, 1983, Rodolfo Sequel, leader of the Confederation of Copper Workers (CTC), called for people to protest from their homes, "with the lights turned out, a candle burning and banging on pots and pans" (M. Silva 1994). People from all sectors of Santiago responded to Sequel's call to demand Pinochet's resignation. Chileans readily recognized the significance of the copper union's involvement: as the largest and most powerful union, the CTC had paralyzed the economy during Allende's last few months in power. People interpreted the CTC's involvement as a signal of widespread discontent. That day, tens of thousands of people kept their children home from school and refused to go to work, ride public transportation, or go shopping. Protests erupted on university campuses. As one activist recalled, "It was no longer the same old two hundred of us in the courtyards, calling for change. That day there were eight hundred, a thousand, twelve hundred voices that shouted, applauded and sang" (quoted in Constable and Valenzuela 1991: 261). That night, people in the shantytowns erected barricades blocking police from entering their neighborhoods while people in the well-to-do neighborhoods drove slowly through the streets, clogging traffic, and blaring their horns. All over the city people banged on empty pots and pans, creating a deafening noise. Broadcasts from opposition radio stations kept everyone informed of what was happening throughout the city (for detailed accounts of the protests, see Maza and Garcés 1985; Garretón 1987; Oxhorn 1995).

People also recognized the significance of the empty pots as symbol of the power of the people to bring down the government, although most of the activists I interviewed disavowed any connection between this protest and the women who had opposed Allende. As Marina Valdés, the leader of the Movement of Shantytown Women (MOMUPO), stated, "Banging on empty pots was a symbol of empty pots. It was to demonstrate your opposition to the [military] government . . . [we banged the pots] because there was massive unemployment, because your family didn't have food to eat" (Valdés 1994). The antimilitary opposition appropriated the *cacerola* as its own and reversed its meaning. Banging on empty pots and pans offered several strategic advantages as a means of protest. The *caceroleo* generated a lot of noise and provided an extremely effective way to express dissent:

When there was a curfew and the entire city lay in silence, and you couldn't drive your car or go out or anything, the *cacerolas* would start. It was a truly wild, wild noise with an incredible impact (Rosetti 1994).

148

In a climate where people did not dare to speak to strangers in public and where even neighbors mistrusted each other, the *caceroleo* provided a way to identify your allies, at least within the small radius of your own neighborhood.[2] In a *New York Times* article (June 29, 1986) Chilean writer Ariel Dorfman recalled a story a friend had told him about the first protest: "It was wonderful. We had always been suspicious of our neighbors. I timidly knocked two spoons together. Next door they answered me. Then another apartment joined in. We went out into the corridor and we all began hugging each other. You're also against him? You too? The whole building poured into the street. Suddenly we recognized that everybody was against Pinochet."

The regime did not refrain from repressing the demonstrations. On the first day of protest, soldiers killed 2 people, wounded 50, and arrested 300. In one neighborhood, "they arrested all the men and held them in Brazil Park. The secret police arrived next. They destroyed entire houses and terrorized families" (Schneider 1995: 158). The military aimed its repressive force at the shantytowns:

Away from the crowded downtown areas and physically segregated from upper- and middle-class neighborhoods, the government showed a complete disregard for even the minimal rights of the urban poor in order to create a climate of fear among the middle and upper classes – not to mention among the *pobladores* themselves (Oxhorn 1995: 218).

Because the *cacerolas* could be banged from inside one's own home, it usually proved a safe way to protest. Some protesters, however, testified that the police "shot and killed people inside their own homes, shooting at you from the windows" to silence the noise (Silva 1994). This depended on where you lived: people in the shantytowns were more vulnerable than those living in wealthier neighborhoods.

Despite the threat of violence, the emergence of the protests crystallized the formation of a movement that joined the three networks of women that had evolved around human rights, self-help, and feminism. On June 20, 1983, twenty-four women's groups formed a coalition

[2] People in many parts of the world have banged on empty pots and pans as an expression of protest, further attesting to its strategic value. Human-rights groups held a *caceroleo* in El Salvador in 1979 (see *El Mercurio* [October 27, 1979]); Venezuelans banged on empty pots to demand the resignation of President Carlos Andres Perez in 1992 (*Fempress* [February–March 1992]); and Russians used them to protest against President Boris Yeltsin in 1993 (*Chicago Tribune* [March 9, 1993]).

called MEMCH-83, invoking the name of the 1935 suffrage organization: the Movement for the Emancipation of Chilean Women. The new alliance saw the sudden mobilization for a return to democracy as an opportunity to promote women's equality. In MEMCH-83, women mobilized along explicitly feminist lines to push for the incorporation of women and women's concerns in public life. The MEMCH-83 executive council made decisions by consensus and self-consciously differentiated their style from that of men: "We're more informal, more focused on relationships and less competitive" (MEMCH-83 leader quoted in Molina 1986: 32).

The monthly protests offered an opportunity for women's organizations to stage their first public appearances. These initial efforts were quite small. The Women's Study Circle decided to participate in the protests on the basis of their identity as feminists, a decision that catalyzed a new direction for the movement (Chuchryk 1989). On the first day of protest, May 11, two members of the women's study circle distributed flyers that said, "Democracy in the country and in the home!" After the second protest, in June 1983, MOMUPO organized "the Marches of the Empty Shopping Bags" in which women would gather at local farmers' markets, held once a week in many neighborhoods, and demonstrate their opposition to high prices, food shortages, and the dictatorship by refusing to buy goods. "We would shout, 'We are women! We are against the dictatorship!' and then we would disperse as fast as we could because the police would arrive and arrest you," recalled activist Marina Valdés (1994). The protests involved a considerable amount of preparation, and usually lasted only a few minutes, but they politicized and empowered the women who participated in them. Protests in well-trafficked public spaces such as the farmers' markets (as opposed to banging on pots and pans from within their homes) helped women overcome the fear engendered by the repression (C. Silva 1993). During the fourth protest, on August 11, "approximately 60 women staged a five-minute sit-in on the steps of Santiago's National Library under a banner which read 'Democracy Now! The Feminist Movement of Chile'" (Chuchryk 1994: 166). This decision – to participate in national political debate on the basis of a autonomous collective identity – would define the strategy of the women's movement throughout the dictatorship.

The emergence of the monthly protests radicalized many of the groups that had been organized clandestinely, including the Women's Study

Circle. The change in the political climate prompted the Academy of Christian Humanism (AHC) to terminate its support of the Women's Study Circle. In November 1983, the AHC asked the group to leave, on the grounds that the group's agenda contravened Catholic Church doctrine. Church officials cited an article supporting divorce that the group had published the year before as cause for its expulsion. Members of the group compared this event to the Spanish Inquisition:

A meeting between representatives of the Circle and the directors [of the Academy] made us understand the Inquisition in flesh and blood and breathe a sigh of relief that we lived in the twentieth century. At least we would not be burned at the stake like witches (Ediciones ISIS 1986: 28).

The antagonisms that developed between the Women's Study Circle and its patron could not be attributed solely to opposition to feminism, however. *All* the study groups under the AHC's wing had to maintain a balance between "their need for protection [and] their fear of control;" while the church provided ample room for various groups to pursue their own intellectual agenda, "blatant attacks on church values could not be tolerated" (Puryear 1994: 45). The national protests prompted many people in the opposition to voice their views about Pinochet publicly, which put them at odds with the AHC's effort to maintain neutrality. After its expulsion from the AHC, the Women's Study Circle split into two new groups: the La Morada Women's Center (Casa de la Mujer La Morada), committed to activism and consciousness raising; and the Center for the Study of Women (CEM), a think tank dedicated to research and publication.

The opposition held eleven protests between May 1983 and October 1984. The protests varied in terms of their success, but "what is certain is that the mobilizations achieved the greatest number of participants only when they had been convoked by groups from across the entire political spectrum of the opposition, and their breadth and impact was diminished if convoked by only one sector of this spectrum" (Garretón 1987: 168). Unity was critical to the opposition's success. The intensity of the protests also varied geographically; the strongest response came from those neighborhoods where the Communist Party enjoyed a strong presence. Political scientist Cathy Schneider (1992: 263) attributes this to the party's "shared political conception" that emphasized a structural analysis of the political crisis and collective action.

Popular Protest and Coalition Conflict

The emergence of the protests took everyone by surprise. The political parties, which had been underground for ten years, moved quickly to assume leadership of the new mobilization. Yet despite public displays of resistance, the opposition parties still faced the daunting problem of agreeing upon an alternative political program. Deep and long-standing conflicts divided the parties of the Left and Center on substantive issues and personal grounds. Activists in the leftist parties distrusted the Christian Democrats for having opposed Allende and supported the 1973 coup. Within the Left, relations among the parties were fraught with conflicts over strategy that had originated long before Allende took office but intensified during the three years of the UP. Defying the regime's ban on party activity, opposition politicians formed two separate alliances. Despite the differences between these two coalitions – which would ultimately prove irreconcilable – both of them sought to assume control over the protests and promoted popular mobilization as a strategy to unseat the military.

On August 7, 1983, the Christian Democratic Party (PDC) joined moderate factions of the Socialist Party and other leftist parties committed to social democracy to form the AD (for a complete list of the parties, see Garretón 1987: 99 n. 11). The Christian Democrats agreed to cooperate with the moderate left on two conditions: acceptance of democratic institutions and support for capitalism. The Christian Democrats refused to form a coalition with the Communist Party until it "unequivocally renounced the use of violence" on the grounds that armed insurrection "would unify the military regime, provoke generalized repression, and narrow the social bases of the protest movement" (Roberts 1998: 125). Despite the official stance of the party, however, individual Christian Democrats had worked closely with members of the Communist Party since the early years of the dictatorship and would continue to do so (Frei 1994). The AD initiated negotiations about the terms of transition with Pinochet's newly appointed Minister of the Interior, Sergio Onofre Jarpa, a leader of the right-wing National Party. The negotiations backfired when it "became evident that Pinochet had used Jarpa to drive a wedge between the business and political oppositions and to diffuse the force of the mass mobilizations" (Silva 1996: 187). It soon became clear that Pinochet had no intention of devolving control back to civilians and that the AD had been premature in its efforts to engage in a dialogue with the government.

The radical left never doubted that Pinochet would resort to this kind of maneuvering. In response to the AD's miscalculation, the Communist Party, a militant wing of the Socialist Party, Movement of the Revolutionary Left (MIR) and a handful of other radical left parties formed the MDP. The MDP coalition favored armed confrontation with the regime over a negotiated return to democratic rule. The Communists wanted to ally with the AD to form an "antifascist front," but were not willing to forgo insurrection. During the UP government, the Communists had maintained a moderate line while the Socialists espoused more radical, extralegal strategies. In 1980, however, the Communists adopted a strategy of popular rebellion and armed confrontation aimed at destabilizing the military regime. The new approach represented the views of a new generation of Communist leaders (most of the old ones had been killed or exiled) who rejected any efforts to negotiate with the military (Oxhorn 1995). In December 1983, a faction of the Communist Party broke off to form a guerrilla group, the Manuel Rodriguez Patriotic Front.

The conflicts that emerged between the two party coalitions represented party politicking at its worst. Philip Oxhorn (1995: 211) cogently describes the kind of infighting that plagued these alliances:

The existence of political blocs such as the AD and the MDP focused the political debate around questions regarding which parties had or had not been included in any given bloc or agreement. Proposals by one bloc were met with counterproposals by other blocs and a spiral ensued that highlighted differences rather than similarities in order to create (or preserve) distinct political identities. Smaller political parties felt threatened by the dominance of alliance partners, leading them to engage in strategies designed to highlight their own uniqueness, which further contributed to fragmentation within the opposition. A single opposition alternative for a democratic transition became an increasingly elusive goal.

For many Chileans, these conflicts confirmed Pinochet's insistence that political parties had caused the country's downfall. In the ten years since the coup, Pinochet had continuously harangued "*los señores políticos*" as being responsible for the election of Allende and the chaos that ensued. Censorship and repression of the media prevented the public expression of any competing interpretations. The "antipolitics" perspective espoused by the military government made it difficult for the parties to reestablish credibility. For Pinochet's supporters, the conflicts that emerged between the AD and the MDP in 1983 proved that Pinochet was right to argue that political parties inevitably violated the national interest in pursuit of their own partisan goals.

Engendering the Opposition

Conflicts among the opposition parties galvanized women. Women's mobilization on the basis of their identity as women took off when these conflicts emerged and when women framed their involvement in the protests as a way to bridge the divisions between the competing partisan coalitions. In late 1983, Women for Life (Mujeres por la Vida [MPLV]) unified women across party lines in order to set an example for their male counterparts. MPLV sought to demonstrate that the opposition parties were not inevitably corrupt, but in fact could articulate a leadership role against the dictatorship. Like Feminine Power, the women in MPLV sought to establish unity among the opposition political parties and claimed that women possessed a superior ability to transcend partisan divisions. MPLV sought to provide an example for men to follow; indeed the group claimed that men must follow their example if the opposition was to succeed in ousting the military. To this extent, women opposed to Pinochet relied on some of the same rhetorical strategies as women opposed to Allende. However, while the nonpartisan mobilization of women against Allende led to the breakdown of democratic institutions, groups such as MPLV helped to restore democracy and promote women's equality.

MPLV formed in November 1983 as a coalition of sixteen women representing each of the various parties within the center-left opposition. These women were sufficiently well known within their respective parties to serve as public signifiers of those parties. As María de la Luz Silva, one of the founding members and a member of the Movement for United Popular Action (MAPU), recalled:

When I joined Women for Life, people from MAPU knew that we approved of this [organization], we were a point of reference for our people. Because we couldn't sign as members of a party, the [founding members of the group] became political referents ... So if I were involved with something, MAPU was involved, if Fanny Pollarolo was there, the Communist Party was there, if Graciela Borquez was there, the Christian Democrats were there (M. Silva 1994).

However, while their individual partisan affiliations were clear, these women did not represent their parties in an official capacity. MPLV was closely associated with the opposition parties, but formally independent from them. The male opposition leaders viewed the organization with considerable skepticism and initially did not support it. Christian

Democratic leader Graciela Borquez describes the deep apprehension she felt about joining MPLV and asserting her autonomy from the party:

When we came up with the idea of [having a] rally, I was a member of the National Directorate of the [Christian Democratic] party. At first [my male colleagues] told me yes, they agreed and they authorized us to go, but in the meantime there was a rally of copper workers where the Christian Democrats fought with the Communists and the Socialists, it came to blows and it turned out badly, so they called me to tell me they wouldn't let me go, because if the men had fought, then it would be worse among the women (quoted in Palestro 1995: 101).

The relationship between male party leaders and MPLV paralleled the dynamic between male party leaders and Feminine Power during the Allende era.

The women who founded MPLV were friends who had come to know one other while participating in human-rights organizations during the early years of the dictatorship. Their decision to organize was precipitated by a terrible event: the suicide of Sebastián Acevedo, a fifty-two-year-old man who lit himself on fire in front of the main cathedral in the city of Concepción to protest the disappearance of his two children. As Silva remembered:

This event struck us all as something extremely painful that could not go on. It was at this point that we women said, "Women support life, against the culture of death that is the dictatorship" (M. Silva 1994).

In response to Acevedo's death, MPLV sought to promote unity among the center-left parties, maintaining that unity that was a "necessary prerequisite for taking decisive action against the dictatorship." As Silva claimed, the group sought

to demonstrate that we, the women, were [in favor of] life, and that life mattered more than the party struggles, the positioning and the strategizing. We were going to demonstrate that when you introduce a higher interest, such as life itself, we can all go forward together (M. Silva 1994).

The women in MPLV claimed they were able to orchestrate a united front by focusing on the issues they shared in common, rather than those specific to their respective parties:

The pain provoked by this system of death and injustice united us, a pain that we transformed into conscience and a fear that we transformed into active solidarity ... we had the conviction that either the end of the dictatorship was imperative or we would all be victims of another collective tragedy. What united us was the

155

conviction that we were all indispensable in the reconstruction of democracy (*Análisis* 1984: 18).

MPLV perceived its agenda in gendered terms: its leaders saw the task of inspiring unity within the opposition as one that women were uniquely qualified to carry out. In the opposition paper *La Época* (January 4, 1988) Communist Party leader Fanny Pollarolo claimed that MPLV's task was "to inspire the spirit necessary to unify the opposition, to overcome the ineffectiveness of the men." The organization drew upon specifically feminine qualities in its efforts to mobilize others. In the same article, Fabiola Letelier, a human-rights lawyer, described the specific contribution that the organization sought to make to the opposition movement: "The active participation of women is of paramount importance because women are the ones who are most affected by the horrors of these years and have been in the front lines of battle." MPLV sought to push the opposition further along in the struggle for democracy.

On December 29, 1983, MPLV held a massive rally in the Caupolicán Theater in downtown Santiago. The event brought together women from all the factions within the opposition, the AD as well as the MDP, and movement activists as well as party members. The women organized the event in response to widespread and deep frustration over the inability of the opposition parties to reach accord regarding how to bring about the end of the regime. As Patricia Verdugo, a well-known journalist and one of the organizers, remarked at the time:

The recent acts sponsored by the Opposition had been characterized by spending more energy in loudly proclaiming divisions and mutually insulting one another than in charging our batteries to put an end to the [military] regime. The challenge was to construct real unity (*Análisis* 1984: 17).

MPLV sought to make united opposition to the regime an immediate moral necessity. A pamphlet distributed prior to the event read:

Today and Not Tomorrow: We come together to express the decision to act and join our determination today and not tomorrow to put an end to the signs of death: torture, hunger and unemployment, *detenidos-desaparecidos*, exile, arbitrary detentions . . . repression and abuses of power.

This gendered appeal struck a nerve. Nearly 10,000 women attended the rally, which became known as the *caupolicanazo*.[3] It served as the bench-

---

[3] The *azo* suffix indicates a blow or explosion: *puñetazo* is a punch with the fist (*puño*), for example. In this case, the *azo* suffix signifies the impact of the event.

mark against which all future opposition events would be measured. Before the *caupolicanazo*, "the Communist Party and the Christian Democrats had never gotten together, and were absolutely incompatible, like water and oil," but the Caupolicán rally brought leaders from these two parties together, said María de la Luz Silva (1994). The rally represented women's unique style of "doing politics." As Graciela Borquez recalled:

The men had always done events with nothing but speeches, then someone would come out and sing a song and then another speech, so to replace this we tried something different, participatory, and in this sense it was pretty important to have created this as women (quoted in Palestro 1995: 101).

The theme of unity was carried out to the most minute detail. The organizers prohibited participants from carrying party flags or banners. Instead, the coordinating council designed a banner in which all the flags of the various parties were arranged in a circle around the national symbol, "so that none would be on top of the others. It was like a wheel that spun around" (M. Silva 1994). They did not permit men to attend the event, because "we were afraid that we would be infiltrated by violent extremists," but also to teach the men a lesson (Chuchryk 1994). Pollarolo confirms this point:

this new style [emphasized] human relationships, it was a group in which we privileged trust from the first moment, nobody was going to say anything on behalf of their party, we would not accept that and I would say we succeeded in imposing total autonomy. And among us we put a lot of value in trust, in terms of transparency in our relations with one another and rejection of the things that we women have criticized so much, the men's way of doing politics, the manipulation, the machinations, the personal vision, saying one thing but doing another (quoted in Palestro 1995: 112).

Several sources affirm the significance of this event. Chilean sociologist Manuel Antonio Garretón (1987: 190 n. 18) refers to the *caupolicanazo* as "the most unified act that the opposition would organize against the regime." Natacha Molina (1986: 27) observes,

This act demonstrated that the women's movement had an enormous ability to mobilize women. There they made public the work of denunciation and mobilization that women's groups had been developing for some time. But the most important thing is that it was so unexpected, by the parties, by the regime and by the very women who organized it. For the parties and the political coalitions, the [*caupolicanazo*] revealed the capacity and efficiency of the women's movement, the creativity and its enormous potential for social mobilization . . .

without disorder and with agreement even down to the signs we carried. The event worried the regime and marked the start of a period of severe repression against women.

As María Elena Valenzuela (1995: 172) notes, "Women for Life became the reference point for political organizations on women's issues as well as the most important arena for convening and discussing the social mobilization of women." The success of the rally won approval from male opposition leaders, but did not prompt them to unite with the Communist Party. Graciela Borquez described how the leaders of the PDC responded:

The night before the Caupolicán I didn't sleep. Some said I should retire [from the party] and others supported me, and my legs were just shaking in fear. After the rally, I arrived at a meeting of the Political Commission [of the party], and all the men applauded me. They saw that it had been a success, but later they began to say unity was not the point. They said one thing, then they said another (*que aquí que alla*) (quoted in Palestro 1995: 101).

MPLV thus failed to forge unity among the men. Afterward, tensions between the two factions would begin to plague the women's movement as well.

Between 1983 and 1988, MPLV organized and participated in more than 170 events, including protests, demonstrations, and hunger strikes, as well as roundtable discussions, meetings with officials, and press conferences.[4] The group provided a safe forum for women's organizations to join together and articulate a common view of women's role in the movement against the military regime. The participation of notable female party leaders played an important role in this regard. Their presence signaled to various organizations that it was safe to attend and that attending might have some impact.

MPLV enjoyed more support than the other coalitions among women's organizations. No other entity proved equally capable of sustaining cooperation among women across the entire spectrum of positions represented by those who opposed the military government. However, MPLV also contributed to divisions within the women's movement. Its dominance within the opposition frustrated some feminists, who saw the group as exemplifying a more traditional way of participating in politics. Some feminist groups viewed it as a vehicle of the parties, rather than a repre-

---

[4] Teresa Valdés, one of the founding members of Women for Life, documented these events in "*Mujeres por la Vida: Itinerario de una lucha.*" Mimeograph. Santiago, 1989.

sentative of women's concerns per se (Lidid and Maldonado 1997). These
tensions were fueled by the fact that MPLV emerged precisely at the point
at which feminists were beginning to articulate a new way of "doing politics." As Patricia Chuchryk (1994: 84) observed, "Mujeres por la Vida had
tremendous convocatory and legitimating power that transcended party
alliances, but some saw it as co-opting the energies, organizational base,
and public visibility of the feminist movement."

It is difficult to discern the precise impact that MPLV had on electoral
politics, largely because so many women's organizations were active at the
time. Up until the plebiscite, it had successfully maintained a coalition that
included women's organizations from all points within the opposition
spectrum. Male party leaders, on the other hand, remained divided
between the two poles represented by the two-party coalitions, the AD
and the MDP. The divisions between these two coalitions resulted from
strategic differences about how to put an end to the dictatorship. The AD
advocated acceptance of the conditions set by the military government,
viewing it as a necessary evil. The isolation of the Communist Party from
the transition, and its subsequent political marginalization following the
transition, constitutes one of the great costs that Pinochet imposed on the
democratization process. The power of MPLV to mobilize women derived
from its ability to maintain alliances among women from all sectors of the
opposition. It used this convocatory power to press for the inclusion of
women's concerns on the opposition agenda.

In November 1984, the military declared a state of siege, prompting
many to retreat from the protests. A year later, women broke the mora-
torium on protests with a massive demonstration, one of two other events
that stood out in their ability to convene women. On October 30, 1985,
hundreds of women marched single file from different points of Avenida
Providencia, Santiago's main thoroughfare, linked with ribbons the colors
of the Chilean flag (Molina 1986: 51). The slogan of the demonstration
was "We are more" (Somos Más). The following month, Archbishop Henriquez convened the parties of the AD, the moderate socialists, and two of
the right-wing parties to sign the National Accord (Acuerdo Nacional), a
document that outlined a list of measures that the regime would have to
implement "in order to create an appropriate environment for political
negotiations" surrounding a transition (Oxhorn 1995: 77). The opposition
staged several protests to publicize the National Accord, including a peaceful demonstration in the Parque O'Higgins that hundreds of thousands of
people attended. However, the Communist Party and other sectors of the

Left were excluded from this event. Shortly afterward, the MDP, the leftist coalition, "sent a public letter to the AD calling for greater opposition coordination and cooperation" (Oxhorn 1995: 77). The refusal of the PDC to negotiate with the Communists prevented the AD from issuing a response until it decided to permit each party within the alliance to develop its own position.

The protests peaked in July 1986 when eighteen social organizations representing different sectoral interests formed the Civic Assembly. This coalition included unions, shantytown organizations, university students, professional associations, women's organizations, and human-rights groups. Feminist activist and party leader María Antonieta Saa represented MPLV. All the opposition parties supported this organization, from the Christian Democrats to the Communists. The Civic Assembly presented the government with a list of demands in a letter called *Demanda de Chile*. Feminist activists considered the inclusion of two demands representing women's interests to be a significant victory. The assembly called for a two-day national strike when the military failed to acknowledge the letter. The military responded to this protest with unprecedented fury in which ten people were killed. The most gruesome incident took place in Los Nogales, a *población* outside Santiago. There soldiers arrested two teenagers, doused them with gasoline, and set them on fire. One of the victims, a young woman named Carmen Gloria Quintana, survived but retained serious scarring that disfigured her face. The other victim, Rodrigo Rojas, died after being taken to the hospital. Rodrigo, a nineteen-year-old Chilean living in Washington D.C., had been taking pictures of the protests.[5]

These events convinced the AD that violent confrontation with the military was doomed to fail given the government's obvious advantages. In the wake of these incidents, the government discovered a large cache of armaments in the north of Chile and traced them to the Manuel Rodriguez Patriotic Front, the Communist-led revolutionary organization. In September, members of this group attempted to assassinate General Pinochet as his entourage headed toward his home in the mountains outside Santiago. The assailants wounded Pinochet and killed several of his bodyguards. In retaliation Pinochet once again declared a state of siege that lasted until January 1987. The AD withdrew from the protests, leaving only a small,

---

[5] For a moving account of Rodrigo's story, see "To Die in Chile," *Washington Post* (November 23, 1986).

radical core of shantytown activists and militant students (Schneider 1992: 261). The decline of the protests prompted the opposition to reevaluate its strategy.

Framing Women's Political Identity

Women's groups responded to the ban on protesting by shifting their focus away from public demonstrations to the more internal work of developing a policy agenda for women. They entered an intense round of "declarations, forums and meetings" and developed a series of initiatives that united the diverse array of women's groups in Chile around a common vision (Molina 1986). Women faced formidable short-term obstacles in organizing against the military regime: economic crisis, fear of repression, and lack of access to the media, for example. But perhaps the most difficult long-term challenge they faced was changing existing cultural norms and creating a new political identity for women. From a social movement perspective, women activists were engaged in the process of developing new frames of action. These frames would facilitate the formation of alliances across diverse groups and organizations – some more successfully than others.

Three different aspects of women's political identity emerged among women's organizations during the first ten years of the dictatorship. I identify these frames as "democracy in the country and in the home," "women as agents of history," and "popular feminism." Clandestine conferences and publications provided the most important venues for the transmission and evolution of these new ideas. Academic research institutes conducted studies that not only publicized women's status and women's history, but legitimated women as autonomous social subjects worthy of political attention.

"Democracy in the Country and in the Home"

In North America and Western Europe, feminist ideology has centered on the gendered distinction between public and private spheres and the possibilities for women's equality within the context of liberal democracy (Elshtain 1981; Pateman 1988; MacKinnon 1989). In Chile, feminist scholars have also drawn upon the concepts of public and private spheres to explain women's subordination, but Chilean feminism emerged out of a critique of authoritarian politics and the failure of the socialist project (Kirkwood 1986; Muñoz 1987; Valenzuela 1987). Chilean feminists

161

criticized the military government for its restrictive notions of gender distinctions and challenged the explicitly gendered vision of the individual disseminated by the military regime. They linked the transformation of gender roles with an end to military rule, comparing the authoritarian system of political rule to the dominant pattern of behavior within Chilean families. They insisted that the struggle for democracy necessitated a fight against *machismo* and discrimination against women. After the coup, the public realm, in the form of the policies and practices of the military regime, intruded upon the private realm, and rendered it impossible for women to run their households in the manner to which they were accustomed. The punitive effects of regime policies – massive unemployment, price increases, and the disappearances of family members – destroyed the private sphere. The fact that the military justified its actions in defense of the family exacerbated this situation and precipitated women's collective action. In other words, women mobilized in response to unwanted incursions by the state into the domestic sphere. These perceived links between authoritarianism in the state and patriarchy within the family became the basis for the slogan for which Chilean feminists would become known worldwide: "democracy in the country and in the home" (Kirkwood 1986; Valenzuela 1987; Chuchryk 1994).

The military government was not the only target of this slogan, however. Feminist discourse about the public and the private also addressed the men in the leftist parties. Repression after the coup virtually destroyed the Left. During the dictatorship, leftist leaders and activists (those who survived) subjected themselves to profound questioning about the causes and consequences of the failure of the UP, a victory for which the Left had struggled for more than fifty years. The Chilean Left embarked on a long process of internal reform. As scholar Manuel Antonio Garretón (1990) remarked, "[The Chilean Left] engaged in a renovation long before the fall of the Berlin Wall." Similar debates raged within the Left in other Latin American countries in the wake of military coups and the decimation of revolutionary guerrilla groups. Numerous studies have examined the crisis of the Latin American Left in this context, focusing on changing alliances among and within parties, the evolution of economic policy, and the search for new bases of support (Walker 1990; Castañeda 1993; Roberts 1998). These changes affected women profoundly and inspired women's efforts to reform the parties – a point that few scholarly accounts have discussed. The crisis of the Left in Latin America provided feminist activists with an unprecedented opportunity to reshape the

162

progressive agenda. The language of the public-private distinction empha-sized the importance of taking everyday life into account in defining the goals of the Left. Women demanded the democratization of the hierar-chical practices of Marxist-Leninist parties. By expanding the paradigm of class-based oppression to include gender-based oppression, feminists opened up the Left to previously untapped bases of support, particularly in the shantytowns and the middle class (Chuchryk 1994).

The experience of repression also shaped women's perspectives on their status in society. The military subjected women in the opposition to severe verbal and physical abuse. The mistreatment of female protesters during the military regime not only went unchecked, but it was far worse in degree and in kind than women had experienced during the Allende era. During protests, for example, soldiers and police brutally insulted women:

The organisms of repression, whether they were soldiers or police, used a language with women that was brutal, absolutely disparaging. They called us whores . . . [They said things like] 'you're fat, your breasts are sagging, you have a big behind' . . . It was a way to make everybody laugh, and to humiliate and degrade you (C. Silva 1993).

Police arrested female protesters and threw them in jail or confined them to detention centers where they were routinely tortured and raped (Bunster 1988).

During the Allende era, women responded to harassment by appealing to men to defend women's honor. In the aftermath of the March of the Empty Pots, newspapers condemned the abuse of women in chivalric terms. Women who had participated in the March testified passionately before Congress, providing details of their mistreatment at the hands of the police in hopes of inciting the opposition parliamentarians to take deci-sive action against the Allende government. Women in the antimilitary movement, however, did not have the luxury of appealing to others to defend them. The men who might have defended them had already been detained. There was no congress or tribunal to hear their case, and the media did not dare to champion their cause. Women were left to them-selves to handle this kind of abuse. Many organizations within the move-ment sought psychotherapeutic responses to repression and organized workshops on dealing with fear, repression, and abuse. In these workshops, women came to see their treatment at the hands of the regime as consis-tent with the sexualized and degrading vision of women in Chilean culture. As Coty Silva, leader of MOMUPO, said, "What is a public man? He is a political man, someone well-known, accomplished. And what is a public woman? Public women, the women in the street, are prostitutes" (C. Silva 1993). Women learned to see the sexual insults and physical abuse to which they were subjected during street protests as an instrument of repression used specifically against women. Workshops on the body, sexuality, and self-esteem provided a way for women to defend themselves psychologically against this kind of mistreatment, as well as to politicize them by identifying the military as responsible. The movement's later focus on issues such as domestic violence represented an extension of this approach.

Women as Agents of History

The women who mobilized against Allende referred to themselves as the direct descendants of Chile's national heroines, women who had played significant roles in the founding of the Chilean nation, such as Inés de Suarez and Paula Jaraquemada. The women who mobilized against the dictatorship also compared themselves to great women from Chile's past – but they focused on a different group of women. Rather than recalling women from Chile's colonial and independence periods, feminists compared themselves to women from the first half of the twentieth century, particularly those who had been active in the struggle for women's suffrage. The decision to name one of the feminist umbrella groups after a suffrage organization, MEMCH-83, provides one example. Two former leaders of the original MEMCh, Olga Poblete and Elena Caffarena, became mentors of the new movement and subjects of frequent interviews, studies, and homages. Women linked themselves with early Chilean feminists in part to counter criticisms that feminism was a foreign ideology that had little bearing on the Chilean reality. This criticism was made by their own counterparts on the Left as well by those affiliated with the military government. The Marxist left tended to view feminism as a bourgeois ideology that would divide the working class, while the regime viewed feminism as Marxism in disguise. By invoking the history of the early feminist movement in Chile feminists in the 1980s sought to legitimize their own actions.

Popular Feminism

During the dictatorship, middle-class feminists and *pobladoras* sought one another out and worked together, each for distinct reasons. The popular

164

feminist organization MOMUPO, for example, looked to feminist organizations for information about feminism, as well as for technical assistance and financial support. MOMUPO leaders brought in feminist psychologists and academics to conduct workshops on domestic violence, political repression, sexuality, and feminism.[6] They also consulted with feminist lawyers on domestic violence issues. Middle-class feminists came to MOMUPO meetings at first out of curiosity, to witness firsthand the explosive levels of mobilization that occurred among poor women. Organizing among *pobladoras* seemed particularly heroic given the intense repression directed at the shantytowns by the military (Oxhorn 1995). Feminists, drawing upon their training as members or former members of leftist political parties, also sought to build the feminist movement by creating alliances with *pobladora* organizations. They introduced feminist concepts to *pobladoras* and sought to link the class struggle with the women's struggle.

Despite this convergence of interests, coalitions between professional feminists and *pobladoras* were not easily forged. Alliances between the two groups remained fraught with disagreement on both sides. A series of seminars on feminism that MOMUPO organized exemplify this tension. At one point, MOMUPO invited Julieta Kirkwood, the intellectual leader of the feminist movement, to talk about gender discrimination and the history of feminism in Chile. MOMUPO members initially resisted the idea that they were engaged in feminist activities. As Marina Valdés (1994) explained:

At first we insisted that we were not feminists in any way, and didn't want to be. We saw feminists as women who were making demands on their own behalf... who felt sexually discriminated against and wanted equality, to go out and work and come home the same time as the men.... After a few meetings with [the feminists], in which we had real disagreements with them and really fought it out, we realized that what we were doing was feminism.

While they eventually embraced the feminist label, the women of MOMUPO maintained that feminism could not be considered outside the context of life in the *poblaciones*. Many of the conflicts between the *pobladoras* and the "professional" feminists centered on different notions about the family that reflected stark class differences. Coty Silva maintained that

[6] Some women pointed out to me that workshops on sexuality provided women with basic information about reproductive health and body awareness, and had nothing to do with sexual technique.

165

poor women tend to have a more traditional and conservative perspective on the family than their middle-class counterparts. In one of MOMUPO's workshops on feminism, for example, members raised strong objections to the way feminists depicted the notion of family responsibility. Silva (1993) recalled:

At one time the feminists were going around saying, "your children are a backpack that society imposes on you, so you have to take off the backpack." The *pobladoras* said, "For me it's not a backpack, and furthermore, they [feminists] can take it off because they can pay for a domestic servant."

Regarding domestic violence, *pobladoras* argued that they faced greater constraints than other women. Middle-class feminists have always encouraged women to leave abusive relationships, an option not available to *pobladoras*:

Women from the popular sectors have no other options, nowhere else to go. [If your husband beats you] you can't go to your parents' house because they are so poor. Many couples already live with their parents. You have to keep sleeping with the man who just beat you. . . . Other feminists can maintain their dignity more readily. They can sleep in separate bedrooms, or she can leave if she wants to (C. Silva 1993).

The women of MOMUPO maintained that under conditions of poverty, the family unit is essential to survival in a way that it is not for elite women. Despite these conflicts, Coty Silva credits the feminists for having introduced ideas about self-esteem and self-awareness: "To work with women in popular organizations along the lines of personal development, valorization and self-esteem," she stated, "was absolutely new, new, new" (C. Silva 1993).

Conclusion

In retrospect, it is easy to identify the women's groups that formed during the first ten years of the military regime as part of an incipient women's movement – but the formation of such a movement was not inevitable. The women's movement coalesced in 1983 in response to two conditions: the emergence of new coalitions among the opposition parties and the decision to frame women's participation in terms of their ability to transcend male partisanship. Women may frame their participation in many ways, but the frame most likely to resonate with people casts women as political outsiders, mobilizing in opposition to conventional and male-dominated modes of political engagement. In this case, women framed their actions as a response to men's inability to agree upon strategies to resolve a pressing political crisis: the end of the dictatorship.

What the anti-Pinochet and anti-Allende women's movements shared was a common way of "doing politics," a style of political engagement that located them in opposition to conventional mechanisms of negotiation and compromise. In both movements, women explicitly differentiated themselves from men. In both cases, they attributed the political crisis to the competition and horsetrading characteristic of the traditional male approach to party politics. Unlike its anti-Allende predecessor, however, the anti-Pinochet women's movement eventually used its ability to mobilize women on behalf of the opposition to demand support for a policy agenda that advanced women's equality. As the 1980s progressed, the coherence and increasing visibility of the women's movement prompted the Pinochet government to try to capture some of this constituency by modifying its strategies toward women.

8

Democracy in the Country and in the Home

WOMEN FOR AND AGAINST DEMOCRATIC TRANSITION

In the late 1980s, the opposition moved away from popular mobilization and gradually accepted the electoral timetable established by the Constitution of 1980. Women's organizations leveraged their ability to mobilize supporters into demands for policy change on the agenda of the opposition. They achieved a level of political clout unprecedented for Chilean women. Both the opposition and the military government embraced the demands of the women's movement in the context of strenuous competition to secure women's votes in the plebiscite of 1988 and the elections of 1989.

Yet within the women's movement, tremors began to surface along the fault lines established during the days of national protest in the mid-1980s. These fissures widened after the formal transition to civilian rule in 1990. Since then, the women's movement has demobilized and women's policy agenda has been only partially implemented (Cáceres 1993; Centro de Estudios de la Mujer 1993; Provoste 1995; Molina and Provoste 1997). Many of the organizations that formed in the context of dictatorship continue to exist today, but they lack the influence they had prior to the transition. Until the election of Socialist Ricardo Lagos to the presidency in 1999, women found themselves largely excluded from positions of political authority. Ironically, while the suppression of "politics as usual" during the military regime allowed new groups to gain prominence, the return of democracy has pushed these groups back out of the political arena (Waylen 1993; Jaquette 1994; Frohmann and Valdés 1995; Matear 1996; Schild 1998; Valenzuela 1998). It has proven difficult to sustain the women's movement as an autonomous political force. Women's organizations have proliferated in number and in kind, but they lack a set of shared goals and a discursive frame to unite their activities.

168

The women's movement shaped the political agenda of the opposition – and the military government – during the process of democratic transition from 1987 to 1989. In the ten years that followed the transition (from 1989 to 1999), women sought to carve out "a space in the state" in terms of positions of political power and policy implementation – as well as to maintain an autonomous movement. The divisions that appeared within the movement in the late 1980s have limited the success of these endeavors – and will continue to do so in the absence of a major party realignment and a heresthetic frame that unites the diverse interests that women represent.

The Democratic Transition and a Partial Realignment (1987–1989)

After the assassination attempt on General Pinochet in 1986, the Democratic Alliance (AD) abandoned the strategy of relying upon popular mobilization as a means of destabilizing the regime. The forces affiliated with this coalition came to the conclusion that they had little choice but to adhere to the schedule of elections stipulated by General Pinochet's constitution. The Popular Democratic Movement (MDP), the leftist coalition, however, persisted in the belief that any elections the regime held would be inevitably fraudulent and that participating in them would legitimize the regime. Nonetheless, in February 1987, both sides formed "Committees for Free Elections" to pressure the military to hold democratic elections and to mobilize people to register to vote. Voter registration would prove to be a Herculean task: the military had destroyed the Electoral Registry in 1973 so they had to start from scratch. Voting was expensive: voter identification cards cost $1.50, "the equivalent of half a day's wages for many people" (Constable and Valenzuela 1991). The process was time consuming: people often had to wait several hours in line to register, missing work and family responsibilities. Moreover, many simply did not believe the regime could be ousted through a democratic vote and thought it useless to register. Seven months later, as of September, only one-quarter of eligible voters had registered, and women at a much lower rate than men. That month a group of notable women associated with the opposition formed a separate organization to mobilize female voters, called Independent Women for Free Elections (MIEL, the Spanish word for honey). MIEL persuaded women to register by organizing fashion shows, holding raffles with cash prizes, and giving away coupons to buy meat. By October 1988, 92 percent of all eligible voters had registered, "the highest number of registrations in Chilean electoral history" (Garretón 1995: 230). In the end, women outregistered men by more than 200,000: *El Mercurio* (September 17, 1988) put the total at 3,826,459 women and 3,609,454 men. This meant that women's votes would be likely to determine the outcome of the election.

Victory for the Opposition

In March 1987 Pinochet signed a decree allowing non-Marxist and "pro-family" political parties to register. Within a year, all the opposition parties except the Communists agreed to participate in the plebiscite stipulated by the Constitution of 1980. The playing field for this election was hardly level. Pinochet had not yet announced the date for the plebiscite and had not indicated who would run as the regime's candidate – yet he began to campaign in earnest, with elaborate television spots, personal appearances throughout Chile, and massive public expenditures on housing and services. *El Mercurio* ran several articles in July 1988 announcing that women's groups wanted Pinochet to be the regime's candidate, echoing women's call for the military to intervene in 1973.

The situation for the opposition looked grim. The military subjected its opponents to intimidation, threats, and arrests: 1,780 people were arrested for political reasons in the first six months of the year (Constable and Valenzuela 1991: 302). People remained afraid to express dissident views. The conditions of extreme uncertainty surrounding the vote plunged the opposition parties into deeper turmoil – which Pinochet exploited to his advantage. At the end of August, Pinochet announced that he would be the regime's candidate, despite outspoken opposition from his own camp. The government scheduled the vote for October 5, 1988. Voters would choose from two options: vote *Sí* to approve Pinochet and allow him to remain in power until 1997, or vote *No*, in which case elections for a new president would be held in 1989. The plebiscite thus cast a return to democracy as a negative option, putting the opposition in the challenging position of persuading voters to support the *No*. The AD refashioned itself as the Coalition of Parties for the No (Concertación de Partidos por el No). It would later become the Coalition of Parties for Democracy (Concertación de Partidos por la Democracia), the alliance that would take power after the return to civilian rule in 1990.

Polls suggested that a majority of women would support the *Sí*. Pinochet probably believed he would win the majority of women's votes because a majority of women had always voted against the Left. In addition, Pinochet had dedicated significant government resources toward consolidating women's support over the course of his fifteen years in power, through the mothers' centers, the voluntariat, and a myriad of other programs created for women. The *Sí* campaign framed the vote as a choice between the status quo and a return to the Popular Unity (UP). The government's efforts to recruit women revived the fear campaigns of the past, substituting images of Allende's Chile for Castro's Cuba. "The UP was an interminable line for bread," began one of a series of ads with the title "Just 15 Years Ago." At a campaign rally for women in Antofagasta, rightwing leader José Miguel Otero urged women to tell their children what it was like during the UP. "Many of the young people out in the streets shouting 'No' do not realize that they owe their lives to the Pinochet government," he said, according to *El Mercurio* (September 22, 1988). Feminine Power even reemerged, with new branches that corresponded with electoral district boundaries. Carmen Saenz, the former Feminine Power leader, encouraged women not be afraid of voting in the plebiscite, "because we women were so brave during the Popular Unity." First Lady Lucia Hiriart tried to create her own women's movement, the "Women's Movement for Chile," and claimed to represent 35,000 women. Rightwing politician Hermógenes Pérez de Arce personally attested to women's passionate support for Pinochet. During a speech to members of mothers' centers in 1988, Pérez de Arce casually suggested that the opposition had a chance of winning the plebiscite. In response to his comments, the women in the audience physically attacked him and security guards had to escort from the auditorium (Pérez de Arce 1994). The government made some efforts to issue new appeals to women. On June 9, 1988, it announced the passage of a long-awaited reform to the civil code but even Pinochet's supporters criticized it as inadequate.

Given the historic division of the Chilean electorate into "three thirds" (one-third each for the Left, Center, and Right parties), Pinochet probably figured he could count on at least 33 percent of the vote. He sought to divide the opposition by identifying the Left with the failure of the UP, in the hopes of persuading voters on the Center to support him. The government constantly invoked images of the "chaos" of the Allende years in the hopes of replicating the center-right coalition that had supported the

171

coup. Pinochet portrayed the Left as extremist, violent, and committed to revolutionary socialism in order to dissuade moderate voters from supporting the *No*. Yet the relationship between the military government and the center-left opposition differed significantly from the relationship between the Allende government and the center-right opposition during the UP. Unlike Pinochet, Allende did not try to drive a wedge between the opposition parties. When Allende was president, both the government and the opposition had an interest in unifying the opposition parties. Leftists hoped that an alliance between the centrist Christian Democrats and the rightist National Party would lead more of the middle classes to support the Allende government. More radical factions of the Left believed that an alliance between the Center and the Right – "*los fascistas*" – would heighten conflicts between the working classes and the bourgeoisie and thus hasten what they considered to be the historically inevitable process of revolution. The opposition parties also favored an alliance that united them – the National Party eagerly so and the Christian Democrats somewhat less eagerly. The two parties agreed on strategy; they believed (mistakenly, as it turned out) that forming a center-right coalition would give them the votes they needed to control congress and impeach Allende. Divisions between the Nationals and the Christian Democrats did exist, but they would remain latent until after the coup.

The Coalition of Parties for the No had a clear interest in uniting against the dictatorship. Its campaign emphasized unity across partisan lines to counter Pinochet's portrayal of the opposition as sowing dissension. As Manuel Antonio Garretón (1995: 229) affirms, "unity seemed to be the capital that the coalition could count on, and, according to public opinion polls, it was the most valued aspect of the opposition campaign." Their slogan was "happiness is coming" (*viene la alegría*). As the main proponents of unity throughout this period, women played a highly visible role in the campaign. The coalition relied upon women's organizations to legitimize the center-left alliance, and women took advantage of the leverage they had to press for the incorporation of gender-specific demands on the political agenda.

At the same time, conflicts within the opposition forced social movement organizations to take sides. The Civic Assembly, the coalition of party and civil society forces, fell apart; "it lost its unity and its capacity to call different groups together" (Garretón 1995). The decision to participate in the 1988 plebiscite also split Women for Life (MPLV). The group continued to exist but no longer represented the same broad-based, cross-partisan constituency it once had. Most of its leaders left to join the party coalition, so the organization remained in control of a smaller group of women sympathetic to the radical left. MPLV began to focus exclusively on human-rights issues. It adopted a critical stance toward the upcoming vote and organized a campaign that emphasized the military regime's responsibility for human-rights abuses, in counterpart to the more upbeat tenor of the *No* campaign. Scholar Teresa Valdés (1989) describes the goals of MPLV campaign:

In the midst of the debate within the opposition, this campaign seemed to us a great support for the NO, insofar as it made present the feelings of many Chileans that they were not represented by the plebiscite strategy. We tried to suffuse the NO with the spirit of those who had suffered so severely during the dictatorship. We took out an ad that had a picture of a fingerprint on it, with the words "Where do they vote: the exiled, the political prisoners, the disappeared, the dead? They cannot vote. Do not forget them when you vote NO."

Celebrations of International Women's Day in 1988 reflected tensions within the opposition, and illustrated the government's efforts to exploit them. On March 8, party leaders urged compliance with the government's ban on protests. The military authorized women's groups to hold an event in the Don Bosco Auditorium in downtown Santiago, but prohibited all other "demonstrations, marches, meetings or any kind of public act." The day before these events were to take place, the police reneged permission for the Don Bosco event and issued a stern warning against all protests. The police statement, which appeared in *La Tercera* on March 7, 1988, linked women's activism to extremist violence:

We have not issued authorization of any kind, because we know from past experiences that these kinds of demonstrations, especially street protests, have only resulted in acts of violence against people and vandalism to public and private property. . . . We have the duty and the obligation to prevent and impede the planning and realization of whatever illegal act.

In this context, female opposition leader Liliana Mahn urged women to subordinate their gender-specific demands to other concerns and to participate in broader movements for equality and rights. On International Women's Day (March 8) she wrote an editorial in the opposition paper *La Época* that celebrated the life of Margarita Yourcenar, an activist who "declined to participate in the feminist movement because of the aggressiveness of its adherents." The opposition parties wanted women's votes but sought to prevent women from mobilizing autonomously.

Nonetheless, women went ahead with the Don Bosco demonstration. The police energetically repressed them. With an estimated 1,000 women inside the auditorium, those still outside chanted slogans and briefly blocked traffic. *La Época* reported that police responded by spraying the protesters with water cannons and throwing tear gas into the auditorium. They arrested fifty people. The organizers reconvened the women on the patio of a nearby school and the speeches proceeded as planned, only thirty minutes behind schedule. Afterward, organizers denounced the police's use of violence and blamed the disturbances on "outside elements" who had infiltrated the event "in an attempt to make us look responsible." This incident illustrates how the government sought to discredit the women's movement by associating it with violence and disorder.

Ultimately, however, the opposition rallied despite tremendous obstacles to defeat the regime. Voters rejected the plebiscite with a decisive majority – 55 percent for the *No* and 44 percent for the *Sí*. Among female voters, a slender majority, 52.5 percent, voted "No" (Figure 8.1). The vote revealed a 7 percent gender gap: 47 percent of women voted for the *Sí*, compared to 40 percent of men. This difference would ensure that both sides would court women's support assiduously in the upcoming presidential election. The plebiscite victory gave opposition leaders the confidence to demand that Pinochet resign, even though the constitution did not require him to do so. The general refused to step down, but agreed to negotiate a series of reforms to the constitution. By July 1989, the two sides had agreed to fifty-four changes in the Constitution of 1980, which voters approved in another plebiscite.

Attention then turned to the presidential and parliamentary elections scheduled for December 14, 1989. The opposition alliance, known as the Concertación, nominated Christian Democratic leader Patricio Aylwin as its candidate for the presidency. Aylwin was a seventy-one-year-old man, a grandfatherly figure "whose conciliatory style had won wide respect" (Constable and Valenzuela 1991). The pro-military coalition nominated Hernán Büchi as its presidential candidate. Büchi had served as Pinochet's Minister of Finance and won acclaim for restoring the economy after the 1982 recession. The thirty-nine-year-old Büchi cut an odd figure and certainly represented something "new" for the Right. Constable and Valenzuela (1991: 315) describe him as "a dedicated runner and yogurt fanatic with a Prince Valiant haircut [who] projected a youthful image far removed from the darker side of the dictatorship." It was hoped he would appeal to the ladies. One of his campaign ads in *El Mercurio* on

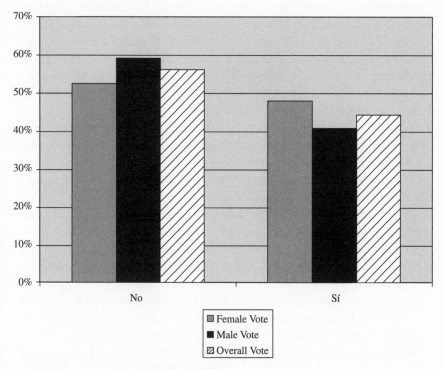

Figure 8.1. Results of 1988 Plebiscite.

November 19 seemed deliberately ambiguous: "More women, every day more women for Büchi." Francisco Javier Errázuriz, known as "Fra Fra" because of a stutter, ran as a third candidate for the Unión de Centro-Centro, a conservative party.

The Coalition of Women for Democracy

The period between the plebiscite and the elections in December 1989 marked a new phase of mobilization for the women's movement. Female party leaders and independent women's organizations took advantage of the gender gap in the plebiscite vote to pressure the opposition parties to incorporate women's demands on their agenda. In December 1988, forty opposition women created the Coalition of Women for Democracy (CMD). The group included women from political parties, social organizations, and feminist groups, as well as independents. The CMD developed a women's policy agenda for the opposition and sought to ensure that opposition leaders took women's rights into account in the upcoming elections. With a budget of nearly $100,000 donated by the Norwegian and Swedish governments, the CMD organized conferences on women's issues and generated a list of policy recommendations in eleven areas, including political participation, civil law, labor law, healthcare, and education (Montecino and Rossetti 1990).

During the 1989 campaign, the CMD highlighted the status of women by issuing frequent public statements about how current events affected Chilean women. One press release published in *La Época* condemned Pinochet's attempt to do away with free TV time for the opposition, comparing it to women's "history of absence from the public sphere" and "forced silence." In January 1989, the U.S. government placed an embargo on Chilean fruit after customs officials discovered two cyanide-laced grapes in a shipment. The CMD held a press conference to condemn the embargo and explain how the embargo affected women. As Josefina Rossetti, the organization's executive secretary, stated: "We women are the ones who do most of the shopping for our families. To the housewives of North America, Japan and European Community, we guarantee that Chilean grapes are in good condition." Her comments in *La Época* (March 18, 1989) condemned the U.S. embargo as a "grave threat to a sector of labor dominated by women," referring to Chile's fruit-export industry.

To promote women's participation in politics, the CMD proposed a list of 100 women willing and able to be named as candidates for political office. The CMD list was so inclusive that it even included women from right-wing parties, such as Feminine Power leader Carmen Saenz, on the grounds that "the country requires a great reconciliation, which includes those from the right and those who supported the military regime," according to a statement that appeared in *La Época* (April 29, 1989). The breadth of the CMD's list illustrates women's efforts to appeal to cross-partisan unity even while engaging in the most partisan of all political activities – choosing candidates for the electoral lists. This move infuriated male party leaders, who considered it an encroachment of their power to create electoral lists (Rosetti 1994). Several years later, leftist leader María Antonieta Saa acknowledged the limitations of the CMD's strategy: "We couldn't agree among ourselves about our strategy for getting power. We tried to create a front to support women in the government and women candidates, but we should have generated a list of 10 women that were well-positioned to be candidates. Instead we made a list of 150

Democracy in the Country and in the Home

[*sic*] women" (quoted in Hola and Pischedda 1993: 228). Nonetheless, the parties did nominate several of the women from the list, including Socialist Adriana Muñoz; Communist Fanny Pollarolo; and Christian Democrats Eliana Caraball and Carmen Frei. Looking back on the role the CMD played, Saa recalled:

I am convinced that if we hadn't formed the Concertación de Mujeres por la Democracia there would be no agenda for women in this government, no [government agency for women], nothing. And that is due more to the *fuerza* of the feminists than to the parties (quoted in Hola and Pischedda 1993: 228).

Conflict between women from feminist organizations and political parties increased as the 1989 elections drew near. Many of CMD's members left to campaign on behalf of the Concertación, while others remained outside the party system. Rossetti claimed that the party coalition co-opted the women's coalition in terms of programmatic work, members, and budget. When candidate Patricio Aylwin's campaign created a women's front, it requested that the CMD contribute $17,000 of its budget to the new organization. The Aylwin campaign "practically obligated us to give them the money," said Rossetti (1994). This example illustrates the Concertación's efforts to limit autonomous organizing within civil society.

To celebrate International Women's Day that year, women's groups organized a huge demonstration in the Santa Laura stadium in Santiago. The event paralleled the 1983 *caupolicanazo* in terms of size, unity, and creativity. Organizers billed the celebration as an artistic-cultural rally, with dancing, singing and theatrical performances, centered on the theme "democracy works because women are there" (*la democracia va, porque la mujer está*). Graciela Borquez, one of the leaders of MPLV, described what set this demonstration apart from previous ones. Her views appeared in *La Época*, the opposition paper, on March 8, 1989:

[There won't be any speeches] because we have found that speeches are so boring; we can say the same thing in visual form, with another language, which today will be *muy de mujer*, with our affective side, our feelings. Let me sum it up by saying it will be an event with an open heart, with our heads in the stars and our feet on the ground.

Indeed, this demonstration was not a typical political rally. Participants took their seats in one of four quadrants in the stadium, representing different aspects of women's roles. The west represented culture: "the witches with their brooms, singers, pianists, violinists, and dancers." The other three sections represented women as workers, students, and mothers, respectively. The event ended with the enactment of the birth of the "new woman," performed by two enormous puppets. As *La Época* reported, "These figures, in the midst of a dialogue about the importance of birth, the loss of fear and the hope of giving birth, told the story of the role of women in Chilean history, beginning with Mapuche women, the colonial era, Independence, the Republic and 1973." The Santa Laura rally celebrated women's efforts to oust the dictatorship and epitomized what Chilean feminists envisioned when they talked about "a new way of doing politics." The event also demonstrated the strength of the women's movement; an estimated 20,000 women attended, making it the largest event that the movement had organized since 1983.

While women's organizations sought to promote alternative political practices, they were also cognizant of the need to promote gender-related policy issues through more conventional channels. The day before the Santa Laura rally, for example, the CMD sponsored a breakfast with politicians from the Concertación to lobby for the adoption of gender-based policies for women. The CMD succeeded in persuading the Aylwin campaign to incorporate the following demands onto its platform: the creation of a cabinet-level ministry for women; positive discrimination measures to increase women's political representation, programs for poor women; and legislation on equal employment opportunities and equal pay. It consciously left abortion, divorce, and reproductive rights off the list. Thus, on the eve of democratic transition, Chilean women's organizations had created a vibrant, creative, and powerful political force. The women's movement united a large constituency of women across party lines and negotiated a series of concrete demands onto the agenda of the soon-to-be-elected democratic government.

The loss of 1988 plebiscite made the Right realize that it had to extend its support beyond the anti-Allende coalition. In the Right's presidential campaign, substantive policy proposals supplanted references to the past, especially regarding women. On November 3, the government announced it would ratify the United Nations Convention to End All Forms of Discrimination Against Women (CEDAW), an international declaration of women's human rights.[1] Just the day before, the CMD had sent a letter to the junta asking for an explanation of the government's failure to ratify the convention. On December 6, 1989 – eight days before the election – Pinochet signed CEDAW, making Chile the ninety-seventh country

---

[1] Pinochet also signed the United Nations Convention Against Torture (Arrate 2001).

to do so. His rationale for doing so represented a radical departure from his earlier views on the status of women. In an article in *El Mercurio* (December 6, 1989) Pinochet stated: "Women's true vocation does not have to be restricted to the family sphere, especially when she becomes aware of her immense capabilities and responsibility for contributing to the development of the nation."

Abortion and divorce – both of which are illegal in Chile – figured prominently in the 1989 campaign. The Concertación tried *not* to address these issues – recall that the CMD did not include them on its list of demands – and as a result came under fire from both the Left and the Right. Women in the MDP, the coalition of leftist parties outside the Concertación, announced their support for a proposal to legalized abortion and divorce in a press conference, as *El Mercurio* reported on March 6, 1989. Meanwhile, the Right stated its unequivocal opposition to legalization, but framed its position in terms of women's equality. The last item on Büchi's list of twenty campaign promises was "more equality for women." He borrowed the phrase from the women's movement but defined it in a way that bore little resemblance to the feminist agenda. His statement appeared in *La Época* (October 1, 1989):

We will promote the full capacity of **married women**. We will promote **flexible work hours** that allow women to combine their domestic labor with work outside the home. We will strengthen the family. **We will not legalize abortion or divorce**, but we will protect single mothers and their children. We will also protect those who have been affected by broken marriages [emphasis in original].

National Renovation leader Fernanda Otero articulated the conservative view on this issue, which identified the legalization of abortion as a "Gramscian" strategy. *El Mercurio* (March 6, 1989) quoted her statement:

In Western societies, this permits communists to gain access to power by way of conquering culture, which it considers essential in order to destroy Western Christian values. The most expeditious way to achieve this is by destroying the family, the basic nucleus of society.

Büchi sent a letter to all the parliamentary candidates asking them to sign a statement opposing the legalization of abortion. The Pinochet government retrenched its position by issuing a change in the abortion law. Under the new law, released just before the election, abortion is illegal even in cases where the mother's life was threatened. Women who get abortions and medical professionals who perform them face three to five years in prison, while nonmedical practitioners who perform abortions face terms of eighteen months to three years.

Despite these efforts to define the campaign in terms of issues, advocates of Büchi's campaign made a few predictable appeals to the Allende era. The day before the election, Pinochet supporter Sara Navas issued a desperate appeal to the "empty pots" brigade. Her statement appeared as a letter to the editor in *El Mercurio* (December 13, 1989):

On this day on which we celebrate the patriotic event that honors the Chilean woman, we see on the political scene the same people from the Popular Unity of yesterday, who will try, by way of the [electoral] lists of the Concertación, to recuperate the power they lost to initiate once again the "Allende path" . . . Where is the woman who protested in the march of the *cacerolas*? . . . What remains of the bitter and painful experience of the 1,000 days of the UP government? The rejection of the candidates of the Concertación and the support of Büchi and his parliamentarians in the next elections is the only response that the authentic Chilean woman can give.

To lock in the support of the mothers' centers for Pinochet, the president issued a decree that the commander-in-chief of the armed forces would remain in charge of the mothers' centers. Widespread criticism eventually forced Lucía Hiriart to back down from her plan and relinquish the mothers' centers. Despite these efforts, on December 14, 1989, Concertación candidate Patricio Aylwin won the battle for women's votes and defeated the regime (Figure 8.2).

"A Space in the State"

Many activists in the women's movement were optimistic about their ability to get their demands met by the new civilian government. Yet they expressed dismay that the women's movement fell apart precisely at the moment it stood a chance at getting its demands translated into concrete policy gains. The disunity that emerged within the movement came as a shock to many. In 1990, Natacha Molina, a leading feminist activist, remarked, "no one anticipated that the movement would fail to achieve its goals, much less fall apart as it has" (Molina 1990). Researcher Eugenia Weinstein echoed this lament: "During the dictatorship, everyone was together. Now it's a fight, a battle. [She pauses]. There *was* a movement. Now there's just confusion and disorganization" (Weinstein 1990). From a more distanced perspective, explanations for the dissolution of the women's movement after the transition to democracy abound. But fallen

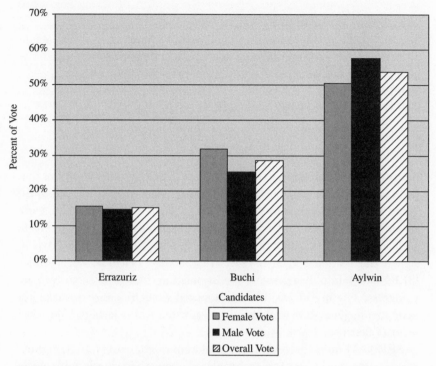

Figure 8.2. Results of 1989 Presidential Election.

expectations generated lasting bitterness among activists, especially among the poor (Ellison 2000).

President Aylwin's cabinet provided one of the first indications that the return to democracy had not brought about a change in parties' attitudes toward women. When the official photograph of the all-male cabinet appeared in newspapers, some remarked, "All that's missing is a sign that says 'No girls allowed!'" (Molina 1990; Pisano 1990). Aylwin eventually made the Director of the National Women's Service a cabinet-level position and appointed Christian Democratic leader Soledad Alvear to it. When President Eduardo Frei took office in 1994, he appointed three women to ministerial posts and two to undersecretary positions. In 2000, President Ricardo Lagos appointed five women ministers and eight under-secretaries Table 8.1).

Activists in the women's movement had long envisioned a government agency dedicated to carrying out their goals. The desire to create a

Table 8.1. *Women's Appointments to the Executive Branch, 1990–2000.*

Year	Female Ministers	% Women	Female Subsecretaries	% Women
1990 President Aylwin	1	4.8%	3	11.1%
1994 President Frei	3	14.3%	2	7.1%
2000 President Lagos	5	31.3%	8	29%

Source: Valdés and Gomáriz 1992, 1995; *Santiago Times* March 8, 2000.

ministry for women stemmed from the experiences of other countries that had recently restored democracy – especially Argentina, Brazil, and Spain – and reflected the concerns spelled out in CEDAW (Valenzuela 1998). President Aylwin moved quickly to honor his campaign promise to create such an agency. Two months after taking office, in May 1990, Aylwin signed the National Women's Service (Servicio Nacional de la Mujer [SERNAM]) into being, with the stipulation that it be approved by Congress. The president's decision honored women's desire to make it a permanent agency that could not be eliminated with a change of government (Valenzuela 1998).

SERNAM immediately became a fulcrum of controversy. The rightist parties strenuously opposed the proposed agency, viewing it as a vehicle for the dissemination of antifamily policy and radical feminist propaganda. Women in shantytown organizations expressed concerns that the new agency would be an elitist institution and doubted that it would embrace their concerns; the fact that its agenda did not include human rights fueled their skepticism. Some feminist activists resented the predominance of Christian Democratic leaders and perspectives within SERNAM: Soledad Alvear, for example, had not participated in the women's movement. Others considered the agency to be a product of the movement, "the child to whom they had given birth," while some Christian Democratic leaders found it to be too radical for their tastes (Barrig 1998). In short, SERNAM officials not only had to navigate between the Scylla of the conservative opposition and the Charybdis of the feminist movement, but among numerous other rocky shoals within the government (Baldez 2001).

Women's representation in political office since the transition has been low. Women have been the most successful in getting elected at the municipal level. Yet several activists in the feminist movement now find themselves in positions of political power. Perhaps the most prominent is María Antonieta Saa, whom President Aylwin appointed mayor of Conchalí, a working-class suburb of Santiago, in 1991. Saa, a member of the Party for Democracy (PPD), has sought to infuse feminist sensibilities into her political work. At a Socialist Party (PS) conference held in 1993, Chile 2000, Saa insisted that the party pursue feminist goals: democratize the party; eliminate hierarchical relations of power; treat socialism as a process rather than an end; and develop leadership training programs for women. Yet even Saa has had to fight to get on the ballot. In 1993, the PPD did not nominate her as a candidate for the House of Deputies. This prompted female leaders from the Concertación to organize a protest to demand that Saa be given a spot. "The women from all the parties of the Concertación succeeded in getting the party to hold a special session to reconsider the issue" and PPD president Sergio Bitar responded by nominating Saa on his party's list, according to PPD member Sandra Cepeda (1994).

Between 1990 and 1997, Congress introduced twenty-four bills that pertained directly to gender equality issues. Of these, half have passed – 11 laws out of a total of 693 new laws overall, or 1.6 percent of the total (Siavelis 2000). The other half of the women's bills remain dead in committee (Haas 2000). Those that have passed have been amended to replace the feminist tenor with a discourse that focuses on women's role as mothers, in the context of the family (Valenzuela 1998). The limited success of the women's movement to achieve its goals must also be understood in the context of pressure from the Catholic Church. The church led the struggle against the military, but apparently demanded a high price for this support in terms of vetoes over changes in family policy once the transition occurred (Waylen 1993; Haas 2000; Htun forthcoming).

The Struggle to Maintain the Women's Movement

The status of the women's movement after the transition can be evaluated in both positive and negative terms. From one perspective, the return to democracy has been accompanied by the expression of different perspectives and increased diversity within the women's movement. "Feminist spaces" have proliferated within Chile. They include *mujer/fempress*, a journal that reports feminist activity throughout Latin America; *Radio Tierra*, a feminist radio station that broadcasts 117 hours per week and reaches more than one million women (Quevedo 1994); Las Lilas, a feminist bookstore in Santiago; and even Agenda Mujer, a popular feminist datebook. Numerous academic institutes and nongovernmental organizations (NGOs) conduct research on the status of women. Women's studies programs have flourished in Chile's public and private universities (Oyarzún 2000). To a certain extent, these diverse spaces constitute part of what Sonia Alvarez (1990: 273) identifies as "a flexible, multidimensional feminist strategy – one that organizes gender-conscious political pressure *at the base*, both within and outside the state."

However, the effectiveness of a "multidimensional" strategy presumes that various organizations within a movement share a common vision of what they are trying to achieve. In Chile, conflicts within the movement have intensified rather than diminished in the years since the transition. Increasing divisiveness within the movement has stymied the accomplishment of goals that women set out for themselves on the eve of the transition. Several events have proved to be pivotal in the evolution of the women's movement in the 1990s, including the Latin American regional feminist *encuentros*, policy conflicts with the conservative opposition, and the Fourth World Conference on Women sponsored by the United Nations in Beijing in 1995 (Waylen 1993; Chuchryk 1994; Frohmann and Valdés 1995; Matear 1996; Baldez 1997; Barrig 1997; Lidid and Maldonado 1997; Franco 1998; Schild 1998; Valenzuela 1998). One of these events was the decision to mount a campaign for an independent, autonomous feminist candidate for congress in 1993. The factors leading up to this campaign, the conflicts that unfolded during it, and the consequences that flowed from it illustrate in precise terms the difficulties that Chilean feminists have faced in maintaining a movement that combines autonomy and political presence.

A Feminist in Congress

By 1991, women's organizations appeared to have recouped their energy somewhat in preparation for the "First National Feminist Conference" in Valparaíso. The goal of the conference was to reflect on the status of the women's movement and develop new strategies. The 556 participants approved a document that outlined 11 goals centered on "strengthening the feminist movement locally and regionally." The most concrete of these goals was to schedule another *encuentro* for the following year. Outside funding helped make the conference run smoothly. The total budget for the conference was $14,000, nearly half of which came from the

International Women's Health Coalition.[2] Another third of this amount came from registration fees, and the rest came from organizations and individuals in Chile. After the conference, the organizers regrouped under the name Feminist Initiative.

In 1993, Feminist Initiative decided to put its ideas about "democracy in the country and in the home" into practice by forwarding an independent feminist candidate for Congress. Activists associated with the Feminist initiative did not consider the women currently in Congress to represent their views. "María Antonieta Saa says she's part of the women's movement but not a feminist," one woman remarked. The decision to run an independent candidate thus constituted a definitive rupture with *las políticas*, feminists affiliated with the parties; it would prove difficult to maintain "double militancy" on this issue.

Each step of the campaign involved considerable debate and conflict: developing a platform, picking a candidate, choosing an electoral district. The decision to run an independent candidate forced the women in the Feminist initiative to confront electoral laws that protect the interests of existing political parties. They knew they needed 1,300 signatures to get on the ballot, but the electoral tribunal failed to inform them that signatures from party members do not count on petitions for independent candidates. Ultimately, the campaign failed to get enough valid signatures and the electoral tribunal rejected their petition. But this proved to be only one of many roadblocks surrounding the campaign.

The campaign heightened conflicts between *pobladoras* and *profesionales*, the middle-class feminist activists. The choices for electoral districts came down to San Joaquin, a working-class district, and Ñuñoa/ Providencia, a progressive, middle-class area. The campaign chose the latter (District 21) because it was a more liberal district where "there were likely to be more feminists" and the Humanist and Green parties had done well there in the previous elections (Walker 1994). Plus the woman chosen to be the candidate, Isabel Carcamo, lived there – a helpful but not necessary qualification for representing the district. Carcamo's background was typical of middle-class feminist activists. As her campaign brochure

---

[2] This organization is a nonprofit organization based in New York City that "promotes women's reproductive and sexual health and rights" in Africa, Asia, and Latin America. This amount equals 6,813,491 Chilean pesos at the October 1991 exchange rate of 493 pesos per dollar.

says, "I am a teacher. I was part of the generation of '68, the dreamers and rebels." She served as a student government leader at the University of Chile in 1970. After the coup, she went into exile in West Germany and became involved in the Chile Solidarity movement. She joined the feminist movement when she returned to Chile. At the time of the campaign, she worked for the Women's Institute, an NGO devoted to women's policy issues.

Carcamo's platform did not include the concerns that *pobladora* feminists cared about. As one woman, the head of the Casa de la Mujer in Lo Espejo, stated, "The feminists are not aware (*consciente*) of the problems of *pobladoras*: getting light, electricity, homes, access to health clinics. They're not interested in the issue of political prisoners. Several of my friends are still in various jails throughout Santiago. The feminists no longer voice opposition to this problem, but it's very important to *pobladoras*. The feminists are concerned only with gender, they're not interested in class-related problems – but those are the problems that are part of our reality [as *pobladoras*]" (Henriquez 1994).

Legalization of abortion became one of the main planks of Carcamo's platform. Although abortion remains illegal in all Latin American countries except Cuba, it is not rare. Approximately 160,000 abortions are performed in Chile each year, or an estimated 4.5 percent of all women between the ages of fifteen and forty-nine each year (compared with 2.7 percent in the United States). According to the *New York Times* (April 12, 1994) "any well-to-do woman can safely have an abortion in a private clinic or hospital for $1,000 to $2,500 – a price out of the range of most Chileans. But poor women must turn to abortionists who lack medical training, who may charge about $200 and who use wires or primitive rubber probes." The *New York Times* (August 9, 1998) also reported that Chilean courts convict approximately fifty women for this crime each year, but usually give them reduced sentences.

The abortion issue constrained the feminist campaign in an extremely significant way. Three of the women who worked at the Women's Institute, the main organization sponsoring the campaign, were nurses who had been jailed for performing abortions. The story behind their arrest graphically illustrates the conditions under which women get abortions in Chile and merits repeating at length:

The [nurses] ran a program on women's reproductive health, but when women had problems [the nurses] would perform abortions for them. They had a whole network set up, with an arrangement with a hospital that would take the women.

Democracy in the Country and in the Home

I don't know if this story is true or false, but they say that a Peruvian woman here in Chile got pregnant while she was working as a maid. She wanted to get an abortion and went to these ladies for help. They did the abortion, but later the woman started hemorrhaging so she went back to the hospital. They seized her [the patient] because there were no papers documenting her previous visit, and that's how they found the nurses and had them arrested. But they paid some good lawyers and got them out of jail (Mendoza 1999).

The campaign directors feared that the nurses would generate negative publicity, so the Women's Institute fired them. This decision provoked violent debates among the organizers and produced an immediate, definitive, and, as it has turned out, lasting split within the movement between "those who wanted to have an impact and those who criticized the relationship between institutions and the movement" (Walker 1994). The campaign became a struggle between women who envisioned it as a consciousness-raising effort and those who viewed it as a vehicle to promote concrete policy change (and wanted to win). "When the campaign started, I was so happy, because finally we were going to have a feminist in the congress, someone who was going to represent our views," recalled María Mendoza (1994), "but for the majority, the success of the candidacy became an end in itself" rather than a part of a process of building awareness about feminism.

Assessments of the campaign afterward were mixed. Many participants viewed it as a valuable experience, but others considered it a disaster. One woman referred to it as "nightmare numero uno." "You can't get anyone excited about politics, or getting involved right now," said another. For still others, the campaign detracted from the tasks of organizing and consciousness raising: "We forgot the importance of constructing the movement." The dynamics of decision making during the campaign defied the consensual style feminists had come to take for granted: "a few tried to impose a decision that affected all of us, with the conviction that they were farther along in their thinking than others." Some concluded that the campaign forced women to embrace a masculine style of politics: "the process trapped us, put us in the position of having to choose between the logic of dominating male politics and . . . the logic of collaboration" (all quotes from Lidid and Maldonado 1997).

On the positive side, the campaign proved to be an important learning experience. One activist, Betty Walker, found it challenging to translate what she had learned from years of participating in the feminist movement into something outsiders could readily understand:

You have two minutes to tell someone why they should listen to you and then get them to sign [the petition] so that a feminist candidate could run for office . . . The contact with people in the street was so important. To meet total strangers, charm them into stopping to talk to you and then getting to the heart of the matter (Walker 1994).

The campaign raised public awareness about feminist issues. "We talked to thousands of people in the process of collecting signatures . . . and we broke away from the interminably self-referential nature of feminism," affirmed another one of the organizers. In the end, however, the tensions that emerged during the campaign divided the "*institucionales*" committed to working within the political arena from the "*autónomas*" who wanted to preserve the movement.

Institucionales and Autónomas

The women who thought the Carcamo campaign was a disaster split off to form their own group, the Autonomous Feminist Movement (MFA). The MFA is a loose coalition of approximately twenty feminist collectives of between ten and twenty members each. Most of the groups are from the Santiago area. The MFA portrays itself as "questioning the values and institutions of the [neoliberal economic] system" (Lidid and Maldonado 1997: 3). The MFA openly criticizes the government, especially SERNAM and the NGOs that work with SERNAM, on the grounds that these institutions support policies that deepen the level of poverty in Chile. As the leaders of the movement wrote in 1993, "Today it is undeniable that [SERNAM] responds to the government's global policies that are part of the consolidation of the neoliberal system, implemented by the International Monetary Fund" (ibid.: 16). Implicit in the MFA's agenda is a socialist vision of Chile independent of foreign capital and not subservient to international markets. This is a radical nationalist perspective of development, one imbued with a gendered understanding of social justice. The MFA objects to the degree to which many women's NGO organizations are linked to the state and to international agencies, on the grounds that these sources of funding compromise their commitment to women in Chile.

Funding that the United States Agency for International Development (USAID) made available for the NGO community prior to the Beijing Conference constituted a central concern for autonomous feminists, in Chile and throughout the region. The manner in which USAID channeled resources caused tremendous conflict among feminist organizations. As Sonia Alvarez notes, "in a highly controversial move, [USAID] insisted on disbursing funds through 'focal points' consisting of a single NGO or a consortium of NGOs in each of six subregions" throughout Latin America (Alvarez 1998: 308). This procedure tended to favor the more profession-alized NGOs, the ones "skilled in the art of lobbying and who possessed policy-specialized staff, who had previous experience in the U.N. process, and who earned handsome foreign funding" (ibid.). MFA activists saw the USAID project as an effort to derail the feminist movement and "silence women's real concerns" (Lidid and Maldonado 1997: 89). Nonetheless, the MFA relies on international funding from private foundations to finance its own projects: the group published a book about the movement with a grant from the Global Fund for Women, for example.

Celebrations of International Women's Day in the 1990s illustrate the tensions between *institucionales* and *autónomas*. Each year since the transi-tion, the Concertación government has sponsored official celebrations of International Women's Day. Yet while these official ceremonies take place, other women's groups have held protests and demonstrations that have been repressed by police, often with tear gas and arrests. The irony behind the repression of these parallel celebrations is that speakers at the official events have often referred to the March 8 protests that took place under the military regime. In 1991, President Aylwin became the first Chilean president to give a speech to honor International Women's Day. While he gave his speech, members of Women for Life demonstrated outside to demand the release of political prisoners. Police dispersed the protesters by spraying them with water cannons, according to *La Tercera* (March 9, 1991). On International Women's Day in 1994, Jaime Ravinet, the mayor of Santiago, addressed women gathered in the Municipal Theater. He recalled how the military had violently repressed International Women's Day marches in the past and reveled in the fact that now they "celebrated in the most important theater in Chile." And yet outside the theater, a few blocks away, in a democratic Chile under civilian rule, police arrested demonstrators from the MFA. As Edda Gaviola, one of the organizers of this protest, recalled:

What happened there is a precise example of our political will to express ourselves as autonomous feminists. The act was scheduled to begin at 7:00 p.m. At 6:30 police impetuously began to detain women who arrived at the [plaza] with signs. Their objective was clear: to prevent the march from happening, at all costs. By 7 p.m. they had detained six women. Our slogan "this democracy is a disgrace" (*"esta democracia es una desgracia"*) became all the more significant. We formed a circle of force and energy to declare our political statement, and we did it. . . . Before too long we were 300 women shouting, singing, walking toward the police station. The police had to stop once we got there. For more than two hours we autonomous feminists exercised our freedom to think, to meet, to declare our views publicly, to speak and shout from a position of rebellion (Gaviola 1994).

Why would police arrest women staging a protest on International Women's Day in a democratic regime? The answer seemed obvious to the women who had organized the protest. "Autonomous movements are not permitted. You have to be linked with a political party. That's why this democracy is a disgrace," said Margarita Pisano (1994).

The nature of foreign support for organizations in the women's movement has changed significantly over time. International funding to women's organizations prior to 1989 funded three kinds of projects: research on women's issues; service provision; and citizen mobilization against the military regime. Since the end of the dictatorship, funding has been directed primarily toward policy formation and implementation. At the same time, international donors reduced their funding to Chile as the world's attention shifted away from Latin America and toward Eastern Europe and the former Soviet states (Barrig 1997).

Scholarship on gender-based issues in Latin America has reflected these changes. During the 1970s and 1980s, gender researchers in Chile compiled diagnostic studies of women's status and presented this information to the public. Chilean researcher Claudia Serrano has referred to this project as "politicizing the everyday," or demonstrating the links between the personal and the political (quoted in Hola and Pischedda 1993: 85). In the 1990s, gender research has become more policy oriented. As Serrano notes, "with the return of democracy, we made a complete 180 degree turn. Now our interest is the State and public policy, where we put this enormous accumulation of knowledge and our professional development to practical use" (ibid.). Sonia Alvarez (1998) has identified this shift in focus as the "NGO-ization" of women's movements, a phenomenon that has occurred throughout Latin America. Feminist organizations now tend to function more as technical experts rather than as rights advocates. Evidence from Chile confirms Alvarez's findings, although researchers view this evolution toward pragmatism in both positive and negative terms (Hola and Guzmán 1996).

Divisions between policy elites and grass roots supporters have impeded the movement's ability to lobby for policy change. On the one hand, women at the grass roots do not feel that their concerns are adequately represented by NGOs, which they view as the pawns of international agencies. On the other hand, when NGOs forward their policy agendas through SERNAM and in congress, they cannot rely on movement activists to rally in support of specific proposals. This has become a vicious circle: without a base of popular support to push for the adoption of feminist policies, lobbyists are forced to accept weak versions of their programs. Without a track record of policy successes on issues that feminists at the grass roots level care about, activists are increasingly unwilling to cooperate with NGOs. Debates between *institucionales* and *autónomas* became particularly fierce during the Seventh Annual Latin American Feminist Encuentro, held in Cartagena, Chile, in December 1996.

Coalition Politics and the Women's Movement

It is not the return of political parties per se that causes social movements to decline. Instead, the struggle for dominance among parties within a particular institutional context prompts parties to encourage (or at least tolerate) some kinds of mobilization while suppressing others. In Chile, the fate of social movements following the transition must be understood within the context of coalition politics on three levels: in terms of conflicts between the government coalition (the center-left Concertación) and the opposition (the center-right Unión por Chile); between the Concertación and the Communist Party; and within the Concertación.[3] After the transition to democracy in 1990, the Chilean government adopted policies that weakened the ability of the women's movement to establish an institutional foothold in the government and prevented movement organizations from building upon their existing base of popular support. Two goals motivated these policies, one pertaining to relations between the government and the pro-military opposition, the other to relations among the parties within the governing coalition. First, the government sought to maintain political stability by limiting conflict with the opposition. In the name of pursuing political stability and "consensual democracy," the Concertación sought to reach agreement on social policy with the center-right coalition,

[3] As of June 1999, the parties of the Concertación are the PDC, the PS, the PPD, and the Radical Social Democratic Party (PRSD). The two main parties in the opposition are the Independence Democratic Union (UDI) and the National Renovation (RN). The rightist coalition is currently called Unión Por Chile; it has also gone by Democracia y Progreso and Unión por el Progreso.

which has controlled a majority in the Senate. This severely limited the range of policies for women that the government pursued. Second, the leading party within the Concertación sought to protect its interests and limit competition with its more progressive counterparts. Specifically, the PDC sought to prevent leftist parties – particularly its main coalition partners, the PS and the PPD – from claiming the women's movement as an electoral constituency. As the dominant party in the governing coalition, the PDC used the extensive powers of office afforded to the executive branch to demobilize the women's movement, limit the movement's impact on policy, and build an alternative base of support among women. Strategic decisions made by the leftist parties compounded these forces. After the transition, the PS "very consciously eschewed the path of grass-roots mobilization to create social and political pressure for more far-reaching reforms," a decision that resulted in a process of reform that "has been elite-initiated and highly divorced from grass-roots collective action" (Roberts 1998: 121).

The organizations within the women's movement, and the CMD as the movement's policy arm, claimed to represent a crosspartisan constituency. In fact, however, the political sympathies represented by the movement were weighted decidedly toward the Left. Stronger ties between the government and women's movement organizations would have enhanced women's support for the leftist parties – the PS/PPD bloc. This would have threatened the dominance of the PDC within the ruling coalition and potentially destabilized the coalition overall. Moreover, implementation of the gender-based policies advocated by the CMD would have provoked the right and threatened the politics of consensus between the Concertación and the conservative opposition. To stave off these possibilities, the centrist PDC promoted policies that weakened the influence of organized, grass roots feminism in the government.

The CMD expected that its ability to mobilize large numbers of women from the Left and Center would make it an important constituency for the Concertación overall. The strength of the women's movement derived from its ability to convene women across party lines and to mobilize outside the realm of party politics. In this sense, the movement both crossed and transcended party lines. From the perspective of the political parties, however, the movement represents and always has represented a primarily leftist constituency, particularly at the grass roots level. The three distinct kinds of organizations that made up the women's movement during the dictatorship – human-rights organizations, economic subsis-

Democracy in the Country and in the Home

tence organization, and feminist groups – all lean to the Left in terms of their political sympathies. This is perhaps most clear with the human-rights organizations, which had relatively strong ties to leftist parties in comparison to other women's organizations. As María Elena Valenzuela (1995: 167) notes, "The close links of [human rights] groups to the proscribed [i.e., Marxist] political parties, out of whose ranks most of the victims of the repression came, led these organizations to give higher priority to partisan activities." Economic subsistence groups, such as soup kitchens, shopping collectives, and craft workshops tended to be organized in shantytowns whose affiliation with the Left was well known (Oxhorn 1995; Schneider 1995). The majority of feminist activists also sympathized with the Left, although they sought to establish a measure of autonomy from the political parties (Chuchryk 1984; Kirkwood 1986; Muñoz 1987; Molina 1989).

This is not to say that women with more centrist political orientations did not participate in the women's movement, or that all members of the PDC view the women's movement as an electoral threat. Graciela Borquez, as you will recall, was one of the founding members of Mujeres por la Vida (MPLV). Several female leaders in the PDC actively partici-pated in the CMD, including Senator Carmen Frei (daughter of the former President Frei and sister of the current President Frei); former Congresswomen Wilna Saavedra; and Mariana Aylwin, the daughter of President Aylwin. Many male PDC leaders have supported feminist con-cerns, especially Ignacio Walker, one of the leading proponents of divorce legislation in congress. Nonetheless, few of the grass roots–level organi-zations within the women's movement sympathize with the Christian Democrats. As one feminist activist commented,

The PDC wasn't linked to the struggle during the dictatorship, and lacked a strong connection with people at the base; moreover, people at the base didn't have faith in [the PDC] ... Women's organizations had spent more than a decade working with poor women (*pobladoras*) all over the country. But when [SERNAM] Minister Soledad Alvear traveled around Chile to publicize the government's pro-grams for women, people would come up to me and say hello, greet me enthusi-astically, but they had nothing to say to her (Norero 1994).

Despite its appeal to crosspartisan unity, the bridge built by the women's movement reached relatively few women on the center right of the politi-cal spectrum.

To my knowledge, no one in the women's movement supported the rightist parties. Conservatives tend to view the women's movement, and

193

feminism in particular, as a cultural cover for the traditional Marxist-Leninist left and an unacceptable threat to the social order. In an article discussing SERNAM, for example, Lucía Santa Cruz (1994), a leading conservative pundit, describes feminists as a special interest group that seeks to use the state to further its own concerns, "at the expense of the general interest of the country, especially the poor."

This acknowledgment of the predominantly leftist orientation of the women's movement will come as a surprise to no one, given the context in which the movement emerged and the issues around which women mobilized. Nonetheless, this point is critical to understanding the fate of the movement's demands in the period following the transition to democracy in Chile. The predominant party within the Concertación, the centrist Christian Democrats, had little to gain by meeting the demands of the women's movement and much to lose by sustaining the movement as an autonomous political force. The Concertación's policy toward women in the 1990s can be explained as the result of efforts by the PDC to regain control of women's political agenda, to mobilize a new constituency of women loyal to the party, and to limit the ability of the leftist parties to be perceived as representing women's interests.

Conclusion

Many activists in the anti-Pinochet women's movement had high hopes that the democratic transition would bring significant changes in the status of Chilean women. The CMD established an alliance of activists and party leaders from all the parties of the ruling coalition. It developed a precise and tractable list of demands; and, with SERNAM, succeeded winning permanent, institutional access to the powerful executive branch of the Chilean government. Divisions existed within the movement, but women's organizations had proved capable of bridging their differences in the struggle against the dictatorship; certainly they could do at least that well under democratic rule. Nonetheless, women's hopes for policy advances and crosspartisan cooperation have not been fully borne out in the period since 1990. The agenda forwarded by the CMD has been weakly implemented and the movement has, for the most part, demobilized.

It is difficult for any social movement to make the switch to more conventional approaches to political change. The women's movement was more than an interest group that wanted access to government resources. Activists in the movement had sought to introduce a "new way of doing politics" into the public arena, one premised on erasing the boundaries between the private and the public and uprooting authoritarian practices from all aspects of life. Women's lives had been profoundly changed by participating in the movement and risking their safety to protest against the dictatorship. Their perspective put them at odds with the electoral imperatives of the incoming democratic regime.

Coalition governments present unique constraints for the status of organized groups in civil society. In a coalition context, activists looking to establish "a space in the state" need to pay close attention to party competition within the governing coalition. The outcome for the women's movement in Chile echoes the status of women's movements elsewhere in terms of its limited impact on public policy and tendency to fragment, but my explanation focuses on factors specific to the Chilean political system. The evidence provided here is suggestive, but not conclusive. The next step is to examine the dynamics of women's movements in other countries in an effort to validate these claims.

9

Why Women Protest

COMPARATIVE EVIDENCE

It is common to think of women's movements, particularly those in the West, in terms of three phases of development: a first-wave movement centered on the demand for suffrage, followed by period of relative quiescence, and then a second-wave women's movement focused on women's equality. This approach predominates within contemporary historiography of women's movements. In Chile, for example, the first-wave movement began when women organized around the right to vote in the late 1800s and ended when women won full voting rights in 1949. Next came a period characterized by a dearth of mobilization among independent women's organizations, which Chilean scholar Julieta Kirkwood (1986) called "the feminist silence." The second-wave women's movement began in the 1970s and remains active today. A similar pattern characterizes women's mobilization in the United States. The suffrage movement began with the Seneca Falls Convention in 1848 and ended with the nineteenth amendment in 1920, and the second-wave movement began in the late 1960s and continues to the present day. Women did not altogether retreat from public life in the forty-year period between the first- and second-wave movements, as recent scholarship has shown (Andersen 1996; Mettler 1998; Wolbrecht 2000). Yet relatively low levels of organizing among women prompted Leila Rupp and Verta Taylor (1987) to refer to this period as "the doldrums."

I invoke the categorization of movements into first and second wave as a way to return to the starting point of this book: some periods foster the mobilization of women and others do not. This book seeks to identify those conditions. To do so, my approach centers on three relatively straightforward concepts: tipping, timing, and framing. *Tipping* is defined as a protest that triggers the coalescence of an array of diverse organizations into a

196

coherent social movement. *Timing* and *framing* identify the two conditions that set the tipping process in motion and precipitate the formation of a movement: partisan realignment and women's decision to frame their activities in terms of their status as political outsiders. In short, during periods of partisan realignment, new coalitions form around a new set of issues. This provides an opportunity for organized groups within civil society to press for the incorporation of their demands onto the political agenda. If leaders of women's organizations respond to realignment by framing their activities in terms of women's exclusion, a women's movement is likely to emerge. The movement may gain additional support when leaders of the new partisan coalition respond to women's demands in an effort to establish new bases of popular support. In the absence of these factors, a women's movement will not materialize. Women's organizations may certainly form, but they will prove unable to transcend the myriad differences among them in order to mobilize on the basis of a shared gender identity. Political entrepreneurs may try to catalyze a movement, but their efforts will fall short if they do not coincide with partisan realignment.

In both of the movements examined in this book, women framed their participation in similar ways, emphasizing their status as political outsiders. In the 1980s, Chilean feminists maintained they were practicing a new way of "doing politics" that sought to erase the gendered boundaries between the private and the public. Yet the anti-Allende activists also wanted to lessen the distance between everyday life and formal politics by insisting that male politicians address issues such as food shortages and children's safety. In both cases, women demanded a place inside the political arena, albeit a transformed version of politics. In both cases, the appeal to women's status as political outsiders fostered participation among women who had never been active in politics before. Their reliance on practices and rhetoric that effectively placed them outside politics proved to be an important source of leverage. Yet the discourse of these movements also contributed to women's eventual marginalization.

This framework accounts for similarities between two movements that differ dramatically in terms of ideology and historical context. The two cases closely resemble one another in terms of the moment at which women's movements coalesced and the way in which women framed their concerns and demands. But these two cases both took place in Chile – a single country with a unique history. To what extent can the theory presented here be used to explain the emergence of women's movements in other countries?

The conceptual simplicity of the framework outlined in this study begs comparison across other cases. The explanation directs scholars of women's movements to do two things: first, identify moments of partisan realignment and second, determine whether female political entrepreneurs respond to realignment by mobilizing on the basis of gender identity. These are fairly simple instructions. Yet identifying these two factors with precision requires intimate and detailed knowledge of a particular case. The analysis of the comparative cases presented in the following text represents a broad-brushed effort to confirm the plausibility of this approach based on secondary literature. I defer to other scholars to provide a conclusive evaluation of these claims with respect to other countries.

Countries in South America and the former Communist bloc constitute an important set of cases against which to examine this argument. Throughout South America – Argentina, Brazil, Peru, and Uruguay, as well as Chile – transitions to democracy in the 1970s and 1980s fueled the formation of mass movements among women. Women mobilized across class and party lines to demand that a return to civilian rule be accompanied by greater opportunities for women to participate as equals in political life. Women viewed periods of regime change as opportunities and seized them in an effort to advance their own agendas, with greater and lesser success. Women in the former Soviet states, on the other hand, responded to democratic transitions very differently (Tatur 1992; Einhorn 1993; Havelkova 1993; Marody 1993; Siklova 1993; Matynia 1995; Marsh 1996; Sawa-Czajka 1996; Buckley, M. 1997; Jaquette and Wolchik 1998; Siemienska 1998; Wolchik 1998; Sperling 1999). Granted, the starting points and the dynamics of the transitions differed dramatically across the two regions. Some women in Russia and Eastern and Central Europe did mobilize as women on the grounds that "there is no democracy without women." Yet for the most part, their claims failed to resonate. Women's movements in Russia and Eastern and Central Europe remained (and remain) small, fragmented, and ineffective in shaping the agendas of post-Soviet governments. Why did transitions to democracy generate the formation of broad, visible women's movements in South America but not in the former Soviet states? I pose this as an empirical question rather than a normative one, to explain variation across cases rather than to suggest that women in the former Communist countries have false consciousness. Addressing this question will highlight both the strengths and limitations of my approach and (hopefully) will raise interesting questions for future research. In the following text I examine the emergence of women's movements in three countries: Brazil, Russia, and the former East Germany. In each case, the analysis focuses on two factors: the formation of new coalitions during the process of transition and women's responses to them.

Brazil

Brazilian women formed a mass movement in the 1970s and 1980s amidst the transition away from authoritarianism. The Brazilian case confirms the importance of partisan realignment in explaining the emergence of the women's movement. The tipping point for the Brazilian women's movement coincided with the realignment of the party system in 1979. However, female activists do not appear to have framed their actions in terms of their status as political outsiders. They framed their demands in terms of specific issues instead. This discrepancy can be explained in terms of differences between the institutional arrangements that guided party competition in Brazil and Chile.

Women began to mobilize at the local level in Brazil in the 1970s but official repression ensured that their initial efforts remained relatively isolated. As the military regime became increasingly tolerant of opposition activities, women formed local networks around specific issues such as food prices and day care. Many women's organizations initially framed their demands in classic Marxist terminology but gradually came to insist on the importance of giving equal weight to class and gender. Middle-class professional women formed numerous feminist organizations in 1975, following a conference held to commemorate the United Nations International Women's Year (Hahner 1990; Tabak 1994; Soares, Costa et al. 1995).

The tipping point for the Brazilian women's movement came in 1979 – the same year that a partisan realignment occurred there. From 1965 to 1979, the military government had permitted only two parties to exist: the progovernment Alliance for National Renovation (ARENA) and the opposition Brazilian Democratic Movement (MDB). In 1979, then President General João Batista Figueiredo dissolved these two parties and decreed a law that permitted the formation of new parties out of the MDB. In so doing, the military government hoped to weaken support for the opposition by dividing it and forcing various factions to compete against one another. Five new opposition parties formed between 1979 and 1981: the Popular Party; the Brazilian Labor Party; the Party of the Brazilian Democratic Movement; the Democratic Workers' Party; and the Workers' Party.

Thus a realignment occurred in Brazil in 1979, albeit a realignment imposed from above.

Women's organizations coalesced into a movement at the same time. Sonia Alvarez (1990) emphasizes the significance of this period for the women's movement at several points:

By 1979, women activists had sparked a burgeoning political movement that appeared to span all social classes, races, and ideologies (p. 113).

1979 through 1981 were *the* peak mobilizational years of the contemporary Brazilian women's movement. Feminist groups multiplied . . . and dozens of new neighborhood women's associations blossomed in Brazil's urban periphery (p. 110).

[In 1980] it finally seemed as if feminism, as a distinctive transformational project, had the potential to become a mass-based, cross-class political movement (p. 148).

Realignment spurred the formation of the women's movement because of a convergence of interests between the new parties and women's organizations: "during *abertura*, the opposition actively courted women's support. And women's movement organizations overwhelmingly supported the opposition, mobilizing thousands of women for electoral participation and promoting antiregime mass rallies" (Alvarez 1990: 11). Instead of weakening the opposition, the regime's strategy strengthened the links between politicians and the grass roots. As a result, all the political parties included at least some of women's demands on their agendas (Alvarez 1990: 161). However, the dynamics of the *abertura* period proved difficult to sustain once elections took place. The women's movement began to split apart almost as soon as it formed, as women's organizations allied themselves with competing parties. Splits also emerged between those who collaborated with political parties and those who advocated autonomy.

How did women frame their activities during this critical period? Alvarez (1990) argues that women framed their issues in terms of feminine, feminist, and antifeminist concerns. Her account provides no indication that women framed their efforts in terms of women's status as political outsiders, although further research on this issue may be required to know for sure. This choice of strategy may instead reflect a rational response to the rules of partisan engagement decreed by the regime. In 1981, the Figuieredo regime introduced a series of electoral reforms aimed at limiting the opposition's potential to gain a majority in the upcoming election. One of these reforms prevented parties from forming coalitions with one another in the gubernatorial elections. Another required voters to vote a straight ticket. Because the electoral reforms explicitly prohibited the formation of cross-party coalitions, it would have made little sense for women's organizations to try to encourage (mostly) male party elites to transcend partisan differences to form a broad alliance. The electoral rules in place in Brazil at the time stand in contrast to those of Chile. Chilean electoral laws encourage the formation of multiparty coalitions, particularly in order to win control of the presidency and the executive branch. Thus the Brazilian case suggests a need to define, as precisely as possible, the institutional environment in which realignment occurs.

Russia

In Russia, women's organizations mobilized amidst a context of political realignment – but the dynamics of that realignment and of women's mobilization differed dramatically from other cases. As Steve Fish (1995) argues, a vacuum of state authority that emerged between 1989 and 1991 distinguished the Russian transition from other cases in Latin America and Eastern and Central Europe. The transition away from the Communist regime in Russia occurred in several complicated stages. The process of reform began in 1985 with the selection of Mikhail Gorbachev as the General Secretary of the Communist Party and Gorbachev's policies of *glasnost* (political reform) and *perestroika* (economic restructuring). Organized opposition groups began to emerge on the public scene in 1988, but only one – the Democratic Union – identified itself as a political party and criticized the regime openly. The other groups that formed at this time framed their actions in terms of reform of the existing system. Opposition activity reached a "crucial takeoff phase" in 1989, when elections for the Soviet Congress of People's Deputies took place. Fish (1995: 35) affirms the significance of this event: although not completely free, this election "was the first even partially open and competitive national election in the history of the Soviet Union." After the election, opposition forces formed a handful (five or six) loose coalitions that functioned as democratic movements or "proto-parties." Despite intense divisions among them, the coalitions all supported a set of general goals: abolish the Communist regime, democratize the political system, and adopt a market-based economy.

The formation of these coalitions in mid-1989 thus appears to constitute a moment of realignment in the Russian political system. The emergence of opposition groups challenged the seventy-year-old hegemony of the Communist Party. However, the collapse of the economy and the political system constrained the possibilities for these coalitions to become viable alternatives to the Communist Party. The opposition "had been formed exclusively in the course of a relatively short-lived, unidimensional conflict with the only regime they had ever known" and thus proved unable to generate an alternative political program (Fish 1995: 214). Unlike in Latin America, the parties that emerged at this point were not resurfacing after one or two decades underground. They were completely new, which put them at a tremendous disadvantage.[1] The collapse of the Russian state meant that the opposition movements had little means and little incentive to build popular support or to become institutionalized. In other words, a realignment occurred but the weakness of the state prevented new political actors from being able to reach out to new constituencies. Thus, we should not expect that these new coalitions would have an interest in fostering the mobilization of women – or that women's groups would look to the state in order to meet their demands.

How did women respond to the transformations that occurred in Russia during this period? Political scientist Valerie Sperling (1999: 18) maintains that independent women's groups first formed in the late 1980s, a handful of "tiny feminist organizations . . . that took on the function of consciousness-raising groups." Women's organizations officially registered with the state starting in October 1990, when it became legal to do so. The first opportunity for forming a network among these groups took place at the First Independent Women's Forum in March 1991, which was followed by the Second Forum in late 1992. These conferences constituted the "moment of madness" for the Russian women's movement: the point at which a diverse array of organizations came together under a common umbrella. Over the next several years, three additional networks of women's organizations emerged: the Union of Russia's Women replaced the Soviet Women's Committee after the Soviet collapse in 1991; the Women's League was established in 1993; and women in Russia and the United States formed the U.S.-N.I.S. Consortium in 1994. By 1994, more than 300 women's groups had registered officially. While separate from one another, they enjoyed some common ground: "all the networks shared the goal of improving women's status in Russia, all were to varying degrees involved in politics, and all asserted their independence from the state" (Sperling 1999: 21).

---

[1] I am grateful to Valerie Sperling for this insight.

The convocation of the First and Second Independent Women's Forums may be as close as Russian women have come to achieving a tipping point. Nonetheless, a broad-based women's movement has yet to emerge. Sperling's account emphasizes this point. She writes that "there have been no large national demonstrations or confrontational protests for women's rights," "there is little cooperation between groups in Moscow," and women's organizations "seem almost disinterested in attracting new members" (Sperling 1999: 42). The "movement" in Russia consists of a network of several hundred women's organizations located throughout the country who are loosely coordinated by a central information center, the Independent Women's Forum. The women's movement in Russia does not constitute a *mass* movement.

Sperling suggests that the frequency of new political alliances and continuous emergence of new institutional arrangements during the transition period actually limited the possibilities for the creation of a strong women's movement. Constantly changing conditions fostered a lack of transparency in the political system, which in turn impeded the efforts of groups within civil society to develop coherent strategies for getting their demands met.

Moreover, Russian women's organizations lack a "resonant frame" that unites them and communicates their message to the public in a way that generates widespread support. Feminist ideology carries negative connotations in Russia, and other plausible frames have done little to precipitate a groundswell of support for women's issues. Attempts to link women's concerns with democracy (as feminists in Latin America have done) have not proven fruitful because many Russians have come to associate democracy with "corruption, inflation, privilege, crime, Western incursions . . . and so on" (Sperling 1999: 93). Other concepts like "'discrimination' do exist [in the Russian language, but] they are often perceived as being foreign, bourgeois and irrelevant to the Russian situation" (ibid.: 88). In Russia and many of the former Soviet states, the one thing that might ostensibly link women – their status as political outsiders – has been discredited by its association with the Soviet regime, which claimed to have emancipated women and incorporated them fully into the political system (Einhorn 1993; Waters and Posadskaya 1995).

In Russia, one of the two conditions required for the formation of a mass women's movement (political realignment) is present, but the other (framing) is not. The first condition for women's mobilization – partisan realignment – is present in the former Soviet Union. The fall of

Communism and the emergence of opposition reform parties definitely constitutes a realignment – although in Russia at the time of the transition the state lacked the capacity to meet the demands of organized groups. As the cases of Chile and Brazil suggest, the institutional context in which realignment occurs must be taken into account. Yet, for the most part, women did not perceive this moment in gendered terms.

East Germany

Women in the former East Germany have come the closest of all the East Bloc countries to forming a mass movement among women. Their success was fostered by the fact that women's organizations responded to partisan realignment in terms of women's exclusion from political decision making. Networks of small, independent women's organizations began to emerge in East Germany in the 1980s (Young 1999: 69). The level of independence that these groups achieved prior to 1989 surpassed that of comparable groups elsewhere in the region (Einhorn 1993). The most prominent of these, Women for Peace, formed in the early 1980s as a group of friends that organized a support network for the families of dissidents. Women for Peace became more firmly established in 1983 when the Soviet government deployed nuclear weapons on East German soil, in response to the deployment of Pershing II and Cruise missiles in West Germany. Independent women's organizations remained active in East Germany during the rest of the 1980s. They consistently framed their activities in terms of female opposition to a male-dominated state, but they could not be said to constitute a movement at this point (Young 1999: 73). These groups formed the organizational infrastructure upon which a women's movement could be constructed.

The timing of women's mobilization in East Germany suggests that women organized amidst a climate of political realignment. In the first few weeks of September 1989, four distinct "citizens' movements" emerged, each offering a different set of proposals for constructing a new state. New Forum, the largest of the four, called for democratic dialogue but did not offer a clear programmatic alternative to Communist rule. It had more than 200,000 members. Dissidents loosely affiliated with the Protestant Church formed Democracy Now. This group included approximately 4,000 people and supported the democratic renovation of socialism. A group of Protestant Church leaders organized Democratic Awakening, which also called for a renewal of socialism, but along more conservative lines. A fourth group, United Left, was more tolerant of the ruling Communist Party and "openly identified itself as a Marxist leftist, socialist group" (Young 1999: 84). As in Russia, these groups did not constitute formal political parties, but rather proto-parties that articulated alternatives to the Communist system. The formation of these movements marked the emergence of a cleavage between the ruling party and reformist groups and can be characterized as a period of realignment.

September 1989 was a moment ripe for a "tip" among women's organizations. In East Germany, this is precisely what happened.[2] Women mobilized quickly in response to the absence of women's issues on the agendas of the new coalitions. As Brigitte Young (1999) affirms, "virtually none of the citizens' movements included women's issues in their platforms." Female political entrepreneurs responded publicly to this situation just a few weeks later and "organized in virtually every city" around the goal of participating in the political process as women (Young 1999: 3). On October 11, 1989, a group called Lila Offensive staged a protest during a government-sponsored rally in which they called for women to participate as equals in society and politics. Their slogans demanded that women have a place in political decision making (Young 1999: 82). On November 6, prominent feminists began to circulate a public letter that demanded a series of measures to increase women's participation. The letter publicized the feminists' cause and spread the word. On December 3, a month after the collapse of the Berlin Wall, women's groups came together to form the Independent Women's League (UFV), a coalition that represented a wide array of organizations, including radical feminist groups, lesbians, socialist organizations, groups with national visibility, and local grass roots organizations (Einhorn 1993: 203; Young 1999: 74). The main slogan of the demonstration, "Without Women There is No State," drew twelve hundred women to attend. The UFV alliance appeared to herald the formation of a women's movement in East Germany. Young (1999: 5) invokes Zolberg's notion of a "moment of madness" to identify its significance. Barbara Einhorn (1993: 204) confirms this perspective:

initially, it had seemed as if the UFV would become a mass movement, with considerable influence and a large presence in the mainstream political process. There

---

[2] Scholar Brigitte Young (1999) explicitly rejects partisan realignment on the grounds that "shifts in ruling alignments" constrained the women's movement as much as they fostered it. The evidence she provides, however, suggests a link between the emergence of a new dimension in East German politics and the emergence of the women's movement.

was a feeling of exhilaration and the hope that, inadequate as [East Germany's] approach to "emancipation" had been, it nevertheless provided a basis upon which demands for measures which they saw as guaranteeing real equality of opportunity for women could build.

Adherents of the organization saw their main task as "organiz[ing] women's politics among women's groups independent of political party structures" (Young 1999: 89). Nonetheless, feminists' efforts to shape the outcomes of the transition period rested on an assumption that East Germany would continue to exist as a separate state. With the reunification of East and West Germany, the UFV and many other East German organizations found themselves on the margins of an arena dominated by West German parties.

Conclusion

The framework presented in this book represents an effort to make sense of an important and widespread phenomenon: the mobilization of women. This study differs significantly from the approach followed by most other studies of women's movements. First, I define women's movements as those that mobilize on the basis of gender identity, rather than on the basis of particular issues. I do so in part to underline the importance of right-wing mobilization and in part to illustrate similarities among all kinds of women's movements that would otherwise be missed. Second, I argue that women's movements coalesce ("tip") when the political system provides an opportunity – specifically, when realignment brings about new alliances among political elites. At that point, female political entrepreneurs can exercise considerable initiative, using women's exclusion from political decision making to frame their claims in gender terms. This in turn provides an additional opportunity for the movement, when party elites become motivated to respond to mobilized women's groups in an effort to find bases of popular support under conditions of uncertainty.

These dynamics show not only the conditions under which movements emerge, but why, despite often spectacular success, they inevitably decline. Organizing on the basis of their exclusion from politics is the one factor that brings diverse groups of women together, uniting them across classes, political ideologies, and other forms of identity. But this unity cannot be sustained once women enter the political arena: women cannot maintain their status as political outsiders once they gain access to political power. At the very least, they can no longer maintain the "big tent" of unity. They will be divided by the need to take responsibility for specific policy choices. Thus mobilizing as women is a double-edged sword that provides access to women as a mass constituency but limits their ability to gain collective representation within the political system.

The inevitable dissolution of women's movements may appear as grim news – but only if sustained unity is perceived to be the desired outcome.[3] How effective is united mobilization among women as a strategy for attaining substantive goals? What are the policy consequences of mobilizing on the basis of a shared gender identity? Despite the similarities in the way they framed their activities, the two movements in Chile differ in terms of outcomes. Mobilization on the basis of women's status as political outsiders led to very different consequences in these two cases. Anti-Marxist women's claims to transcend partisan politics appealed to ordinary housewives as well as women inside the political parties. But their rhetoric fed easily into the "antipolitics" solution of the Chilean military. In fact, General Pinochet took women's claims more seriously than they did. He purged the anti-Allende movement of women who actually were party members and recast women as the natural allies of the military as part of his effort to destroy the party system entirely. In the case of the anti-Pinochet movement, the rhetoric of "political outsiders" did not serve women's organizations well after the democratic transition when it came time to negotiating for positions on electoral lists, lobbying for cabinet posts, or shaping the legislative agenda of the new government. Framing women's participation in terms of an outsider status, combined with women's inexperience in partisan politics, left women without an effective strategy in the formal political arena. These findings contrast directly with research that suggests women's ability to achieve policy gains is highest when they organize autonomously. The very factor that led to the success of these movements – mobilizing as outsiders – allowed male politicians and "antipoliticians" to marginalize women. Studies of women's movements frequently conclude with a call to consolidate women's mobilization, but that recommendation may prove self-defeating when it comes to meeting women's particular demands. This book has examined the conditions that foster women's mobilization. The natural next step focuses on

[3] I thank Gary King for this insight.

which strategies lead to the most significant and sustained policy gains for women. It is far from self-evident that unified organizing among women is the best way to pursue their (our) collective interests. I suggest a different tack in terms of the direction of future research, one that looks at issues of women's representation in the formal political arena.

References

Ackelsberg, Martha A. (1991). *Free Women of Spain: Anarchism and the Struggle for the Emancipation of Women*. Bloomington: Indiana University Press.

Agosín, Marjorie (1987). *Scraps of Life*. Trenton, NJ: Red Sea Press.

(1996). *Tapestries of Hope, Threads of Love: The Arpillera Movement in Chile, 1974–1994*. Albuquerque: University of New Mexico Press.

Alessandri, Silvia (1994). Personal interview. Santiago, Chile, March 22.

Alvarez, Sonia E. (1990). *Engendering Democracy in Brazil: Women's Movements in Transition Politics*. Princeton: Princeton University Press.

(1998). "Latin American Feminisms 'Go Global': Trends of the 1990s and Challenges for the New Millennium." *Cultures of Politics, Politics of Cultures*. Sonia E. Alvarez et al., eds. Boulder, CO: Westview Press.

Alvarez, Sonia E., Evelina Dagnino, et al., eds. (1998). *Cultures of Politics, Politics of Cultures: Re-visioning Latin American Social Movements*. Boulder, CO: Westview Press.

Análisis (1984). "Las mujeres irrumpen, marcando el camino," January 16.

(1988). "La unidad en peligro," March 14.

Andersen, Kristi (1996). *After Suffrage: Women in Partisan and Electoral Politics Before the New Deal*. Chicago: University of Chicago Press.

Angell, Alan and Benny Pollack (1993). *The Legacy of Dictatorship: Political, Economic and Social Change in Pinochet's Chile*. Liverpool: Institute of Latin American Studies, University of Liverpool.

Antezana-Pernet, Corinne (1994). "Peace in the World and Democracy at Home: The Chilean Women's Movement in the 1940s." *Latin America in the 1940s: War and Postwar Transitions*. David Rock, ed. Berkeley: University of California Press.

Arrate, Jorge (2001). Personal interview. St. Louis, MO, February 23.

Arriagada, Genaro (1988). *Pinochet: The Politics of Power*. Boston: Unwin Hyman.

Astelarra, Judith (1986). "Democracia y feminismo." *La Otra Mitad de Chile*. M. Angelica Meza, ed. Santiago, Chile: Centros de Estudios Sociales, Instituto para el Nuevo Chile.

209

Baldez, Lisa (1997). "In the Name of the Public and the Private: Conservative and Progressive Women's Movements in Chile, 1970–1996." Ph.D. diss., University of California, San Diego.
   (2001). "Coalition Politics and the Limits of State Feminism." *Women and Politics* 22 (4): 1–28.
Banaszak, Lee Ann (1996). *Why Movements Succeed or Fail: Opportunity, Culture, and the Struggle for Woman Suffrage*. Princeton: Princeton University Press.
Barrig, Maruja (1997). De cal y arena: ONGs y movimiento de mujeres en Chile. Unpublished manuscript.
   (1998). "Los Malestares del Feminismo Latinoamericano: Una Nueva Lectura." Paper presented at the Latin American Studies Association Annual Meeting, Chicago, September 24–26.
Bashevkin, Sylvia (1998). *Women on the Defensive: Living Through Conservative Times*. Chicago: University of Chicago Press.
Basu, Amrita (1995). *The Challenge of Local Feminisms: Women's Movements in Global Perspective*. Boulder, CO: Westview Press.
Beckwith, Karen (1996). "Lancashire Women Against Pit Closures: Women's Standing in a Men's Movement." *Signs* 21 (4): 1034–68.
Bello, Walden F. (1975). "The Roots and Dynamics of Revolution and Counterrevolution in Chile." Ph.D. diss., Princeton University.
Bernhard, Michael H. (1993). *The Origins of Democratization in Poland: Workers, Intellectuals, and Oppositional Politics, 1976–1980*. New York: Columbia University Press.
Bitar, Sergio (1987). *Isla 10*. Santiago, Chile: Pehuén.
Black, Naomi (1989). *Social Feminism*. Ithaca, NY: Cornell University Press.
Blee, Kathleen M. (1991). *Women of the Klan: Racism and Gender in the 1920s*. Berkeley: University of California Press.
Blee, Kathleen M., ed. (1998). *No Middle Ground: Women and Radical Protest*. New York: New York University Press.
Boeninger, Edgardo (1998). *Democracia en Chile: lecciones para la gobernabilidad*. Barcelona: Editorial Andrés Bello.
Boyle, Catherine (1993). "Touching the Air: The Cultural Force of Women in Chile." *"Viva": Women and Popular Protest in Latin America*. Sarah A. Radcliffe and Sallie Westwood, eds. London: Routledge.
Brady, David, John Ferejohn, et al. (2000). "Constitutional Moments and Congressional Preferences: What Happened in 1964?" Paper presented at the Conference on Critical Elections and Constitutional Quandaries, Center for Political Economy at Washington University, St. Louis, December 8–10.
Brunner, Jose Joaquin and Alicia Barrios (1987). *Inquisición, mercado y filantropía: ciencias sociales y autoritarismo en Argentina, Brasil, Chile y Uruguay*. Santiago, Chile: FLACSO.
Buckley, Mary, ed. (1997). *Post-Soviet Women: From the Baltic to Central Asia*. New York: Cambridge University Press.
Buckley, Sandra (1997). *Broken Silence: Voices of Japanese Feminism*. Berkeley: University of California Press.

References

Bunster, Ximena (1988). "Watch Out for the Little Nazi Man That All of Us Have Inside: The Mobilization and Demobilization of Women in Militarized Chile." *Women's Studies International Forum* 11 (5): 485–91.

(1993). "Surviving Beyond Fear: Women and Torture in Latin America." *Surviving Beyond Fear: Women, Children and Human Rights in Latin America.* Marjorie Agosín and Monica Bruno, eds. Fredonia, NY: White Pine Press.

Butler, Judith P. (1990). *Gender Trouble: Feminism and the Subversion of Identity.* New York: Routledge.

Bystydzienski, Jill M. and Joti Sekhon, eds. (1999). *Democratization and Women's Grassroots Movements.* Bloomington: Indiana University Press.

Cáceres, Ana (1993). *Cómo les ha ido a las mujeres chilenas en la democracia?: Balance y propuestas mirando al 2000.* Santiago, Chile: Instituto de la Mujer.

Carey, John M. (2000). "Parchment, Equilibria, and Institutions." *Comparative Political Studies* 33 (6/7): 735–61.

Castañeda, Jorge G. (1993). *Utopia Unarmed: The Latin American Left after the Cold War.* New York: Knopf (distributed by Random House).

Centro de Estudios de la Mujer (1993). *Los contenidos de la políticas públicas hacia la mujer; Las Propuestas de la Concertación de Mujeres por la Democracia y las acciones del SERNAM.* Santiago, Chile: Centro de Estudios de la Mujer.

Cepeda, Sandra (1994). Personal interview. Santiago, Chile, February 23.

Chafetz, Janet Saltzman, Anthony Gary Dworkin, et al. (1986). *Female Revolt: Women's Movements in World and Historical Perspective.* Totowa, NJ: Rowman and Allanheld.

Chai, Sun-Ki (1997). "Rational Choice and Culture: Clashing Perspectives or Complementary Modes of Analysis?" *Culture Matters: Essays in Honor of Aaron Wildavsky.* Richard J. and Michael Thompson Ellis, eds. Boulder, CO: HarperCollins Publishers, Inc.

Chaney, Elsa (1979). *Supermadre: Women in Politics in Latin America.* Austin: Institute of Latin American Studies by University of Texas Press.

Chatty, Dawn and Annika Rabo, eds. (1997). *Organizing Women: Formal and Informal Women's Groups in the Middle East.* Oxford: Berg.

Chong, Dennis (1991). *Collective Action and the Civil Rights Movement.* Chicago: University of Chicago Press.

Christian Democratic Leaders (1994). Personal interview. Santiago, Chile, May 27.

Chuchryk, Patricia (1984). "Protest, Politics, and Personal Life: The Emergence of Feminism in a Military Dictatorship, Chile 1973–1983." Ph.D. diss., York University.

(1989). "Subversive Mothers." *Women, the State, and Development.* Sue Ellen M. Charlton, Jana Matson Everett, and Kathleen A. Staudt, eds. Albany: State University of New York Press.

(1994). "From Dictatorship to Democracy: The Women's Movement in Chile." *The Women's Movement in Latin America.* Jane S. Jaquette, ed. Boulder, CO: Westview.

Clark, Ann Marie, Elisabeth J. Friedman, and Kathryn Hochstetler (1998). "The Sovereign Limits of Civil Society: A Comparison of NGO Participation in

UN World Conferences on the Environment, Human Rights, and Women." *World Politics* 51 (1): 1–35.

Cohen, Cathy J., Kathleen B. Jones, et al., eds. (1997). *Women Transforming Politics: An Alternative Reader.* New York: New York University Press.

Collier, Simon and William F. Sater (1996). *A History of Chile, 1808–1994.* New York: Cambridge University Press.

Constable, Pamela and Arturo Valenzuela (1991). *A Nation of Enemies: Chile Under Pinochet.* New York: W.W. Norton.

Corradi, Juan E., Patricia Weiss Fagen, et al. (1992). *Fear at the Edge: State Terror and Resistance in Latin America.* Berkeley: University of California Press.

Correa, María (1974). *La guerra de las mujeres.* Santiago, Chile: Editorial Universidad Técnica del Estado.

——— (1993). Personal interview. Santiago, Chile, December 4.

Costain, Anne N. (1992). *Inviting Women's Rebellion: A Political Process Interpretation of the Women's Movement.* Baltimore: Johns Hopkins University Press.

Cox, Gary W. (1997). *Making Votes Count: Strategic Coordination in the World's Electoral Systems.* New York: Cambridge University Press.

Cusack, David F. (1977). *Revolution and Reaction: The Internal Dynamics of Conflict and Confrontation in Chile.* Denver: University of Denver Graduate School of International Studies.

Davies, James C. (1962). "Toward a Theory of Revolution." *American Sociological Review* 27 (1): 5–19.

De Grazia, Victoria (1992). *How Fascism Ruled Women: Italy, 1922–1945.* Berkeley: University of California Press.

Donoso, Teresa (1974a). *Breve historia de la unidad popular: documento de "El Mercurio."* Santiago, Chile: El Mercurio.

——— (1974b). *La epopeya de las ollas vacías.* Santiago, Chile: Editora Nacional Gabriela Mistral.

Dooner, Patricio (1985). *Crónica de una democracia cansada: el Partido Demócrata Cristiano durante el gobierno de Allende.* Santiago, Chile: Instituto Chileno de Estudios Humanísticos.

Drake, Paul W. (1978). *Socialism and Populism in Chile, 1932–1952.* Urbana: University of Illinois Press.

Drake, Paul W. and Iván Jaksić, eds. (1995). *The Struggle for Democracy in Chile.* Lincoln: University of Nebraska Press.

Dulles, John (1970). *Unrest in Brazil: Political-Military Crises 1955–1964.* Austin: University of Texas Press.

Ediciones ISIS (1986). *Movimiento feminista en américa latina y el caribe.* Santiago, Chile: Ediciones ISIS.

Einhorn, Barbara (1993). *Cinderella Goes to Market: Citizenship, Gender, and Women's Movements in East Central Europe.* London: Verso.

Ellison, Susan (2000). "Doing Ants' Work: The Evolution of Chile's Popular Movement." Senior thesis, Washington University.

Elshtain, Jean Bethke (1981). *Public Man, Private Woman: Women in Social and Political Thought.* Princeton: Princeton University Press.

References

Elster, Jon (1989). *Nuts and Bolts for the Social Sciences*. New York: Cambridge University Press.

Enloe, Cynthia H. (1993). *The Morning After: Sexual Politics at the End of the Cold War*. Berkeley: University of California Press.

Eva (1972a). "Aniversario del cacerolazo," December 1.

——— (1972b). "El poder femenino," September 5.

Farrell, Joseph P. (1986). *The National Unified School in Allende's Chile: The Role of Education in the Destruction of a Revolution*. Vancouver, Canada: University of British Columbia Press (in association with the Centre for Research on Latin America and the Caribbean York University).

Faúndez, Julio (1988). *Marxism and Democracy in Chile: From 1932 to the Fall of Allende*. New Haven, CT: Yale University Press.

Feijoo, María del Carmen (1994). "Women and Democracy in Argentina." *The Women's Movement in Latin America*. Jane S. Jaquette, ed. Boulder, CO: Westview.

Fernandez, María Luisa (1996). "Beyond Partisan Politics in Chile: The Carlos Ibañez Period and the Politics of Ultranationalism Between 1952–1958." Ph.D. diss., University of Miami.

Fischer, Kathleen B. (1979). *Political Ideology and Educational Reform in Chile, 1964–1976*. Los Angeles: UCLA Latin American Center, University of California, Los Angeles.

Fish, M. Steven (1995). *Democracy from Scratch: Opposition and Regime in the New Russian Revolution*. Princeton: Princeton University Press.

Fontaine, Arturo (1999). *Todos querían la revolución: Chile 1964–1973*. Santiago, Chile: Zig-Zag.

Foweraker, Joe and Todd Landman (1997). *Citizenship Rights and Social Movements: A Comparative and Statistical Analysis*. New York: Oxford University Press.

Franco, Jean (1998). "Defrocking the Vatican: Feminism's Secular Project." *Cultures of Politics, Politics of Cultures*. Sonia E. Alvarez, Evelina Dagnino, and Arturo Escobar, eds. Boulder, CO: Westview Press.

Frei, Carmen (1994). Personal interview. Santiago, Chile, May 24.

Friedman, Elisabeth J. (2000). *Unfinished Transitions: Women and the Gendered Development of Democracy in Venezuela, 1936–1996*. University Park, PA: Pennsylvania State University Press.

Frohmann, Alicia and Teresa Valdés (1995). "Democracy in the Country and in the Home: The Women's Movement in Chile." *The Challenge of Local Feminisms: Women's Movements in Global Perspective*. Amrita Basu, ed. Boulder, CO: Westview Press.

Fuentes, Manuel (1999). *Memorias secretas de Patria y Libertad: algunas confesiones sobre la guerra fría en Chile*. Santiago, Chile: Grijalbo Grupo Grijalbo-Mondadori.

Garcés, Joan E. (1972). *Revolución, congreso y constitución: el caso Tohá*. Santiago, Chile: Quimantú.

——— (1976). *Allende y la experiencia chilena: las armas de la política*. Barcelona: Ariel.

Garretón, Manuel Antonio (1987). *Las complejidades de la transición invisible, movilizaciones populares y régimen militar en Chile.* Santiago, Chile: FLACSO.

(1989). "Popular Mobilization and the Military Regime in Chile: The Complexities of the Invisible Transition." *Power and Popular Protest: Latin American Social Movements.* Susan Eckstein, ed. Berkeley: University of California.

(1990). Personal interview. Santiago, Chile, August 1.

(1995). *Hacia una nueva era política: estudio sobre las democratizaciones.* México, D.F.: Fondo de Cultura Económica.

Gates, John B. (1987). "Partisan Realignment, Unconstitutional State Policies and the U.S. Supreme Court, 1837–1964." *American Journal of Political Science* 31 (2): 259–80.

Gaviola, Edda (1986). *Queremos votar en las próximas elecciones: historia del movimiento femenino chileno, 1913–1952.* Santiago, Chile: Centro de Análisis y Difusión de la Condición de la Mujer.

(1994). "Por un gesto urgente de libertad, 8 de marzo 1994." Paper presented at the II Foro Nacional Feminista, Movimiento Feminista Autónomo, Santiago, Chile, March 19–20.

Gazmuri, María Olivia (1994). Personal interview. Santiago, Chile, April 19.

Gelb, Joyce (1989). *Feminism and Politics: A Comparative Perspective.* Berkeley: University of California Press.

Gill, Anthony James (1998). *Rendering Unto Caesar: The Catholic Church and the State in Latin America.* Chicago: University of Chicago Press.

Gilmartin, Christina K. (1995). *Engendering the Chinese Revolution: Radical Women, Communist Politics, and Mass Movements in the 1920s.* Berkeley: University of California Press.

Guilladat, Patrick and Pierre Mouterde (1998). *Los movimientos sociales en Chile 1973–1993.* Santiago, Chile: Ediciones LOM.

Gurr, Ted Robert (1970). *Why Men Rebel.* Princeton: Princeton University Press.

Haas, Liesl (2000). "Legislating Equality: Feminist Policymaking in Chile." Ph.D. diss., University of North Carolina.

Hahner, June Edith (1990). *Emancipating the Female Sex: The Struggle for Women's Rights in Brazil, 1850–1940.* Durham, NC: Duke University Press.

Hall, Clarence W. (1964). "The Country That Saved Itself," *Reader's Digest.* November, 133–160.

Halperin, Ernst (1965). *Nationalism and Communism in Chile.* Cambridge: MIT Press.

Hardin, Russell (1989). "Why A Constitution?" *The Federalist Papers and the New Institutionalism.* Bernard Grofman and Donald Wittman, eds. New York: Agathon Press.

Harvey, Anna L. (1998). *Votes Without Leverage: Women in American Electoral Politics, 1920–1970.* New York: Cambridge University Press.

Havelkova, Hana (1993). "A Few Prefeminist Thoughts." *Gender Politics and Post-Communism.* Nanette Funk and Magda Mueller, eds. New York: Routledge.

Henriquez, Elizabeth (1994). Personal interview. Santiago, Chile, April 14.

References

Hipsher, Patricia (1997). "Democratization and the Decline of Urban Social Movements." *Comparative Politics* 28 (3): 273–98.

Hite, Katherine (2000). *When the Romance Ended: Leaders of the Chilean Left, 1968–1998*. New York: Columbia University Press.

Hola, Eugenia and Virginia Guzmán, eds. (1996). *El conocimiento como un hecho político*. Santiago, Chile: Centro de Estudios de la Mujer.

Hola, Eugenia and Gabriela Pischedda (1993). *Mujeres, poder y política: nuevas tensiones para viejas estructuras*. Santiago, Chile: Ediciones CEM.

Horne, Alistair (1972). *Small Earthquake in Chile: A Visit to Allende's South America*. London: Macmillan.

Htun, Mala (forthcoming). *Dictatorship, Democracy and Gender Rights*. New York: Cambridge University Press.

Hurley, Patricia A. (1991). "Partisan Representation, Realignment and the Senate in the 1980s." *Journal of Politics* 53 (1): 3–33.

Jaksić, Iván (1989). *Academic Rebels in Chile: The Role of Philosophy in Higher Education and Politics*. Albany: State University of New York Press.

Jaquette, Jane S., ed. (1994). *The Women's Movement in Latin America: Participation and Democracy*. Boulder, CO: Westview Press.

Jaquette, Jane S. and Sharon L. Wolchik, eds. (1998). *Women and Democracy: Latin America and Central and Eastern Europe*. Baltimore: Johns Hopkins University Press.

Jarpa, Sergio Onofre (1973). *Creo en Chile*. Santiago, Chile: Sociedad Impresora Chile.

Jayawardena, Kumari (1986). *Feminism and Nationalism in the Third World*. New Delhi, India: Kali for Women.

Jelín, Elizabeth (1991). *Family, Household and Gender Relations in Latin America*. London: Kegan Paul International (in association with UNESCO).

Jetter, Alexis, Annelise Orleck, et al., eds. (1997). *The Politics of Motherhood: Activist Voices from Left to Right*. Hanover, NH: Dartmouth College – University Press of New England.

Jónasdóttir, Anna, G. and Kathleen B. Jones, eds. (1988). *The Political Interests of Gender: Developing Theory and Research with a Feminist Face*. London: Sage Publications.

Kampwirth, Karen and Victoria Gonzalez, eds. (2001). *Radical Women in Latin America: Right and Left*. University Park, PA: Pennsylvania State University Press.

Kaplan, Temma (1982). "Female Consciousness and Collective Action: The Case of Barcelona, 1910–1918." *Signs* 7 (3): 545–60.

(1985). "Commentary: On the Socialist Origins of International Women's Day." *Feminist Studies* 11 (1): 163–71.

(1992). *Red City, Blue Period: Social Movements in Picasso's Barcelona*. Berkeley: University of California Press.

(1997). *Crazy for Democracy: Women in Grassroots Movements*. New York: Routledge.

Katzenstein, Mary Fainsod and Carol Mueller, eds. (1987). *The Women's Movements of the United States and Western Europe: Consciousness, Political Opportunity, and Public Policy*. Philadelphia: Temple University Press.

References

Kaufman, Robert R. (1972). *The Politics of Land Reform in Chile, 1950–1970.* Cambridge: Harvard University Press.

Kawato, Sadafumi (1987). "Nationalization and Partisan Realignment in Congressional Elections." *American Political Science Review* 81 (4): 1235–50.

Kay, Diana (1987). *Chileans in Exile: Private Struggles, Public Lives.* Houndmills, Basingstoke, Hampshire: Macmillan.

Keck, Margaret E. and Kathryn Sikkink (1998). *Activists Beyond Borders: Advocacy Networks in International Politics.* Ithaca, NY: Cornell University Press.

Kessler, Suzanne J. and Wendy McKenna (1978). *Gender: An Ethnomethodological Approach.* New York: J. Wiley.

Kirkwood, Julieta (1986). *Ser política en Chile: las feministas y los partidos.* Santiago, Chile: FLACSO.

Kitschelt, Herbert (1986). "Political Opportunity Structures and Political Protest: Anti-Nuclear Movements in Four Democracies." *British Journal of Political Science* 16: 57–85.

Klatch, Rebecca E. (1987). *Women of the New Right.* Philadelphia: Temple University Press.

   (1999). *A Generation Divided: The New Left, the New Right, and the 1960s.* Berkeley: University of California Press.

Klimpel, Felicitas (1962). *La Mujer Chilena (el aporte femenino al Progreso de Chile) 1910–1960.* Santiago, Chile: Editorial Andres Bello.

Klubock, Thomas Miller (1998). *Contested Communities: Class, Gender, and Politics in Chile's El Teniente Copper Mine, 1904–1951.* Durham, NC: Duke University Press.

Knight, Jack (1992). *Institutions and Social Conflict.* New York: Cambridge University Press.

Koonz, Claudia (1987). *Mothers in the Fatherland: Women, the Family, and Nazi Politics.* New York: St. Martin's Press.

Kyle, Patricia and Michael J. Francis (1978). "Women at the Polls: The Case of Chile, 1970–1971." *Comparative Political Studies* 11 (3): 291–310.

Laitin, David D. (1998). *Identity in Formation: The Russian-Speaking Populations in the Near Abroad.* Ithaca, NY: Cornell University Press.

Lavrín, Asunción (1995). *Women, Feminism, and Social Change in Argentina, Chile, and Uruguay, 1890–1940.* Lincoln: University of Nebraska Press.

Lechner, Norbert and Susana Levy (1984). *Notas sobre la vida cotidiana III: el disciplinamiento de la mujer.* Santiago, Chile: FLACSO.

Levi, Margaret (1988). *Of Rule and Revenue.* Berkeley: University of California Press.

Levine, Daniel H. (1980). *Churches and Politics in Latin America.* Beverly Hills, CA: Sage Publications.

Lidid, Sandra and Kira Maldonado, eds. (1997). *Movimiento Feminista Autónomo (1993–1997).* Santiago, Chile: Ediciones Tierra Mía.

Linz, Juan J. and Arturo Valenzuela, eds. (1994). *The Failure of Presidential Democracy.* Baltimore: Johns Hopkins University Press.

Lladser, María Teresa (1988). The Emergence of Social Science Research Centers in Chile Under Military Rule. Berkeley: UC Berkeley Center for Studies in Higher Education.

References

Lohmann, Susanne (1994). "The Dynamics of Informational Cascades: The Monday Demonstrations in Leipzig, East Germany, 1989–91." *World Politics* 47 (1): 42–101.

Lorber, Judith (1997). "Night to His Day: The Social Construction of Gender." *Feminist Frontiers IV*. Verta Taylor, Laurel Richardson, and Nancy Whittier, eds. New York: McGraw-Hill.

Loveman, Brian (1976). *Struggle in the Countryside; Politics and Rural Labor in Chile, 1919–1973*. Bloomington: Indiana University Press.

 (1988). *Chile: The Legacy of Hispanic Capitalism*. New York: Oxford University Press.

Loveman, Brian and Thomas M. Davies (1997). *The Politics of Antipolitics: The Military in Latin America*. Wilmington, DE: Scholarly Resources.

Lowden, Pamela (1996). *Moral Opposition to Authoritarian Rule in Chile, 1973–90*. New York: Macmillan Press.

Luker, Kristin (1984). *Abortion and the Politics of Motherhood*. Berkeley: University of California Press.

Lyne, Mona (2000). "Parties as Electoral Agents: The Voter's Dilemma and the Paradox of Reform in Brazil and Collapse in Venezuela." Paper presented at the William W. Brown, Jr., Conference in Latin American Studies, University of North Carolina, Chapel Hill, January 6.

MacKinnon, Catharine A. (1989). *Toward a Feminist Theory of the State*. Cambridge: Harvard University Press.

Mainwaring, Scott and Alexander Wilde (1989). *The Progressive Church in Latin America*. Notre Dame, IN: University of Notre Dame Press.

Maira, Luis (1979). "The Strategy and Tactics of the Chilean Counterrevolution in the Area of Political Institutions." *Chile at the Turning Point: Lessons of the Socialist Years, 1970–1973*. Federico Gil, Ricardo Lagos, and Henry A. Landsberger, eds. Philadelphia: Institute for the Study of Human Issues.

Marilley, Suzanne M. (1997). *Woman Suffrage and the Origins of Liberalism in the United States*. Cambridge: Harvard University Press.

Marody, Mira (1993). "Why I Am Not a Feminist: Some Remarks on the Problem of Gender Identity in the United States and Poland." *Reaction to the Modern Women's Movement, 1963 to the Present*. Angela Howard, Sasha Ranae, and Adams Tarrant, eds. New York: Garland Publishing, Inc.

Marsh, Rosalind (1996). *Women in Russia and Ukraine*. New York: Cambridge University Press.

Marshall, Susan E. (1997). *Splintered Sisterhood: Gender and Class in the Campaign Against Woman Suffrage*. Madison: University of Wisconsin Press.

Martínez, Sergio (1996). *Entre Lennon y Lenin: la militancia juvenil de los años 60*. Santiago, Chile: Mosquito Comunicaciones.

Marx, Karl (1987). *The Eighteenth Brumaire of Louis Bonaparte*. New York: International Publishers.

Matear, Ann (1996). "Desde la Protesta a la Propuesta: Gender Politics and Transition in Chile." *Democratization* 3: 246–63.

217

Mattelart, Armand and Michèle Mattelart (1968). *La mujer Chilena en una nueva sociedad: un estudio exploratorio acerca de la situación e imagen de la mujer en Chile.* Santiago, Chile: Editorial del Pacifico.

Maturana, Lucia (1993). Personal interview. Santiago, Chile, October 27.

Matynia, Elzbieta (1995). "Finding a Voice: Women in Postcommunist Central Europe." *The Challenge of Local Feminisms: Women's Movements in Global Perspective.* Amrita Basu, ed. Boulder, CO: Westview Press.

Maza, Erika (1995). "Catholicism, Anticlericalism, and the Quest for Women's Suffrage in Chile," Kellogg Institute Working Papers, University of Notre Dame.

Maza, Gonzalo de la and Mario Garcés (1985). *La explosión de las mayorías: protesta nacional, 1983–1984.* Santiago, Chile: Educación y Comunicaciones.

McAdam, Doug (1982). *Political Process and the Development of Black Insurgency, 1930–1970.* Chicago: University of Chicago Press.

McAdam, Doug, John D. McCarthy, et al., eds. (1996). *Comparative Perspectives on Social Movements: Political Opportunities, Mobilizing Structures, and Cultural Framings.* New York: Cambridge University Press.

McAdam, Doug, Sidney Tarrow, et al. (1996). "Towards an Integrated Perspective on Social Movements and Revolution," in CIAO Working Papers [database online].

McCarthy, John D. and Mayer N. Zald (1973). *The Trend of Social Movements in America: Professionalization and Resource Mobilization.* Morristown, NJ: General Learning Press.

McCarthy, John D. and Mayer N. Zald, eds. (1987). *Social Movements in an Organizational Society: Collected Essays.* New Brunswick, NJ: Transaction Books.

McGee Deutsch, Sandra (1991). "Gender and Sociopolitical Change in Twentieth-Century Latin America." *Hispanic American Historical Review* 71 (2): 259–306.

Mendoza, María (1994). Personal interview. Santiago, Chile, May 31.

(1999). Personal interview. Santiago, Chile, January 8.

Mettler, Suzanne (1998). *Dividing Citizens: Gender and Federalism in New Deal Public Policy.* Ithaca, NY: Cornell University Press.

Mohanty, Chandra Talpade, Ann Russo, et al., eds. (1991). *Third World Women and the Politics of Feminism.* Bloomington: Indiana University Press.

Molina, Natacha (1986). *Lo femenino y lo democrático en el Chile de hoy.* Santiago, Chile: VECTOR.

(1989). "Propuestas politicas y orientaciones de cambio en la situación de la mujer." *Propuestas políticas y demandas sociales.* Manuel A. Garretón and Cristián Cox, eds. Santiago, Chile: FLACSO.

(1990). Personal interview. Santiago, Chile, July 11.

Molina, Natacha and Patricia Provoste (1997). "Igualdad de Oportunidades para las mujeres: Condición de democracia." *Veredas por cruzar.* Natacha Molina and Patricia Provoste, eds. Santiago, Chile: Instituto de la Mujer.

Molyneux, Maxine (1985). "Mobilization Without Emancipation? Women's Interests, the State, and Revolution in Nicaragua." *Feminist Studies* 11 (2): 227–54.

References

Montecino, Sonia and Josefina Rossetti (1990). *Tramas para un nuevo destino: propuestas de la Concertación de Mujeres por la Democracia.* N.P.

Munizaga, Giselle (1983). *La mujer, el vecino y el deportista en los micromedios de gobierno: un estudio sobre construcción de sujetos políticos a través del discurso oficial.* Santiago, Chile: CENECA.

——— (1988). *El discurso público de Pinochet: un análisis semiológico.* Santiago, Chile: CESOC/CENECA.

Munizaga, Giselle and Lilian Letelier (1988). "Mujer y régimen militar." *Mundo de mujer: continuidad y cambio.* Centro de Estudios de la Mujer, ed. Santiago, Chile: Centro de Estudios de la Mujer.

Muñoz, Adriana (1987). *Fuerza feminista y democrática: Utopia a realizar.* Santiago, Chile: Instituto de la Mujer, Vector.

——— (1994). Personal interview. Santiago, Chile, June 9.

Nardulli, Peter F. (1995). "The Concept of a Critical Realignment, Electoral Behavior and Political Change." *American Political Science Review* 89 (1): 10–22.

Navas, Sara (1993). Personal interview. Santiago, Chile, November 5.

Nelson, Barbara J. and Najma Chowdhury, eds. (1994). *Women and Politics Worldwide.* New Haven, CT: Yale University Press.

Neuse, Steven A. (1978). "Voting in Chile: The Feminine Response." *Political Participation in Latin America.* John A. Booth and Mitchell A. Seligson, eds. New York: Holmes and Meier Publishers.

Norero, Isabel (1994). Personal interview. Santiago, Chile, January 4.

North, Douglass Cecil (1990). *Institutions, Institutional Change, and Economic Performance.* New York: Cambridge University Press.

Oppenheim, Lois Hecht (1999). *Politics in Chile: Democracy, Authoritarianism, and the Search for Development.* Boulder, CO: Westview Press.

Orellana, Patricio and Elizabeth Quay Hutchison (1991). *El movimiento de derechos humanos en Chile, 1973–1990.* Santiago, Chile: Centro de Estudios Politicos Latinoamericanos Simon Bolivar.

Oxhorn, Philip (1995). *Organizing Civil Society: The Popular Sectors and the Struggle for Democracy in Chile.* University Park: Pennsylvania State University Press.

Oyarzún, Kemy (2000). "Engendering Democracy in Chile's Universities." *NACLA Report on the Americas* 33 (4): 24–9.

Palestro, Sandra (1995). "Liderazgo de mujeres: entre el partido politico y el movimiento social." Thesis, Universidad Arcis.

Parikh, Sunita and Charles Cameron (1999). "A Theory of Riots and Mass Political Violence." Paper presented at the Political Economy Mini-Conference on Formal and Historical Comparative Politics, Washington University, St. Louis, MO, December 3–5.

Pateman, Carole (1988). *The Sexual Contract.* Stanford, CA: Stanford University Press.

Pérez de Arce, Hermógenes (1994). Personal interview. Santiago, Chile, May 5.

Petersen, Roger Dale (2001). *Resistance and Rebellion: Lessons from Eastern Europe.* New York: Cambridge University Press.

Petras, James F. and Morris H. Morley (1974). *How Allende Fell: A Study in U.S.–Chilean Relations.* Nottingham: Spokesman Books.

Pinto, Silvia (1972). *Los días del arco iris*. Santiago, Chile: Editorial del Pacífico.

Pisano, Margarita (1990). Personal interview. Santiago, Chile, June 30.

——— (1994). Personal interview. Santiago, Chile, March 20.

Poblete, Olga (1987). *Dia internacional de la mujer en Chile: otro capítulo de una historia invisible*. Santiago, Chile: Ediciones MEMCH-83.

Power, Margaret (1996). "Right Wing Women and Chilean Politics: 1964–1973." Ph.D. diss., University of Illinois at Chicago.

Provoste, Patricia (1995). *La construcción de las mujeres en la política social*. Santiago, Chile: Instituto de la Mujer.

Puga, Carmen (1994). Personal interview. Santiago, Chile, March 24.

Puryear, Jeffrey (1994). *Thinking Politics: Intellectuals and Democracy in Chile, 1973–1988*. Baltimore: The Johns Hopkins University Press.

Qué Pasa (1972). "El miedo barrio por barrio," December 19.

Quevedo, Virginia (1994). "Estrategias comunicacionales feministas: Radio Tierra una experiencia." Paper presented at the II Foro Nacional Feminista, Movimiento Feminista Autónomo, Santiago, Chile, March 19–20.

Ravines, Eudocio (1974). *El rescate de Chile*. México: G. de Anda.

República de Chile (1971). *Diario de sesiones*. Camara de Diputados, Sesión 28, March 30.

——— (1972a). *Boletín de sesiones*. Camara de Diputados, Sesión 22, December 27.

——— (1972b). *Diario de sesiones del senado*. Senado, Legislatura 317a, Sesión extraordinaria, October 13.

——— (1972c). *Diario de sesiones del senado*. República de Chile. Senado, Sesión 47, December 12.

——— (1975). *Chile Lights the Freedom Torch*. Santiago, Chile: República de Chile.

——— (1990). *Memoria de gobierno, 1973–1990*. Santiago, Chile: República de Chile. Presidencia.

——— (1997). Registros de votantes. Senado.

——— (1991). Comisión Nacional de Verdad y Reconciliación. *Informe Rettig: informe de la Comisión Nacional de Verdad y Reconciliación*. Santiago, Chile: La Nación – Ediciones del Ornitorrinco.

Riker, William H. (1986). *The Art of Political Manipulation*. New Haven, CT: Yale University Press.

Riker, William H., Randall L. Calvert, et al. (1996). *The Strategy of Rhetoric: Campaigning for the American Constitution*. New Haven, CT: Yale University Press.

Roberts, Kenneth M. (1998). *Deepening Democracy?: The Modern Left and Social Movements in Chile and Peru*. Stanford, CA: Stanford University Press.

Rodríguez, Victoria Elizabeth (1998). *Women's Participation in Mexican Political Life*. Boulder, CO: Westview Press.

Rohrschneider, Robert (1993). "New Party versus Old Left Realignments: Environmental Attitudes, Party Policies and Partisan Affiliations in Four West European Countries." *Journal of Politics* 55 (3): 682–701.

Rosaldo, Michelle Zimbalist, Joan Bamberger, et al., eds. (1974). *Woman, Culture, and Society*. Stanford, CA: Stanford University Press.

References

Rosemblatt, Karin (2000). *Gendered Compromises: Political Cultures and the State in Chile, 1920–1950*. Chapel Hill: University of North Carolina Press.

Rosetti, Josefina (1983). *La mujer chilena y el feminismo*. Santiago, Chile: Cuadernos del Circulo Mayo.

——— (1994). Personal interview. Santiago, Chile, March 10.

Rupp, Leila J. (1997). *Worlds of Women: The Making of an International Women's Movement*. Princeton: Princeton University Press.

Rupp, Leila J. and Verta A. Taylor (1987). *Survival in the Doldrums: The American Women's Rights Movement, 1945 to the 1960s*. New York: Oxford University Press.

Saenz, Carmen (1993). Personal interview. Santiago, Chile, December 4.

Santa Cruz, Lucía (1994). "Una mirada al momento político." *Libertad y Desarollo* 39: 1.

Santiago Times (2000). "Eleven New Disappeared Cases Presented." March 30.

Sawa-Czajka, Elzbieta (1996). "International Trends: Are There Female Political Elites in Poland?" *Journal of Women's History* 8 (2).

Schelling, Thomas C. (1978). *Micromotives and Macrobehavior*. New York: Norton.

Schild, Veronica (1998). "New Subjects of Rights? Women's Movements and the Construction of Citizenship in the 'New Democracies.'" *Politics of Culture, Cultures of Politics*. Sonia Alvarez, Evelina Dagnino, and Arturo Escobar, eds. Boulder, CO: Westview Press.

Schneider, Cathy Lisa (1992). "Radical Opposition Parties and Squatters Movements in Pinochet's Chile." *The Making of Social Movements in Latin America*. Arturo Escobar and Sonia E. Alvarez, eds. Boulder, CO: Westview Press.

——— (1995). *Shantytown Protest in Pinochet's Chile*. Philadelphia: Temple University Press.

Scott, Joan Wallach (1988). *Gender and the Politics of History*. New York: Columbia University Press.

Shugart, Matthew Soberg and John M. Carey (1992). *Presidents and Assemblies: Constitutional Design and Electoral Dynamics*. New York: Cambridge University Press.

Siavelis, Peter (2000). *The President and Congress in Postauthoritarian Chile: Institutional Constraints to Democratic Consolidation*. University Park: Pennsylvania State University Press.

Siemienska, Renata (1998). "Consequences of Economic and Political Changes for Women in Poland." *Women and Democracy: Latin America and Central and Eastern Europe*. Jane S. Jaquette and Sharon L. Wolchik, eds. Baltimore: Johns Hopkins University Press.

Sigmund, Paul E. (1977). *The Overthrow of Allende and the Politics of Chile, 1964–1976*. Pittsburgh: University of Pittsburgh Press.

——— (1993). *The United States and Democracy in Chile*. Baltimore: Johns Hopkins University Press.

Siklova, Jirina (1993). "Are Women in Central and Eastern Europe Conservative?" *Gender Politics and Post-Communism*. Nanette Funk and Magda Mueller, eds. New York: Routledge.

Silva, Clothilde (1993). Personal interview. Santiago, Chile, December 1.

References

Silva, Eduardo (1996). *The State and Capital in Chile: Business Elites, Technocrats, and Market Economics.* Boulder, CO: Westview Press.

Silva, Julio (1979). "Errors of the Unidad Popular and a Critique of the Christian Democrats." *Chile at the Turning Point: Lessons of the Socialist Years, 1970–1973.* Federico Gil, Ricardo Lagos, and Henry A. Landsberger, eds. Philadelphia: Institute for the Study of Human Issues.

Silva, L. (1994). Personal Interview. Santiago, Chile, March 26.

Silva, María de la Luz (1994). Personal interview. Santiago, Chile, May 25.

Skocpol, Theda (1979). *States and Social Revolutions: A Comparative Analysis of France, Russia, and China.* New York: Cambridge University Press.

(1994). *Social Revolutions in the Modern World.* New York: Cambridge University Press.

Smelser, Neil J. (1963). *Theory of Collective Behavior.* New York: Free Press of Glencoe.

Smith, Brian H. (1982). *The Church and Politics in Chile: Challenges to Modern Catholicism.* Princeton: Princeton University Press.

Snow, David E. (1992). "Master Frames and Cycles of Protest." *Frontiers in Social Movement Theory.* Aldon D. Morris and Carol McClurg Mueller, eds. New Haven, CT: Yale University Press.

Snow, David E. and Robert Benford (1988). "Ideology, Frame Resonance, and Participant Mobilization." *From Structure to Action: Comparing Social Movement Research Across Cultures.* Bert Klandermans, Hanspeter Kriesi, and Sidney G. Tarrow, eds. Greenwich, CT: JAI Press.

Soares, Vera, Ana Alice Alcantara Costa, et al. (1995). "Brazilian Feminism and Women's Movements: A Two-Way Street." *The Challenge of Local Feminisms.* Amrita Basu, ed. Boulder, CO: Westview Press.

SOL Leaders (1994). Personal interview. Santiago, Chile, April 19.

Sota, Vicenta (1994). Personal interview. Santiago, Chile, April 18.

Sperling, Valerie (1999). *Organizing Women in Contemporary Russia: Engendering Transition.* New York: Cambridge University Press.

Stallings, Barbara (1978). *Class Conflict and Economic Development in Chile, 1958–1973.* Stanford, CA: Stanford University Press.

Stephen, Lynn (1997). *Women and Social Movements in Latin America: Power From Below.* Austin: University of Texas Press.

Sternbach, Nancy Saporta, Marysa Navarro-Aranguren, et al. (1992). "Feminisms in Latin America: From Bogotá to Taxco." *Signs* 17 (2): 393–434.

Sundquist, James (1983). *Dynamics of the Party System: Alignment and Realignment of Political Parties in the United States.* Washington, DC: The Brookings Institution.

Taagepera, Rein and Matthew Soberg Shugart (1989). *Seats and Votes.* New Haven, CT: Yale University Press.

Tabak, Fanny (1994). "Women in the Struggle for Democracy and Equal Rights in Brazil." *Women and Politics Worldwide.* Barbara Nelson and Najma Chowdhury, eds. New Haven, CT: Yale University Press.

Tapia, Jorge (1979). "The Difficult Road to Socialism." *Chile at the Turning Point: Lessons of the Socialist Years, 1970–1973.* Federico Gil, Ricardo Lagos, and

References

Henry A. Landsberger, eds. Philadelphia: Institute for the Study of Human Issues.

Tarrow, Sidney G. (1994). *Power in Movement: Social Movements, Collective Action, and Politics.* New York: Cambridge University Press.

Tatur, Melanie (1992). "Why Is There No Women's Movement in Eastern Europe?" *Democracy and Civil Society in Eastern Europe.* Paul G. Lewis, ed. New York: St. Martin's Press.

Taylor, Michael (1987). *The Possibility of Cooperation.* New York: Cambridge University Press.

Terborg-Penn, Rosalyn (1998). *African American Women in the Struggle for the Vote, 1850–1920.* Bloomington: Indiana University Press.

Tétreault, Mary Ann, ed. (1994). *Women and Revolution in Africa, Asia, and the New World.* Columbia: University of South Carolina Press.

Threlfall, Monica (1996). *Mapping the Women's Movement: Feminist Politics and Social Transformation in the North.* London: Verso.

Tilly, Charles (1978). *From Mobilization to Revolution.* Reading, PA: Addison-Wesley Publishing Company.

Tinsman, Heidi Elizabeth (1996). "Unequal Uplift: The Sexual Politics of Gender, Work, and Community in the Chilean Agrarian Reform, 1950–1973." Ph.D. diss., Yale University.

Tomic, Radomiro (1979). "Christian Democracy and the Government of the Unidad Popular." *Chile at the Turning Point: Lessons of the Socialist Years, 1970–1973.* Federico Gil, Ricardo Lagos, and Henry A. Landsberger, eds. Philadelphia: Institute for the Study of Human Issues.

Townsend, Camilla (1993). "Refusing to Travel La Via Chilena: Working-Class Women in Allende's Chile." *Journal of Women's History* 4 (3): 43–63.

United States Congress (1975). Senate. Select Committee to Study Governmental Operations with Respect to Intelligence Activities. *Covert Action.* Washington, DC, December 4–5.

Valdés, Hernán (1975). *Tejas Verdes: Diary of a Chilean Concentration Camp.* London: Gollancz.

Valdés, Marina (1994). Personal interview. Santiago, Chile, April 21.

Valdés, Teresa (1989). "Mujeres por la vida: Itinerario de una lucha." Santiago, Chile: Unpublished manuscript.

Valdés, Teresa and Enrique Gomáriz (1992). *Mujeres latinoamericanas en cifras.* Santiago, Chile: FLACSO.

Valdés, Teresa and Marisa Weinstein (1989). *Organizaciones de pobladoras y construcción democrática en Chile: notas para un debate.* Santiago, Chile: Facultad Latinoamericana de Ciencias Sociales.

(1993). *Mujeres que sueñan: las organizaciones de pobladoras: 1973–1989.* Santiago, Chile: FLACSO.

Valdés, Ximena, Loreto Rebolledo, et al. (1995). *Masculino y femenino en la hacienda chilena del siglo XX.* Santiago, Chile: Fondart – Cedem.

Valenzuela, Arturo (1978). *The Breakdown of Democratic Regimes: Chile.* Baltimore: Johns Hopkins University Press.

Valenzuela, J. Samuel and Timothy R. Scully (1997). "Electoral Choices and the Party System in Chile: Continuities and Changes at the Recovery of Democracy." *Comparative Politics* 29 (4): 511–28.

Valenzuela, María Elena (1987). *La mujer en el Chile militar: todas íbamos a ser reinas.* Santiago, Chile: Ediciones Chile y América-CESOC – ACHIP.

——— (1993). Personal interview. Santiago, Chile, November 15.

——— (1995). "The Evolving Roles of Women Under Military Rule." *The Struggle for Democracy in Chile.* Paul W. Drake and Iván Jaksić, eds. Lincoln: University of Nebraska Press.

——— (1998). "Women and the Democratization Process in Chile." *Women and Democracy: Latin America and Central and Eastern Europe.* Jane S. Jaquette and Sharon L. Wolchik, eds. Baltimore: Johns Hopkins University Press.

Valenzuela, Samuel J. and Arturo Valenzuela (1986). *Military Rule in Chile: Dictatorships and Oppositions.* Baltimore: Johns Hopkins University Press.

Varas, Augusto (1987). *Los militares en el poder: régimen y gobierno militar en Chile, 1973–1986.* Santiago, Chile: FLACSO.

Verba, Ericka Kim (1999). "Catholic Feminism and Acción Social Femenina (Women's Social Action): The Early Years of the Liga de Damas Chilenas, 1912–1924." Ph.D. diss., University of California, Los Angeles.

Verdugo, Patricia (1998). *Interferencia secreta.* Santiago, Chile: Editorial Sudamericana.

Walker, Betty (1994). Personal interview. Santiago, Chile, April 20.

Walker, Ignacio (1990). *Socialismo y democracia: Chile y Europa en perspectiva comparada.* Santiago, Chile: Cieplan-Hachette.

Waters, Elizabeth and Anastasia Posadskaya (1995). "Democracy Without Women Is No Democracy: Women's Struggles in Postcommunist Russia." *The Challenge of Local Feminisms: Women's Movements in Global Perspective.* Amrita Basu, ed. Boulder, CO: Westview Press.

Waylen, Georgina (1993). "Women's Movements and Democratization in Latin America." *Third World Quarterly* 14 (3): 573–87.

Weinstein, Eugenia (1990). Personal interview. Santiago, Chile, July 10.

West, Guida and Rhoda Lois Blumberg, eds. (1990). *Women and Social Protest.* New York: Oxford University Press.

West, Lois A. (1997). *Feminist Nationalism.* New York: Routledge.

Williams, Melissa S. (1998). *Voice, Trust, and Memory: Marginalized Groups and the Failings of Liberal Representation.* Princeton: Princeton University Press.

Winn, Peter (1986). *Weavers of Revolution: The Yarur Workers and Chile's Road to Socialism.* New York: Oxford University Press.

Wolbrecht, Christina (2000). *The Politics of Women's Rights: Parties, Positions, and Change.* Princeton: Princeton University Press.

Wolchik, Sharon L. (1998). "Gender and the Politics of Transition in the Czech Republic and Slovakia." *Women and Democracy.* Jane S. Jaquette and Sharon L. Wolchik, eds. Baltimore: Johns Hopkins University Press.

Wright, Thomas C. (1995). "Legacy of Dictatorship: Works on the Chilean Diaspora." *Latin American Research Review* 30 (3): 198–209.

References

Wright, Thomas C. and Rody Oñate (1998). *Flight From Chile: Voices of Exile.* Albuquerque: University of New Mexico Press.

Yocelevsky, Ricardo (1987). *La democracia cristiana chilena y el gobierno de Eduardo Frei (1964–1970).* Mexico, D.F.: Universidad Autónoma Metropolitana.

Young, Brigitte (1999). *Triumph of the Fatherland: German Unification and the Marginalization of Women.* Ann Arbor: University of Michigan Press.

Zald, Mayer N. and John D. McCarthy (1979). *The Dynamics of Social Movements: Resource Mobilization, Social Control, and Tactics.* Cambridge, MA: Winthrop Publishers.

Zolberg, Aristide R. (1972). "Moments of Madness." *Politics and Society* II (2): 183–207.

Zophy, Angela Marie Howard and Frances M. Kavenik (1990). *Handbook of American Women's History.* New York: Garland Publishing, Inc.

Index

Index

Index

Sigmund, Paul, 76, 103, 105
Silva, Coty, 35, 139, 163, 165, 166
Silva, María de la Luz, 154, 155, 157
Silva Henriquez, Raúl, 94, 130, 159
Silva y Lepe, Domitila, 21
Simon, Marlise, 89, 96
Social Democratic Party, 50
Socialist Party, 24, 35, 43, 50, 66, 73, 84, 130, 152–3, 183, 192
social movement theory
  cultural framing, 5, 10, 11, 16, 17, 147, 161, 196–7, 203
  political opportunities, 8, 145
  resource mobilization, 11, 145
  structural explanations, 13, 145
Solidarity, Order, and Liberty (SOL), 69, 70, 87, 88, 94–5, 116–17
Soviet Union, 53, 203
soup kitchens (ollas comunes), 38, 137, 193
Sperling, Valerie, 202
Statute of Democratic Guarantees, 62, 84, 102
strikes
  copper, 38, 137. *See also* copper industry
  truckers, 105, 137
student movement, 42–4

Tarrow, Sidney, 8
Taylor, Verta, 196
Teitelboim, Volodia, 85
Thayer, William, 108
timing, 5, 17, 147, 196–7
Tinsman, Heidi, 99
tipping, 3, 5, 17, 196–7, 199
Tohá, José, 83, 84, 86, 125
Tomic, Radomiro, 50, 73, 109
Tradition, Family, and Property, 35
transitions to democracy, 198
  in Brazil, 199–200
  in East Germany, 204–6
  in Russia, 201–4

Unión por Chile, 191
United Nations
  Convention to End All Forms of Discrimination Against Women (CEDAW), 178, 182
  World Conferences on Women, 141, 184, 189
United States Agency for International Development (USAID), 188, 189
United States Central Intelligence Agency (CIA), 36, 51, 71, 77, 103
United States government, 36
  foreign policy, 61–2
University of Chile, 43, 56, 74, 92, 132

Valdés, Marina, 139, 148, 150, 165
Valdés, Teresa, 137, 143, 158, 173
Valenzuela, Arturo, 71, 174
Valenzuela, María Elena, 134, 135, 158, 193
Verdugo, Patricia, 112, 156
Viaux, Roberto, 61
Vicariate of Solidarity. *See* Catholic Church

Walker, Betty, 134, 187
Walker, Ignacio, 193
Weinstein, Eugenia, 180
Weinstein, Marisa, 137
Winn, Peter, 53
women
  cabinet appointments, 183
  as legislative candidates, 176, 183, 184–8
  in political parties, 31–2, 51
Women of Chile (MUDECHI), 138
Women for Life (MPLV), 154–60, 172–3, 177, 189, 193
Women's Action of Chile, 36, 50
Women's Institute, 186–7
Women's League, 202
women's legislation, 183

233

Other Books in the Series (continued from page iii)

Torben Iversen, Jonas Pontusson, David Soskice, eds., *Unions, Employers, and Central Banks: Macroeconomic Coordination and Institutional Change in Social Market Economies*

Thomas Janoski and Alexander M. Hicks, eds., *The Comparative Political Economy of the Welfare State*

Robert O. Keohane and Helen B. Milner, eds., *Internationalization and Domestic Politics*

Herbert Kitschelt, *The Transformation of European Social Democracy*

Herbert Kitschelt, Peter Lange, Gary Marks, and John D. Stephens, eds., *Continuity and Change in Contemporary Capitalism*

Herbert Kitschelt, Zdenka Mansfeldova, Radek Markowski, and Gabor Toka, *Post-Communist Party Systems*

David Knoke, Franz Urban Pappi, Jeffrey Broadbent, and Yutaka Tsujinaka, eds., *Comparing Policy Networks*

Allan Kornberg and Harold D. Clarke, *Citizens and Community: Political Support in a Representative Democracy*

David D. Laitin, *Language Repertories and State Construction in Africa*

Mark Irving Lichbach and Alan S. Zuckerman, eds., *Comparative Politics: Rationality, Culture, and Structure*

Doug McAdam, John McCarthy, and Mayer Zald, eds., *Comparative Perspectives on Social Movements*

Scott Mainwaring and Matthew Soberg Shugart, eds., *Presidentialism and Democracy in Latin America*

Anthony W. Marx, *Making Race, Making Nations: A Comparison of South Africa, the United States and Brazil*

Joel S. Migdal, Atul Kohli, and Vivienne Shue, eds., *State Power and Social Forces: Domination and Transformation in the Third World*

Wolfgang C. Muller and Kaare Strom, *Policy, Office, or Votes?*

Maria Victoria Murillo, *Labor Unions, Partisan Coalitions, and Market Reforms in Latin America*

Ton Notermans, *Money, Markets, and the State: Social Democratic Economic Policies since 1918*

Paul Pierson, *Dismantling the Welfare State? Reagan, Thatcher and the Politics of Retrenchment*

Simona Piattoni, ed., *Clientelism, Interests, and Democratic Representation*

Marino Regini, *Uncertain Boundaries: The Social and Political Construction of European Economies*

Yossi Shain and Juan Linz, eds., *Interim Governments and Democratic Transitions*

Theda Skocpol, *Social Revolutions in the Modern World*

David Stark and László Bruszt, *Postsocialist Pathways: Transforming Politics and Property in East Central Europe*

Sven Steinmo, Kathleen Thelan, and Frank Longstreth, eds., *Structuring Politics: Historical Institutionalism in Comparative Analysis*

Susan C. Stokes, *Mandates and Democracy: Neoliberalism by Surprise in Latin America*

Susan C. Stokes, ed., *Public Support for Market Reforms in New Democracies*

Sidney Tarrow, *Power in Movement: Social Movements and Contentious Politics*

Ashutosh Varshney, *Democracy, Development, and the Countryside*

Elisabeth Jean Wood, *Forging Democracy from Below: Insurgent Transitions in South Africa and El Salvador*